CONTEMPORARY SOCIAL RESEARCH SERIES
General Editor: MARTIN BULMER

7

Documents of Life

CONTEMPORARY SOCIAL RESEARCH SERIES

Documents of Life

An Introduction to the Problems and
Literature of a Humanistic Method

KEN PLUMMER

Lecturer in Sociology, University of Essex

London
GEORGE ALLEN & UNWIN
Boston   Sydney

George Allen & Unwin (Publishers) Ltd,
40 Museum Street, London WC1A 1LU, UK

George Allen & Unwin (Publishers) Ltd,
Park Lane, Hemel Hempstead, Herts HP2 4TE, UK

Allen & Unwin, Inc.,
9 Winchester Terrace, Winchester, Mass. 01890, USA

George Allen & Unwin Australia Pty Ltd,
8 Napier Street, North Sydney, NSW 2060, Australia

First published in 1983

British Library Cataloguing in Publication Data

Plummer, Ken
    Documents of life. – (Contemporary social research series)
1. Social sciences – Information services
I. Title   II. Series
300'.7   H62
ISBN 0-04-321029-5
ISBN 0-04-321030-9   Paperback

Set in 10 on 11 point Times by Fotographics (Bedford) Ltd
and printed in Great Britain
by Biddles Ltd, Guildford, Surrey

Contents

Now the blindness in human beings ... is the blindness with which we are all inflicted in regard to the feelings of creatures and people different from ourselves. We are practical beings, each of us with limited functions and duties to perform. Each is bound to feel intensely the importance of his own duties and the significance of the situations that call these forth. But this feeling is in each of us a vital secret, for sympathy with which we vainly look to others. The others are too much absorbed in their own vital secrets to take an interest in ours. Hence the stupidity and injustice of our opinions, so far as they deal with the significance of alien lives. Hence the falsity of our judgements, so far as they presume to decide in an absolute way on the value of other persons' conditions or ideals ...

What is the result of all these considerations ... ? It is negative in one sense, but positive in another. It absolutely forbids us to be forward in pronouncing on the meaninglessness of forms of existence other than our own; and it commands us to tolerate, respect and indulge those whom we see harmlessly happy and interested in their own ways, however unintelligible these may be to us. Hands off: neither the whole of truth nor the whole of good is revealed to any single observer, although each observer gains a partial superiority of insight from the peculiar position in which he stands ... (William James, 'On a certain blindness in human beings', in his *Talks to Teachers*, 1899)

*For Mum
And in Memory of Dad*

Acknowledgements

Many people have been very helpful in writing this small volume. Not all can be mentioned but particular thanks should go to: the Social Science Research Council for sponsoring the research into sexuality from which my interest in 'documents of life' grew; Annabel Faraday for being a critical research officer on that project; the subjects who let their lives be documented – while they may not figure explicitly in this book, they have been vital to my understanding; Terry Tostevin and the library staff at the University of Essex – for providing an endless stream of books and articles; my colleagues and students in the sociology department for support and stimulation; The Fuller Bequest Fund; Stan Cohen and Paul Rock for continuing inspiration; Paul Thompson and Jonathan Stratton for commenting on earlier drafts of this book; Janet Parkin, Linda Hill and Marion Haberhauer for typing various drafts; Brenda Corti and Mary Girling, rarely thanked but always there; Martin Bulmer for support, comments and showing me what a model editor is like; and all friends – but especially my 'bestest friend': Everard Longland.

Editor's Preface

The structure of the social sciences combines two separate elements, theory and empirical evidence. Both are necessary for successful social understanding; one without the other is barren. The *Contemporary Social Research* series is concerned with the means by which this structure is maintained and kept standing solid and upright, a job performed by the methodology of social research.

The series is intended to provide concise introductions to significant methodological topics. Broadly conceived, research methodology deals with the general grounds for the validity of social scientific propositions. How do we know what we do know about the social world? More narrowly, it deals with the questions: how do we actually acquire new knowledge about the world in which we live? What are the strategies and techniques by means of which social science data are collected and analysed? The series will seek to answer such questions through the examination of specific areas of methodology.

Why is such a series necessary? There exist many solid, indeed massive, methodology textbooks, which most undergraduates in sociology, psychology and the other social sciences acquire familiarity with in the course of their studies. The aim of this series is different. It goes beyond such texts to focus upon specific topics, procedures, methods of analysis and methodological problems to provide a readable introduction to its subject. Each book contains annotated suggestions for further reading. The intended audience includes the advanced undergraduate, the graduate student, the working social researcher seeking to familiarise himself or herself with new areas, and the non-specialist who wishes to enlarge his or her knowledge of social research. Research methodology need not be remote and inaccessible. Some prior knowledge of statistics will be useful, but only certain titles in the series will make strong statistical demands upon the reader. The series is concerned above all to demonstrate the general importance and centrality of research methodology to social science.

Kenneth Plummer's *Documents of Life* is concerned with the use in social science research of life histories and other types of personal document which give a first hand account of social experience from the participants' point of view. Such materials are invaluable in providing evidence about the subjective point of view of the social actor, and are congruent with a theoretical approach in terms of action theory or an action frame of reference. The use of personal documents has a long history in social science, going back at least to

W. I. Thomas and Florian Znaniecki's monumental work, *The Polish Peasant in Europe and America* (1918–20). This type of material was extensively used in many of the monographs of the 'Chicago School' of sociology in the 1920s and 1930s. This period also produced classic life histories such as Clifford Shaw's *The Jack Roller* and Edwin Sutherland's *The Professional Thief.* Thereafter, for various reasons which this book discusses, the method fell into general disuse. The use of personal documents has, however, in recent years enjoyed a modest revival, and has been extended to fields other than crime, deviance and urban ethnography in which it was originally developed. *Documents of Life* takes this revival a stage further, providing both an excellent overview of the strengths and limitations of such first-hand accounts of social experience and an original discussion of the practical problems of collecting and analysing such data.

MARTIN BULMER
*London School of
Economics and Political Science*

1

In Pursuit of a Subject

Whether in the field of psychology, sociology, linguistics or history, the human element cannot quite be reduced to a scientific norm; there is always a residuum of uniqueness which does not fit the abstractions and generalisations in which the scientist would like to enclose it. The human being is thus difficult to handle; the best solution, of course, is to suppress him (sic), or to declare that he (sic) no longer exists. In this way, science could really take over and work out theories no human element could contradict. (Chiari, 1975, p. 169)

This short, introductory study is concerned with depicting and discussing a particular and peculiar style of investigating and understanding human experiences, a style which simply advocates getting close to concrete individual men and women, accurately picking up the way they express their understandings of the world around them, and, perhaps, providing an analysis of such expressions. It is a style which constitutes a large underbelly of social science research, but a style which is rarely discussed explicitly. It is exemplified in the studies by Oscar Lewis of family life and poverty in Mexico and Puerto Rico; by the intensive life histories of delinquents gathered by Clifford Shaw in Chicago in the late 1920s; through the *vox populi* gathered together in the studies by Tony Parker of criminals, unmarried mothers, 'street' people and lighthouse keepers; and in the startling films of organisational life produced by Frederick Wiseman – of schools, hospitals, welfare, army. All this research is characterised by a lack of pomposity and pretension about methods: the researcher is merely there in the first instance to give 'voice' to other people; in some circumstances the voices may then be interpreted. Such studies rarely get bogged down in the abstract methodological and theoretical debate which characterises so much social science today. Methodology and theorising is something simply done with a firm problem in mind; it is not something to be endlessly pontificated about. In this sense all the studies to be discussed in this book have in mind C. Wright Mills's dictum: 'Every man his own methodologist! Methodologists get to work!' (Mills, 1970, p. 137).

Yet a book like this does run the risk of fetishising the technique and forgetting the purpose, of elevating form over substance, of worshipping the abstract and denying the concrete – all tendencies that sociologists have described as characterising modern societies (Zijderveld, 1970). More pragmatically: why waste time and trees writing *about* research when one could be simply *doing* it? Surely one reason for sociology's disillusionment, crisis and eclipse in the recent decade has been this distinctive turn away from *doing* research to endless *talk about* it? It has often become arid and empty precisely because it has lost its substance; philosophical presuppositions, theoretical speculation and methodological cookbooks have taken over from sociological work. So it is most certainly not my argument that methods should ever be divorced from concrete problems, theorising and down-to-earth research. Nevertheless, given the existence of certain trends within contemporary sociology, it does seem a fruitful exercise to bring together much of what is so far known about a particular methodological style that is decidedly under-rated and persistently neglected in current research texts. That style has gone by various names – personal documents, the documentary tradition, oral history – but for sociologists it has most regularly, since Thomas and Znaniecki, been identified as 'human documents': 'account(s) of individual experience which reveal the individual's actions as a human agent and as a participant in social life' (Blumer, 1979, p. 29). These accounts embrace a wide range of forms (to be discussed in Chapter 2): letters and diaries, biographies and life histories, dreams and self-observation, essays and notes, photographs and film. There was a moment in sociological history, roughly between 1920 and 1935, when it looked as if such documents would finally establish themselves as a central sociological resource; I will discuss this stage in its history in Chapter 3. But that moment has come and gone, and most contemporary sociologists would not be expected to have even the most passing acquaintance with this research style. It is the 'outsider' of social science research. Whoever, for example, reads Thomas and Znaniecki these days?

The reasons for this neglect are not hard to find. One is the still prevailing trend towards positivism, and whilst personal documents are certainly concerned with the observable facts of social life, they are rarely committed to the 'unity' of science, the search for generalisable laws and the quantification that characterises positivism. If they find unity at all, it is with the humanities; literature and the arts not science and the experiment become the model for personal document research. Secondly, there is the counter-prevailing trend away from positivism towards realism, rationalism and the theoretical heavens, a view which sees a concern with mere epiphenomena as marginal. Such 'data' require well developed theoretical problematics before they may be interpreted; for these critics, the epistemological status of personal documents becomes highly suspect because they cannot embody 'objective truth'. To a considerable extent, both these counter positions – positivism and realism – converge in their refutation of the idea of human subjectivity and individuality: it is this which is the cornerstone of the personal document approach and it is the rejection of this which can unite such seemingly strange bed-fellows as B. F. Skinner and the post-1844 Karl Marx.

This rejection of the human subject highlights one of sociology's core contradictions: an interminable tension between the subjectively creative individual human being acting upon the world and the objectively given social structure constraining him or her. As Alan Dawe has rightly commented, it is a tension to be found not only through 'all varieties of Western social, political, moral and creative thought and work, from philosophy and ethics to the novel and the film', it is also 'a problem central to our everyday experience in vast industrial societies' (Dawe, 1978, p. 364). Just how can we reconcile our own human creativity with a coercive and dehumanising social order? The problem is posed over and over again throughout the history of sociology from Marx to ethnomethodology, and almost invariably the answer is finally achieved by giving primacy to social structure over human agency; the humanistic Marx becomes the scientific Marx, the voluntaristic Parsons becomes the Parsonian system, the 'breaching' Garfinkel becomes the 'deep-ruled' Cicourel. Nor is this surprising:

. . . Although sociology has many potential uses and has been enlisted in support of various political faiths, it is by the nature of its key concepts and approaches intrinsically oriented toward the group rather than the individual, toward the herd rather than the lone stray. In connection with this emphasis, sociology stresses the notion of order, of collectivity, of social organisation, irrespective of political labels such as 'Left' or 'Right'. Thus sociology has an anti-liberal twist, and may even be considered as a critique of the traditional liberal idea of individualism . . . few sociologists have been distinguished by their concern for the individual as opposed to their preoccupation with social disintegration . . . A sociologist who is also a liberal – individualist, then, may encounter theoretical difficulties and contradictions. (Bramson, 1961, pp. 16–17)

The logic of sociology thus strains towards the system's side of the individualist – collectivist tension. Indeed, some recent 'sociologies' have gone so far as to eliminate 'the subject' altogether; the human being becomes an epistemological disaster – an 'idealism of the essence' (Althusser, 1969, p. 228) and a 'myth of bourgeois ideology'

(Althusser, 1976, pp. 52–3) while humanism becomes little more than an ideological construct, which along with bourgeois notions like democracy and freedom permits the maintenance and reproduction of the late capitalist hegemonic state. There is no human being independent of the material and ideological forces that construct 'it'. In such views, 'the final goal of human sciences is not to constitute man, but to dissolve him' (Lévi-Strauss, 1966).

Dissolve the subject! Such statements may be supported by refined theoretical reasoning, but they bring with them the spectre of conservative collectivist idealism which can kill off any concern for the concrete joys and suffering of active human beings; they bring with them a denial of the root tension that has existed within sociology since its earliest days by co-opting 'the subject' into an ideology; they harbour a myopia which can deny insights of other approaches and contrary discipline. In short, they encourage a premature theoretical closure and a tottering towards sure, safe absolutism (cf. E. P. Thompson, 1978, pp. 193–399). Again, C. Wright Mills provides the classic humanistic statement about the need for a triple concern with biography, structure and history:

> Always keep your eyes open to the image of man – the generic notion of his human nature – which by your work you are assuming and implying; and also to the image of history – your notion of how history is being made. In a word, continually work out and revise your views of the problems of history, the problems of biography, and the problems of a social structure in which biography and history intersect. Keep your eyes open to the varieties of individuality, and to the modes of epochal change. Use what you see and what you imagine as the clues to your study of the human variety . . . know that many personal troubles cannot be solved merely as troubles, but must be understood in terms of public issues – and in terms of the problems of history making. Know that the human meaning of public issues must be revealed by relating them to personal troubles and to the problems of individual life. Know that the problems of social science, when adequately formulated, must include both troubles and issues, both biography and history, and the range of their intricate relations. Within that range the life of the individual and the making of society occur; and that within that range the sociological imagination has its chance to make a difference in the quality of human life in our time. (Mills, 1970, pp. 247–8)

This triple focus, on biography, history and structure, which is sociology's heritage can be denied by an exclusive focus on structure; human joy and suffering can simply be left out. There are parallel movements in psychology to remove the subject – from Skinner's behaviourism to Lacan's structuralism. But it is in deep opposition to such anti-humanist views that the main justification for this small study lies. For to resolve the central contradiction of sociology by taking one side and denying the other – of championing system over agency, discourse over doing, structure over consciousness – runs the risk of developing accounts of the world that are simply wild and wrong, untempered as they are with the concrete historical yet human experiences out of which societies are invariably composed.

There is no case here for a sociology without society or for a pre-occupation with individuals or individualism; I am not challenging the helpfulness of many structural accounts, and certainly the concrete human must always be located within this historically specific culture – for 'the individual' becomes a very different animal under different social orders. But in the face of the inherent society –individual dualism of sociology, surely there must always remain a strand of work that highlights the active human subject? It may strain against the logic of sociological inquiry, but it is a positive, if minor, check on its worst excesses.

This corrective sociology may be called 'humanistic' and has at least four central criteria. It must pay tribute to *human subjectivity and creativity* – showing how individuals respond to social constraints and actively assemble social worlds; it must deal with concrete human experiences – talk, feelings, actions – through their *social, and especially economic, organisation* (and not just their inner, psychic or biological structuring); it must show a naturalistic *'intimate familiarity'* with such experiences – abstractions untempered by close involvement are ruled out; and there must be a self-awareness by the sociologist of the ultimate *moral and political role* in moving towards a social structure in which there is less exploitation, oppression and injustice and more creativity, diversity and equality. A list like this is open to detailed extension and revision, but it is hard to imagine a humanistic sociology which is not at least minimally committed to these criteria.

The Humanities Baseline

In his study of *Sociology as an Art Form*, Nisbet reflects 'How different things would be . . . if the social sciences at the time of their systematic formation in the nineteenth century had taken the arts in the same degree they took the physical science as models' (Nisbet, 1976, p. 16). At times it has seemed as though the two cultures have grown irrevocably apart: facts, generalisations and abstractions have become divorced from the imaginative, the inspirational and the idiographic, and – for all its critical ponderings on 'positivism' – it is clear for all to see the path by which sociology has been most moulded. Of course affinities between art and science may be found, and for sure some social scientists see their work as profoundly inspirational (cf. Truzzi, 1973): but the baseline is firm. Its major journals speak to abstractions, hypotheses, explanations, proof, samples, theory, objectivity, distance – and although it is constantly at war with the enemy of positivism, in the very battle it reveals what ultimately matters to it. Nobody wages war with Dostoevski or Dickens, Balzac or Bellow, Austen or Auden. Their mode of experiencing, feeling, interpreting and writing sets no standards, provides no models, makes no sense to a discipline that has always aspired to science.

Table 1.1   A Bridgeable Divide?[1]

	Towards the humanities	Towards the positivistic sciences
Foci	Unique and idiographic	General and homothetic
	Human centred	Structure centred
	The inner: subjective, meaning, feeling	The outer: objective, 'things', events
Epistemology	Phenomenalist	Realist
	Relativist	Absolutist/Essentialist
	Perspectivist	Logical positivist
Task	Interpret, understand	Causal explanation
	Describe, observe	Measure
Style	'Soft' 'Warm'	'Hard' 'Cold'
	Imaginative	Systematic
	Valid – 'real' 'rich'	Reliable 'replicable'
Theory	Inductive and grounded	Deductive and abstract
	'Story telling'	'Operationalism'
Values	Ethically and politically committed	Ethically and politically neutral
	Egalitarianism	'Expertise and elites'

[1] These distinctions are made in many places and are now a commonplace. See e.g. Bruyn (1966, ch. 2); Brown and Lyman (1978, ch. 1); Lee (1978, ch. 4) and Halfpenny (1979). For a discussion of potential synthesis, see Brown and Lyman op. cit., and Cook and Reichardt (1979, pp. 12–16).

There are then 'two orders . . . separate but unequal' (Gouldner, 1962, p. 210). Such differences (documented in Table 1.1) are very broad: it is the chasm between a *compassion* for the sufferer and a *neutrality* towards him or her; between looking inside, exploring, feeling and imagining, or recording externals, measuring, generalising and theorising. The images are starkly opposed: one 'falls in love', the other 'observes love'. In a powerful display of this contrast, *Redeeming the Sin*, Audrey Borenstein remarks:

> Just as genes are not always expressed in material form, so, too, the silent workings of feelings and thought are often hidden from appearance. From the outside looking in, an observer might see a 'common' condition: a son is killed in Vietnam, a daughter's mind is destroyed by LSD, a woman is widowed, a man becomes subject to mandatory retirement, there is a divorce. Yet, in interior life, what happens to one is unique. Life histories, like snowflakes, are never of the same design. The social terrain surveyed by the sociologist is criss-crossed with pathways, each with its crusaders beckoning, its pied pipers and sirens making their invitational music. But it is not given to the social scientist to say which path is to be followed. Nor is it given to anyone to say what another shall make of the journey. In inner life, each of us is solitary ... Wherever one begins, the task is always the same: to follow the labyrinthine corridors between inner and outer reality, without losing one's integrity, one's selfhood, in either. (Borenstein, 1978, p. 30)

The sensitive scientific sociologist has generally acknowledged the need for the inner to be scrutinised with the outer, and the unique with the general (cf. Bruyn, 1966); but in the end, it is always clear that the final solutions lie in grasping general laws from the outside. Ultimately to side with the uniquely subjective is finally to dismantle the model of social science – and to favour the model of the humanities. Here again, as in the structure–action dichotomy, sociology is lodged in a twist – and the logic of sociology is ultimately to side with science. But here again, there must be virtue in sustaining an undercurrent of sociological work that strains against the dominant tendencies and which persistently reminds the scientific sociologist that for all his or her neat abstractions, concrete human beings may not neatly bend before them.

But if the humanities are to be evoked as a baseline, from where will they come? Ballet and mime could throw enormous understanding on the domain of kinetics, and certainly for some 'drama' has provided a marvellous metaphor – Lyman and Scott's (1975) *The Drama of Social Reality* treats the reader to ponderings on Shakespeare's *Macbeth*, *Hamlet*, *Troilus and Cressida* and *Antony and Cleopatra* as a baseline for discussing society – and the early work of Goffman evoking this metaphor is well known (cf. Ditton, 1980). For others, sociology should delve into 'story telling' – modest, elegant but analytic ruminations on social life (cf. Carroll, 1980); and for others, the model may be derived from 'poetics' with its concern for irony, perspective and metaphor (cf. Brown, 1977). All these should have their place, but in this study of life documents the central inspiration comes from the work of biographers and autobiographers.

The Rise of the Personal Tale

The telling of a tale of a life is no new business, and certainly not one confined to the social sciences. Georg Misch (the son-in-law of Dilthey who played an influential part in many of the life histories to be considered later in the chapter) in his classic history of autobiography devotes some 2,724 pages (out of a total of 3,881 pages) to the story of autobiography during the Middle Ages, but takes it at least as far back as the ancient Egyptian tomb inscriptions (Misch, 1951). Likewise Paul Thompson in his much more modest book on oral history remarks: 'Oral history is as old as history itself. It was the *first* kind of history. And it is only quite recently that skill in handling oral evidence has ceased to be one of the marks of the great historian' (Thompson, 1978, p. 19). Nevertheless, it would be quite wrong to suggest that these testaments of personal lives which have existed throughout history have anything like the same meaning as they do now. The roots of individualism and humanism as major forms may be traced back at least to the mediaeval period – the religious confession transcending the penance, the sensitive human portraiture becoming distinguished from the hierarchically observed picture, romantic and courtly love rising from instrumental marriage; through the era of Thomism, with its gradual separation of reason and revelation, the secular and the religious – and on to the Renaissance period; but it is surely with industrialisation that the modern 'Individual' is announced. A new kind of individual with a new kind of 'self' seems to emerge. As Lionel Trilling put it: 'At a certain point in history men became individuals' (Trilling, 1972, p. 24). It is probably at this moment that people start to develop fully a sense of themselves as objects of introspection, of interest, of value; when the individual begins to brood and reflect over his or her inner nature; a time when the individual starts to retreat from the public life into the realms of privacy – the inner thought, the private home, the real self. Much recent sociological writing has testified to this change, indeed some of it has suggested that this individuality has now gone too far and a narcissistic culture of self-absorbed individuals has been created with no sense of public life or outer control (cf. Lasch, 1979). Others have suggested that this brooding introspection – embodied in the 'confessional' – is part of a more general shift in control: from the outer constraints on the *body* to the inner constraints on the *soul* (cf. Foucault, 1977, 1978). There may be much truth in such reflections, but they certainly only tell half the story. For whether we are becoming more 'narcissistic' or more 'controlled', at a certain level we are also probably discovering a broader, more available cultured individuality. The problem, and the virtue, is well stated by Karl Weintraub in the closing paragraph of his 'essay' on autobiographical study, *The Value of the Individual*. He writes:

When understood in the best terms, a view of life resting on a loving admiration for the diversity and the manifold richness of life is a magnificent one. It embodies the deepest respect for the formative powers of man. Even if we can know nothing about ultimate human purpose and the end objectives of this mysterious process of life, we can derive gratification and hope from a conception of cosmic order where creative individuality adds forever to the growing richness of the world. There is nobility in our willingness to understand men on their own terms and to complicate our judgement by giving each man his due. There is a refinement of knowledge in a perspectivist understanding of reality. All matters of great value exact their price. We pay for our commitment to individuality by incurring the dangers of lives floundering in capricious subjectivism, the pursuit of arbitrary whims, the loss of real selves in unrealistic dreams, and by cutting mistakenly the life giving interaction between self-formation and responsible cultivation of our given social and cultural world. Only the future can show whether the price is too high and whether we can live responsibly with the ideal of the self. Perhaps those are right who say that history has no lessons. But historical contemplation may, at least, help us to be wiser. The only admonition that the historian gives us that is worth repeating may well be that, whatever else we do, we ought to live our lives as responsible heirs. (Weintraub, 1978, p. 379)

Until the dawn of the Enlightenment, documents of lives were primarily documents of memorable events (*memoirs*), of great deeds done (*res gestae*), or philosophers' Lives; there were few instances (Saint Augustine's *Confessions* being a notable exception) in which there were ponderings about the nature of one's inner self. Yet for most scholars of the autobiographical form it is precisely this *search for a self* which is the hallmark. This said there are some key figures who signpost the modern personal document.

Thus, when on 1 January 1660 Samuel Pepys sat down to record the first entry in his famous diaries – a task he was to regularly perform for the following nine years – we find the symbolic emergence of the modern diary as a distinctive form. When at the end of the eighteenth century Rousseau published his *Confessions* (1782) and Goethe his *Dichtung und Wahrheit* we have the emergence of the distinctive autobiography, a form 'inspired by a reverence for the self, tender yet severe, [seeing] the self not as a property but as trust' (Pascal, 1960, p. 181); it is motivated by 'Selbstbestimmung' – a search for one's inner understanding – and is a search not a clear answer. Throughout it 'holds the balance between the self and the world, the subjective and the objective' (Pascal, 1960, p. 180) casting light upon both. Biography clearly lacks this unique sense of inner value, but it too has a recent history. The vague foundations flow from the Renaissance (Thomas More) but it failed to develop as a distinctive form until the Victorian era with the writings of Carlyle, Mrs Gaskell and Lytton Strachey (Gittings, 1978, p. 35). The shift in emphasis this time marked a lesser concern with the praise of great men to a stronger concern with accurate research: the modern biographer has a wealth of facts at hand that have to be sifted out, made into theory, carefully checked. He or she is as much of a researcher as a literary writer.

These concerns of the humanities – of understanding the inner pursuit of self, of linking with the outer world, of being accurate – start to be reflected in the emerging social science around the middle part of the nineteenth century. In England, Henry Mayhew's studies begin to give voice to the ordinary people of mid-Victorian England; in France, Frederic Le Play started the painstaking task of documenting family budgets as indicators of family life; and, a little later, in Vienna, Sigmund Freud was to begin his famous explorations into clinical methods. But it was in America – and notably in Chicago – that these concerns were to have a symbolic sociological birth in Thomas and Znaniecki's *Polish Peasant*. I will return to this in Chapter 3.

Conclusion and Aims

My aims in writing this book have been straightforward. In the first instance since this kind of research constitutes the underground of sociological work, I want to bring into the open the major examples, varieties and uses of the approach and provide something of a brief intellectual history of it. A series of appraisals were conducted in the late 1930s under the auspices of the Social Science Research Council in America but since that time, with one or two exceptions, the social scientific literature has remained mute on personal documents. Indeed, most current textbook treatments of methodology give scant attention to such research practices, and it is rarely considered in teaching (cf. Burgess, 1979). My second aim has been to provide an introductory itemisation and discussion of the kinds of problems and dilemmas involved in doing such work. In the space of a small text these discussions are far from exhaustive and I have chosen to focus on three areas: some practical issues in gathering personal documents, the ways in which theory may be related to them, and finally some ethical concerns. My third aim has been to express a kind of surprise at the inherent conservatism of so much social science. While I agree that if we forget our past we are doomed to rediscover it all over again, I also believe that much social science fails to avail itself of the world in which it lives now and will live in the future. Thus, for example, sociology and photography could be dated from the same year – 1839 – when Comte published his key work, and Daguerre made public his method for fixing an image on a metal plate (cf. Becker, 1974). But over the past 140 years, the two have rarely contacted each other. Why? Couldn't photography give a lot to research, writing and teaching in sociology? But even as I write, photography and tape recording is confronting the video revolution. Yet scarcely a sociologist in sight seems to acknowledge this, and its value for doing sociology. In America, some awareness is now taking place of these new media, and in places throughout this book I will comment on such forward-looking tools. But in general, it is time qualitative sociology came into the twentieth century.

In sum, an important approach to understanding human life has been persistently minimised, maligned and rendered marginal by social scientists: they believe that human documents are just too subjective, too descriptive, too arbitrary to help in scientific advance. They may be right: in which case I would argue that 'scientific advance' isn't the only goal of human endeavour, and life documents with their commitment to humanistic sensitivity still have a vital role to play in human progress. But they may be wrong: scientific advance in the social world may actually be contingent upon building a methodology that can take subjectivity and the lived life as its cornerstone. In which case, documents of life must have a central role to play. But in the end, whether we have social studies or social science, life documents are an immensely valuable and vastly under-rated source: this small book is dedicated to this idea.

Suggestions for Further Reading

(Full references are given in the Bibliography at the end of the book.)

The classic introductions to humanistic method are P. Berger's *Invitation to Sociology* (1966) along with the student text, *Sociology: A Biographical Approach* (1976), and C. W. Mills's, *The Sociological Imagination* (1970). The latter contains a diatribe against the tendencies in sociology towards both grand theory (which now moves in the name of French structuralism not Parsons) and abstracted empiricism. Mills's distinctive blend of pragmatism and Marxism is discussed in J. Scimecca, *The Social Theory of C. Wright Mills* (1977). A more recent espousal of humanism in sociology is

A. M. Lee's *Sociology for Whom?* (1978) which also describes the rise of the American Association for Humanist Sociology (in ch. 9). A very central text on methodology and humanism is S. T. Bruyn's classic, *The Human Perspective in Sociology*, which although published in only 1966 seems to have become neglected far too quickly. It is a gold mine of analysis and advice, and strongly recommended (even though its main technical concern is participant observation).

On the positivist and realistic epistemologies which largely stand opposed to personal document research, see B. Aune's *Rationalism, Empiricism and Pragmatism* (1970) which is sympathetic to pragmatism; and R. Keat and J. Urry's *Social Theory as Science* (1975) and Ted Benton's *Philosophical Foundations of the Three Sociologies* (1977), which are sympathetic to realism. The major attacks on humanism in sociology can be found in Althusser's *For Marx* (1969) and Lévi-Strauss's *Structural Anthropology* (1977) whilst helpful defences of the humanist position may be found in Brittan's *The Privatised World* (1977) and E. P. Thompson's *The Poverty of Theory* (1978). The latter is a highly significant Marxist–humanist critique of the Althusserian anti-humanist position by the most celebrated of contemporary English Marxist historians. Of great value too is Alan Dawe's 'Theories of social action' (1978) which both reviews the main tendencies of social theory and makes a plea for a proper concern with action which such theories ultimately negate.

On individualism, see Lukes's *Individualism* (1973) which provides a critical inventory of the uses of the term. On the need to sustain both the personalist and the collectivist tradition, see Halmos's last work *The Personal and the Political* (1978). The changing nature of the individual under industrialisation is discussed in many places, but most recently in Lasch's *The Culture of Narcissism* (1979) and Sennett's *The Fall of Public Man* (1974).

On art and social science, see Nisbet's *Sociology as an Art Form* (1976), M. Truzzi (ed.) *The Humanities as Sociology* (1973) and Borenstein's *Redeeming the Sin* (1978). Helpful discussions on biography and autobiography include K. Weintraub *The Value of the Individual* (1978), J. Olney *Autobiography* (1980), R. Pascal *Design and Truth in Autobiography* (1960), A. Shelston's *Biography* (1977), and R. Gitting's *The Nature of Biography* (1978). On letters in literature, see R. D. Altick's *Lives and Letters* (1969), and on diaries see the classic by A. Ponsonby, *English Diaries* (1923) and the more recent study by R. A. Fothergill, *Private Chronicles* (1974).

2

On the Diversity of Life Documents

... any research procedure which can tell us something
about the subjective orientation of human actors has a
claim to scholarly consideration. (Blumer, 1979, p. xxiii)

The world is crammed full of personal documents. People keep
diaries, send letters, take photos, write memos, tell biographies,
scrawl graffiti, publish their memoires, write letters to the papers,
leave suicide notes, inscribe memorials on tombstones, shoot films,
paint pictures, make music and try to record their personal dreams.
All of these expressions of personal life are hurled out into the world
by the millions and can be of interest to anyone who cares to seek
them out. They are all in the broadest sense 'documents of life', and
the aim of this chapter is to explore a little of this diversity.

In part this diversity comes about because such documents straddle
different disciplines with divergent aims. Cavan (1929) recognised
this long ago, and today there is the oral historian primarily
concerned with using documents to throw light upon the past, the
psychiatrist primarily concerned with seeing how the documents can
be used to throw light upon unconscious motivation, and the anthropologist making the prime target of investigation the culture of which
the document is a part. For the sociologist, the human document is
'an account of individual experience which reveals the individual's
actions as a human agent and as a participant in social life' (Blumer,
1939, p. 29); for the literary biographer the prime task is to explore
the relationship of the self to the past life and the outer world; for the
genealogist, as in Alex Haley's *Roots* (1977), the task is to dig out the
ancestral history (cf. Steel, 1980). Sometimes the approach is broadly
interdisciplinary, attempting to establish general criteria for the
appraisal of life histories which cross academic boundaries – particularly those of sociology, anthropology, medicine and psychiatry
(Dollard, 1935). Sometimes it is simply eclectic – many literary
biographies for example nowadays have to be heavily researched and
rely on 'psychological, medical, economic, political, geographical
and religious' materials (Gittings, 1978, ch. 2, p. 63). Sometimes, too,
the discipline may be a new hybrid, like 'the literature of fact' (cf.
Weber, 1981) where real life events may be fictionalised as in
Truman Capote's *In Cold Blood* (1966) and *Music for Chameleons*

(1981) or the voices of others may be simply recorded and repeated (as in the work of Studs Terkel, e.g. 1977).

Although each of these approaches may differ, they all have in common a concern to present the naturalistic, subjective point of view of a participant. There are many definitions of the field, but Robert Redfield's sensitising one will suffice:

> the essential element in every definition is the same: a human or personal document is one in which the human and personal characteristics of somebody who is in some sense the author of the document find expression, so that through its means the reader of the document comes to know the author and his views of events with which the document is concerned. (Redfield, in Gottschalk *et al.*, 1942, p. vii)

I am taking the vagueness and openness of Redfield's terms to be a virtue, allowing this book to move freely between a range of contrasting forms. It is however clear what they are not: they refuse to be social scientists' second-order accounts that claim to be external and objective truth (though this is not to say that life documents cannot ultimately be used for such purposes). They all attempt to enter the subjective world of informants, taking them seriously on their own terms and thereby providing first hand, intimately involved accounts of life. In what follows my aim is simply to introduce the reader to a few examples of the range of forms of 'documents of life'.

1   The Life History

The cornerstone of social science life document research is akin to the literary biography and autobiography: it is the full length book account of one person's life in his or her own words. Usually, it will be gathered over a number of years with gentle guidance from the social scientist, the subject either writing down episodes of life or tape-recording them. At its best, it will be backed up with intensive observation of the subject's life, interviews with friends and perusals of letters and photographs. It is, of course, a purely subjective account – a detailed *perspective* on the world – and requires serious examination on its own terms. It does not matter if the account can later be shown to be false in particulars – most accounts, even so-called 'scientific' ones, are context-bound and speak to certain people, times and circumstances. What matters, therefore, in life history research is the facilitation of as full a subjective view as posible, not the naïve delusion that one has trapped the bedrock of truth. Given that most social science seeks to tap the 'objective', the life history reveals, like nothing else can, the subjective realm.

Table 2.1   *Life Stories: The Social Science Cast*

Agnes	A male to female hermaphrodite (Garfinkel, 1967)
Mrs Abel	A woman dying of terminal cancer (Strauss and Glaser, 1977)
Ann	A prostitute (Heyl, 1979)
Herculine Barbin	A nineteenth-century hermaphrodite (Foucault, 1980)
Chic Conwell	A professional thief (Sutherland, 1937)
Cheryl	A young woman in love (Schwartz and Merten, 1980)
Janet Clark	A heroin addict who commits suicide (Hughes, 1961)
Jane Fry	A male to female transsexual (Bogdan, 1974)
Arthur Harding	An East End underworld figure (Samuel, 1981)
Don Juan	A Yacqui Indian magician (Castaneda, 1968)
Harry King	Another thief (Chambliss, 1972)
Pierre Rivière	A nineteenth-century French family murderer (Foucault, 1978)
Manny	A 'hard core' heroin addict (Rettig, *et al.*, 1977)
The Martin Brothers	Five delinquent brothers in Chicago in the 1920s (Shaw, 1938)
The Martinez Family	A poor rural Mexican family (Lewis, 1964)
Sam	A career thief (Jackson, 1972)
The Sanchez Family	A poor urban Mexican family (Lewis, 1970)
Stanley	A Chicago delinquent in the 1920s (Shaw, 1966)
James Sewid	A Kwakiutl Indian (Spradley, 1969)
Sidney	Another Chicago delinquent (a rapist) (Shaw, 1931)
Vincent Swaggi	A professional fence (Klockars, 1975)
Don Talayesa	A Hopi Indian chief (Simmons, 1942)
William Tanner	A drunk (Spradley, 1970)
Henry Williamson	A hustler (Keiser, 1965)
Wladek Wisniewski	A Polish emigré to Chicago (Thomas and Znaniecki, 1958)

Most of the above characters are reintroduced and discussed in more detail later in the text. The most significant omission, however, is Ann (Heyl, 1979) which came to my attention too late to be included but which looks like a seminal life history study.

There are many examples of such stories. In anthropology, for instance, there is a well-established tradition of presenting the fullest accounts of American Indians and their problems of acculturation. Paul Radin's Winnebago autobiography of *Crushing Thunder*

(Radin, 1926) is generally taken to mark 'the beginning of rigorous work in this field' (Kluckhohn, 1942, p. 87), and was followed by many others including studies of Navajo culture (Dyk's (1938) *Son of Old Man Hat*), of Kwakiutl culture (Ford's (1941) *Smoke from their Fires*, and Spradley's (1969) *Guests Never Leave Hungry*) and of Hopi culture (Simmons (1942) *Sun Chief*). In psychology, a major interest has been in case histories of 'abnormal development', although in many cases the biographies are not presented to the reader on their own terms but are translated by the analyst, such as Freud's accounts of 'Dora' and 'Little Hans' (Freud, 1925, 1977), as instances of a more general theory.

In sociology the method was established with the 300-page story of a Polish emigré to Chicago, Wladek Wisniewski, written in three months before the outbreak of World War I. It was one volume of the massive study by W. I. Thomas and F. Znaniecki *The Polish Peasant in Europe and America*, first published between 1918 and 1920, and which I will describe more fully in the next chapter. Broadly, Wladek describes the early phases of his life in the Polish village of Lubotyn – born the son of a rural blacksmith, his early schooling, his entry to the baker's trade, his migration to Germany to seek work, and his ultimate arrival in Chicago and his plight there. Following from the classic work, life histories became an important tool in the work of Chicago and Polish sociologists (cf. Shaw, 1931, 1938, 1966, and Chalasinski in Bertaux, 1981, p. 120). Some of the major instances of this approach are chronicled in Table 2.1.

A very good modern illustration of this sociological life history research is the story of Jane Fry, a transsexual born a 'biological male' but believing she was in fact a woman. It was gathered by Robert Bogdan largely through 100 hours of informal and unchronological discussions with Jane Fry several times a week for three months. The discussions were recorded, transcribed into 750 pages, and then edited by Bogdan to exclude materials that seemed either repetitious or of little sociological value. The work thus becomes a collaboration – Jane's words are filtered through Bogdan's sociology.

In the final book, Jane's story has been organised into seventeen chapters and 200 pages. It takes the reader through her life – from her earliest memories of herself and her family to her life in high school, the navy and psychiatric hospitals, and on to marriage, suicide attempts and her involvement in the gay movement. Like all such documents, the importance of Jane's story lies in the text, no summary can do it justice. Here are two extracts to convey the flavour:

I'm not very moralistic concerning other people's sex. If it turns you on, do it – as long as it doesn't hurt anybody. Life among the freaks and the people at the Crisis (centre) was a beautiful thing. It is really a nice thing they had going, and it was only through my own choice that I was left out. It was because of the situation I was in. For one thing, I just couldn't participate in sex. I couldn't go to bed with a female because I am not 'homosexual', and I couldn't go to bed with a male because he would treat me as if I was a male. There is no way I could function as a female in bed, so I wouldn't be satisfied. So, therefore, I just steer clear of all sex. (Bogdan, 1974, p. 177)

Such a quote opens up the significance of people's subjective inter-pretations of sexuality: no matter that Jane was an 'objective' male – subjectively, she was female: and her actions followed from this. Or consider this almost classical illustration of the self-fulfilling prophecy:

Society is funny – first people put you in a position to make you withdraw, and the people get angry because you are withdrawing. That getting angry with you builds a higher wall between you and the society. The person who is pushed out has a tough time seeing what was happening. That's what was happening to me at this point. I was being tormented by the kids for being feminine so I withdrew, but the more I tried to withdraw the odder I became, and the more they tormented me the more I withdrew. An eight year old kid doesn't have the knowledge to understand what is happen-ing to him – why he does what he does. Somebody might have pointed it out to me, and that might have helped. Well anyway, these are my first feelings of being pushed out of society. (Bogdan, 1974, p. 41)

One is tempted to ask just what a sociologist could add to this formulation? In any event, the two quotes above are fairly random – the biography is splattered with such insights; the whole story has to be read for the greatest understanding.

Although I will be dealing with other forms of life document throughout this book, a central place is to be given to the life history in the chapters that follow.

2   The Diary

For Allport (1942, p. 95), the diary is the document of life *par excellence*, chronicling as it does the immediately contemporaneous flow of public and private events that are significant to the diarist. The word 'contemporary' is very crucial here, for each diary entry – unlike life histories – is sedimented into a particular moment in time:

they do not emerge 'all at once' as reflections on the past, but day by day strive to record an ever-changing present. As Fothergill (1974, p. 9) remarks in his helpful study of English diaries, every diary entry declares, 'I am here, and it is exactly now'. Yet whilst this is true it would also be naïve to believe that each day's entry is that alone: for at least in sustained diary-keeping, the diarist will eventually come to perceive the diary as a whole and to plan a selection of entries according to this plan. Indeed, as Fothergill comments:

. . . As a diary grows to a certain length and substance, it impresses upon the mind of its writer a conception of the completed book that it might ultimately be, if sustained with sufficient dedication and vitality. If, having written regularly and fully for, let us say, several months, he were to abandon the habit, he would be leaving un-written a book whose character and conventions had been established and whose final form is the shape of his life. (Fothergill, 1974, p. 44)

Such an issue is clearly raised by the diaries of Pepys – there was little of significance before his daily nine-year venture (which led to 1,250,000 words in some 3,100 pages) and today it is generally deemed to 'fulfil all the conditions of what a diary should be' (Ponsonby, 1923, p. 82). Yet whilst it is common to believe that Pepys simply 'sat down every night for nine years just scribbling with effortless frankness the little incidents which [he was] honest enough to record as having caught [his] attention at the moment' (Fothergill, 1974, p. 42), it becomes clear from the new revised Latham-Matthews *Pepys* that it was not produced daily, but rather evolved: 'a product fashioned with some care, both in its matter and style' (Pepys, 1970, p. ciii). Diaries, then, are certainly valuable in talking to the subjectivity of a particular moment; but they usually will go beyond this to a conception of some whole.

Whilst there are a good number of literary diaries – many of which are discussed in the classic study by Ponsonby (1923) and the more recent study by Fothergill (1974) – there still remains remarkably little sociological usage. Park employed them in his Race Relations Survey in the 1920s (cf. Bogardus, 1926) and Palmer's research text *Field Studies in Sociology* (1928) can cite two other studies – Cavan's (1928) analysis of two suicide diaries and Mowrer's (1927) case study of Miriam Donaven, a young woman whose marriage gradually fell apart. Both these studies involve the use of diaries in only a very limited way, and subsequent reviews have hardly been able to depict any sustained refinement of the method (cf. Allport, 1942, ch. 8; Denzin, 1978, pp. 223–6), not least perhaps because the diary as a form of writing seems to be going out of fashion.

Nevertheless, there are three apparent forms of diary research that social scientists could use. (See Allport's discussion of the intimate journal, the log and the memoir (1942) for a slightly different classification.)

The first is simply for the sociologist to ask informants to keep diaries. Thus Maas and Kuypers (1974) as part of a statistical, longitudinal study of adjustments to old age in the lives of 142 upper-class San Franciscans asked a number of their respondents to keep diaries for a week. The subjects were given booklets with a day allocated to each page (each page subdivided into morning, afternoon and evening) and were given the following instructions:

> We would like you to keep a daily diary to help us get some idea of how you spend your time during a typical week. We are especially interested in the kinds of things you do, when you do them, for how long and whether you do them with other people. As you write your diary, be sure to include the time of the day when you get up, have your meals, go out of the house, and any other major activity. Also be sure to include whom you met, what you did with them. You may also want to include some of the thoughts and feelings that you had during the day. At the end of the week, look over the diary to see if you have described a pretty typical seven days. Make any comment you want about what you have written . . . (Maas and Kuypers, 1974, p. 218)

Their study is subsequently richly documented with extracts from these diaries. In their instructions the authors have attempted to get round two central weaknesses – selectivity (by indicating what should be included) and typicality (by asking their respondents to comment upon this) – but it is essentially a somewhat flat method, for their concern was more with creating ideal types and statistical probabilities than with insights into specific lives.

Closely allied to this approach is the gathering of 'logs' and 'time budgets'. Sorokin pioneered this method when he asked informants to keep detailed 'time-budget schedules' showing just how they allocated their time during a day (Sorokin and Berger, 1938) and others have used similar approaches in documenting the events of 'One Boy's Day' (Barker and Wright, 1951). But perhaps the most celebrated use is that of Oscar Lewis.

Lewis's particular method focused on a few specific families in Mexico, and the analysis of a 'day' in each of their lives. Of course his actual familiarity with each family was in no way limited to a day – nothing of value could possibly be gained from that. He 'spent hundreds of hours with them in their homes, ate with them, joined in their fiestas and dances, listened to their troubles, and discussed with them the history of their lives' (Lewis, 1959, p. 5). But in the end he decided that it would be analytically more valuable, for both humanistic and scientific purposes, to focus upon 'the day' as a unit of study. Thus each family – Martinez, Gomez, Gutierez, Sanchez and Castro – is first presented as a 'cast of characters' and then followed through one arbitrarily chosen but not untypical day of their life. Lewis believed that a study of a day had at least a threefold value: practically, it was small enough to allow for intensive observation, quantitatively it permitted controlled comparisons across family units, and qualitatively it encouraged a sensitivity to the subtlety, immediacy and wholeness of life.

A third type of diary study has been dubbed 'the diary–diary interview method'. Here, Zimmerman and Wieder, in the course of examining the Californian counter–culture, found considerable difficulties in observing the full daily pattern of activities of their subjects. In place of observation they instituted a method in which respondents were paid a fee of $10 to keep a full diary for seven days. As they comment:

The diary writer was asked to record in chronological order the activities in which he or she engaged over the course of seven days. We provided the formula: who? what? when? where? how? We asked them to report the identity of the participants in the activities described not by name, of course, but by relationship to the writer e.g. room-mate, girlfriend, etc. using initials to differentiate individuals and noting the sex of those involved. The question 'what?' involved a description of the activity or discussion recorded the diarists' own categories. 'When?' involved reference to the timing of the activity, with special attention to recording the actual sequence of events. 'Where?' involved a designation of the location of the activity, suitably coded to prevent identification of individuals or place. The 'How?' involved a description of whatever logistics were entailed by the activity, e.g. how transport was secured, how marijuana was obtained. (Zimmerman and Wieder, 1975, pp. 15–16)

Of particular interest in their method is not just the rich documentation they gained about seven days of a person's life, but the fact that the person is subsequently interviewed step by step on each facet of the diary that has been presented.

The above three forms of diary – the requested, the log and the 'diary–diary interview' – all entail the social scientist soliciting diaries and are comparable to the social scientist soliciting life histories. But just as the life historian could also turn to pre-existing biographies to analyse, so the diary researcher could turn to pre-existing diaries. Hanlan's (1979) diary could throw light on dying, Cleaver's (1968) on racial oppression, Anne Frank's on adolescent growth and Nazi occupation, Crossland's on cabinet government (Howard, 1979) and Dharamsi's (1979) on a local authority children's home. In each case an original subjective story is told from which the social scientists could start to learn a great deal.

3 The Letter

Letters remain a relatively rare document of life in the social sciences. Without doubt, the most thoroughgoing use of letters is still to be found in Thomas and Znaniecki's *Polish Peasant* where on discovering that there was extensive correspondence between Poles and Polish emigrés to America, an advertisement was placed in a Chicago journal offering to pay between 10 to 20 cents for each letter received. Through this method they were able to gain many hundreds of letters, 764 of which are printed in the first volume of their study, totalling some 800 pages and arranged in fifty family sequences. Each sequence is prefaced with a commentary that introduces the family members and the main concerns. The letters, highly formal, are designated 'bowing letters' and exist primarily 'to manifest the persistence of familial solidarity in spite of separation' (p. 303). In addition to this, Thomas and Znaniecki suggest that the letters perform five main functions corresponding to five main types of letters. These are:

(1) Ceremonial letters – 'sent on such familial occurrences as normally require the presence of all the members of the family – weddings, christenings, funerals, Christmas, New Year, Easter. These letters are substitutes for ceremonial speeches.'

(2) Informing letters – providing 'a detailed narration of the life of the absent member of the family group'.

(3) Sentimental letters – which have 'the task of reviving the feelings in the individual, independently of any ceremonial occasion'.

(4) Literary letters – which have a central aesthetic function, and

(5) Business letters – (cf. Thomas and Znaniecki, 1958).

The letters are used inductively to arrive at a more general characterisation of peasant society, particularly its subjective aspects. It remains to this day the most detailed use of letters, and an example is given below. Since 'The Series' is too long to reproduce, I have selected an extract from a concluding section on 'fragments'.

Demoralization of a wife in the absence of her husband. The latter in spite of his emigration, shows more familial feeling, even with regard to the children, than the wife. The letter tends to establish a solidary relation between the husband and the rest of the family as against the wife.)

'Praised be Jesus Christus.'. . .
And now, dear father, what does all this mean that you write me? Why does my wife not wish to come to America, and writes me such stupid things that I am [illegible word] with her? I have sent her a shipticket for all, and she writes me such silly things and is not ashamed of it. When I sent the ticket I sent for all, and not for her alone. Could I leave the children? My heart does not allow me to leave my own children. Then, dear father, if she does not wish to listen it will end badly for her. Dear father, bow to her [ironically] and take the children to yourself, and I will send you directly two hundred roubles for the children, and let her do as she pleases. And if not, then give this shipticket to [sister] Kostka. Let Kostka come with this ticket. She has only to give the name and the age of my wife. Let her come with the children, and when Kostusia [Kostka] comes we will do well together, and my wife, as she was a public woman, so may she remain a public woman. And if the children fear to go, please, father take them to your home; I will send you 200 roubles. Let her not make a fool of me in America, as if I were her servant; this is neither right nor necessary. When someone read me that letter of hers, finally I did not let him finish, because I was ashamed.

If nobody comes with this ticket, I will get the money back and will send it directly to you, father, for the children. And if not, let Kostusia come alone if the children don't want to come.

(B. Leszczyc).

Another vivid use of letters in social science is to be found in Gordon Allport's editing and interpreting of the *Letters from Jenny*, (Allport, 1965). These letters were written by an ageing woman to two friends of her son – Isabel and Glenn – between 1926 and her death in 1937. As Jenny is thwarted by everything around her – especially by her son – and totters from one deep despair to another, she takes time out to write it all down and post it to these remote friends. They rarely meet and the whole story unfolds as a dramatic first person narrative. The readers can tease their way into Jenny's obsessive relationship with her son, into her crises, into her changing reconstructions of things written earlier, to an increasingly predictable series of 'resigned' moments, even happy ones, followed by a long slump into what she calls her 'slough of despond'. The vividness of the letters derives from the way they report life as it happens – each dreadful anxiety is shared with the letter's recipient. And all the way through, too, we get glimpses of the wider social world; she works for some time in a children's home and captures in her letters the appalling conditions where she has to be 'a whipper, a common spanker of little children, a beast, a cur for fifty dollars a month' (p. 32); she ends up her days in an old people's home where she initially feels 'wonderfully well' (p. 97) and finally cries how she is 'hungry to death for a little human companionship' (p. 130).

The case of Frank Moore, an institutionalised alcoholic, in *Escape from Custody* (Strauss, 1974) differs from both the immigrant's and Jenny's letters in so far as the recipient in this case is the sociologist. For over twenty-five years Frank Moore corresponded directly with Robert Strauss about his experiences of drifting in and out of institutions, in and out of work and on and off alcohol dependency – 'the life of a wharf rat' as he puts it. Sometimes, as when he is treated on 'antabuse' to shake him off alcohol, the letters can carry a sense of optimism – 'this antabuse treatment, to my mind, affords the first real test with regards to any constructive treatment. I hope I shall be worthy of the opportunities this place seems to afford', he writes on 17 June.

Such writings indicate that many insights can be gained from the study of letters, yet these materials are only rarely to be found in social science. And in good part this may simply be due to the obvious fact that such letters are increasingly hard to come by – letter-writing appears to be a dying art, and even when letters are sent they are most commonly thrown away rather than stored and collected. Bundles of 300 or so letters from the same person to the same recipient (like Jenny's described above) must today be seen as relatively rare and exciting finds. And even when one recipient keeps all the letters, it is unlikely that both will so that even with the immigrants' letters only one side of the exchange was typically found (cf. Riley, 1963, p. 242). When letters are used these days, they tend to be letters that are written to magazines and newspapers or letters that are solicited by the researcher as in, for example, Nancy Friday's volumes on sexual fantasy (Friday, 1976).

Nevertheless, even when such letters are available, social scientists are likely to remain suspicious of their value on a number of scores. First, as Ponsonby remarks, 'letters may be said to have two parents, the writer and the recipient' (Ponsonby, 1923, p. 2). Consequently, every letter speaks not just of the writer's world, but also of the writer's perceptions of the recipient. The kind of story told shifts with the person who will read it – witness the different letters produced by Robert Burns to his mistress, his friends, his wife on the same day. The social scientist then should view a letter as an interactive product, always inquiring into the recipient's role. In all the studies described above this is largely a mystery; the recipients included unknown family members, a sociologist and two remote friends. What would the stories told look like if the letters had been sent to other recipients: if the Polish peasants wrote to the sociologist, if Frank Moore wrote to remote friends, and Jenny wrote to her family! They would surely look very different indeed.

Another worry about letters concerns what Webb *et al.* referred to as the 'dross rate' (Webb *et al.*, 1966, p. 105). Letters are not generally focused enough to be of analytic interest – they contain far too much material that strays from the researcher's concern. Thus Allport acknowledges that he has cut Jenny's letters down by two-thirds (Allport, 1965, p. vi), presumably because they otherwise would have produced unmanageably boring and repetitive ramblings that would be of little value to social science. Yet of course in cutting out this dross rate, Allport may also be engaged in selecting Jenny's ideas to focus upon issues that interest him. A form of hidden censorship and selective screening may be taking place.

4   'Vox Populi' and Guerrilla Journalism

When many lives are recorded in less depth than life histories, and offered to the reader with little commentary, we can speak of 'guerrilla journalism' – a term coined by one of the leading exponents of this method, Studs Terkel, for himself. Terkel's great skill lies in simply getting people to talk into his recorder: in *Hard Times* they tell of the Depression, in *Division Street: America* they tell of city life in Chicago, in *American Dreams* they talk of aspiration and change in America, and, most celebratedly, in *Working*, 130 Americans speak of their jobs, the violence it does to them and their 'search for daily meaning as well as daily bread' (Terkel, 1968, 1970, 1977, 1978, 1981). Characteristically, this style of work – with its affinity to the naturalistic novels of Zola, the voices to be found in Mayhew, and the reportage of Agee and Evans in *Let Us Now Praise Famous Men* – shuns any claims to being theoretical or scientific: the search for criteria of adequacy like those given by Dollard are of no concern. Thus, Terkel comments in the opening of his oral documentation of city life in Chicago:

Being neither a sociologist nor a research man, motivational or otherwise, I followed no blueprint or book or set of statistics. I played hunches – in some instances, long shots . . . I was on the prowl for a cross section of urban thought, using no one method or technique . . . I realised quite early in this adventure that interviews, conventionally conducted, were meaningless. (Terkel, 1968, pp. 19–21)

Terkel listens, records, transcribes and then publishes, with the minimum of comment and the maximum of content. Whether what the people say is valid is left to the reader, although Terkel's memoirs *Talking to Myself* provide personal accounts of some of the interviews (Terkel, 1978) and elsewhere he has briefly commented on his method (Grele, 1975).

Terkel is far from alone in this style of work. In England, for instance, Jeremy Sandford, Jeremy Seabrook, Ronald Blythe and Tony Parker have all written widely through the voices of others – *The View in Winter* (a study in old age by Ronald Blythe, 1979), *A Lasting Relationship* (a study of homosexuality by Jeremy Seabrook, 1976) or *The Twisting Lane* (a study of sex offenders by Tony Parker, 1969) being good examples. Again no claims to 'social science' are made: 'This is an unscientific study by an untrained observer of an insufficiently understood problem', says Tony Parker at the start of his life history of Charlie Smith – *The Unknown Citizen* (1963) – and one suspects the self depreciation only just masks a healthy sneer at those proper social scientists who spend all their time debating 'the logic of methodology' and 'epistemological breaks' in their ivory towers without ever doing any first-hand talking.

5 Oral History

Closely allied to this tradition has been the development of oral history in the postwar period. It is, of course, no new approach – being as old as history itself – but it is only since the 1940s (with the work of Allan Neins at Columbia University) that an oral history movement has emerged around tape recordings, with its own organisations (The Oral History Association was established in America in 1966 and had 1,300 active members within a decade; The Oral History Society was established in 1970, and had some 600 members by 1980), its own journals (like *Oral History* in England, and the *International Journal of Oral History* established in 1980), and a vast outpouring of research – in 1977 there were some 600 projects in America alone. Much of this oral history work has recently been collated and reviewed in Paul Thompson's *The Voice of the Past* (1978).

It was too recent a period for a satisfactory range of more personal documents to have reached the county record offices. I wanted to know what it was like to be a child or parent at that time; how young people met and courted; how they lived together as husbands and wives; how they found jobs and moved between them; how they felt about work; how they saw their employers and fellow workers; how they survived and felt when out of work; how class consciousness varied between city, country and occupations. None of these questions seemed answerable from conventional historical sources . . . (Thompson, 1978, p. 78)

Thompson's own research, with Thea Vigne (Thompson) on Edwardian England, required the collection of original data. Some 500 Edwardians were interviewed and their recollections gathered in detail. Of course, when the sample becomes so large, and the final study so interwoven with the researchers' comments, we have come a long way from the in-depth case histories associated with Chicago. Others have, however, used oral history in focusing upon one in-depth life. The story of Arthur Harding details life and crime in East London from the end of the nineteenth century (Samuel, 1981) while Kiki tells the life history of a New Guinea politician who was born with a semi-nomadic 'Stone Age' tribe, 'had gone through the dramatic initiation rites of Orokolo, had managed to get an education, had been to Fiji, had qualified as a pathologist, had become a patrol officer, had gone into politics' (Kiki, 1968). As this study's sub-title suggests, we have here 'ten thousand years in a lifetime'.

Despite the growth of oral history, it is viewed by many historians as marginal, suspect and trivial: marginal because it is always limited to the distinctly 'modern' sphere and accessible people; suspect because old folk's tales are likely to say more about the present than the past; and trivial because it indiscriminately amasses mountains of data that will 'never be of use to anyone' (Stewart, 1977). Indeed, Thompson notes how the Social Science Research Council in England has embarked upon 'an openly hostile policy of "containment"' (Thomspon, 1978, p. 60).

6 'The Literature of Fact'

One curious breed of life document, wholly neglected by the social scientist, is the writing which takes on the form of a fictional novel but which is dealing with true events fully researched by the author. Such an approach has a long history – Defoe's *A Journal of the Plague Year* is often cited as an early example – but it gained prominence in America in the postwar period, notably with the publication of Truman Capote's *In Cold Blood* (1966). For this 'murder story' Capote researched a notorious slaying of an entire family by two young men, who were subsequently caught, tried and executed. Whilst the story unfolds, the reader is aware that this is fact not fiction. Yet it is produced with the skill of an artist, not that of the scientist.

It is hard to pinpoint the boundaries of this under-used form of document despite several recent attempts to do so (see Zavarzadeh, 1976, Berger, 1977 and Weber, 1981). It seems to incorporate all those studies which are clearly literary and humanistic but which deal with researched fact rather than fiction. Sometimes this genre can be made to embrace the tradition of oral interview, such as the work of Studs Terkel or the journalist and war correspondent John Hersey whose *Hiroshima* provides six interviews with atomic bomb survivors (1972); sometimes it is signposted as a highly subjective account by an observing writer – Agee's personal tale of share-croppers in the Mid-West during the Depression is a classic here (1965); sometimes the social scientist is actually seen to exemplify it – Oscar Lewis's work for example, is frequently cited; and most commonly it is associated with the literature of Truman Capote and Norman Mailer. There is clearly no firm boundary to this style of work except that it all manages to weave a literary (and literate!) tale around detailed research and analysis of a real life event. It could well assume increasing prominence in the years to come.

7   The Photograph

If diaries and letters became central life documents (as least in the middle classes) during the nineteenth century, they have now been rapidly overtaken by photography. Born at approximately the same time as sociology, photography has gone on to become many things: the democratiser of personal documents (in family albums and holiday shots for all), a major new genre of art, the embodiment of individualism (in the rise of photographic portraiture), a mode of refusing experience, a strategy for conveying immortality upon experience, and last but not least, a form of surveillance and control (cf. Sontag, 1978). Millions of photographs are produced by lay person and professional alike each year, but still sociology remains relatively unscathed by it. It is true that in the earliest days of the *American Journal of Sociology*, photographs were a regular feature in connection with its muck-raking, reformist articles: between 1896 and 1916 thirty-one articles used 244 photographs (see Stasz, 1979a). Likewise many of the early Chicago studies – Thrasher's *The Gang*, for example – included an array of photographs. But in the main sociologists have not taken much interest in what should now be viewed as a major tool for investigation; the lead has primarily come from anthropologists (and in particular the pioneer-ing work of Gregory Bateson and Margaret Mead (1942) who provided a volume devoted entirely to photographic images from the culture of the Balinese, or from journalistic photographers (such as Jacob A. Riis's visual depiction of impoverished styles in New York City's slums (Riis, 1971), and the work of the photojournalists (such as National Press Photographers Association, 1978). It was only during the 1970s that a small group of American sociologists became concerned about its use, organised exhibitions of their photographic work, and coined the term 'visual sociology'.

There are many ways in which photography could be put to work for sociology. Curry and Clark (1977) suggest it may serve as an illustration, as visual information or as source material for analysis, whilst Wagner (1979, pp. 16–19) suggests five modes of photographic research: as interview stimuli, for systematic recordings of social phenomena, for sustained content analysis, for 'native' image making and for 'narrative visual theory'.

Perhaps the most obvious use to date is that of the photograph as documentation – an essentially descriptive task where the photo is designed simply to illustrate a text. Thus, Weinberg and Williams's (1974, p. 50) study of male homosexuals includes a number of photographs of the homosexual communities they studied, providing visual reinforcement to their more wordy descriptions, and Jacobs's (1974) photographs of a retirement community capture the cleanliness and desolation revealed in the ethnographic text. This is an unextraordinary, unremarkable but surprisingly uncommon way in which photographs could be used. This 'documentary tradition' can also be extended to book-length studies. Michael Lesy's *Wisconsin Death Trip* (1973) illustrates the approach. Fortuitously, he gained access to some 3,000 glass negatives taken by a small-town photographer between 1890 and 1910 which, while formally posed, nevertheless represented the ordinary 'events these people, or people like them, once experienced'. Small-town life, the Great Depression, massive incipient change, religion, disease, death: the photos capture vividly these and other themes conveying in one complex image what would take thousands of words to capture. Interspersed with the full-page photographs are direct textual quotations – newspapers, novels, madhouse records of the period – which, taken all together, 'recreate a re-vision of a past time so separated from the present by the cunning sleights of the fearful memories of one human lifetime, that to recall, reveal and recreate such a past is as difficult as driving a tunnel through a granite mountain to the sea' (Lesy, 1973). It is a startling work, and, like most mentioned in this study, has to be 'read' for its substance: I cannot start to do it justice. Yet it signposts a new tradition for personal documents, one that Lesy himself followed further, three years later, in his *Real Life: Louisville in the Twenties*, another rich photographic essay. Lesy's books also illustrate the possibility of gaining a much closer relationship between document and theory, for the photos are fully linked in with the text. They do not merely illustrate: they integrate.

The model for this kind of work is revealed in the classic 1930s' study of average – and thereby poor – white families of tenant farmers in the Southern States of America: *Let Us Now Praise Famous Men* by James Agee and Walker Evans. Here Agee, no sociologist, spent time absorbed in the lives of the tenant families whilst Evans (later to be famed for his *American Photographs* (1938) produces the first volume of the study with photographs of places, objects and people. As Agee says, 'The photographs are not illustrative. They, and the text, are co-equal, mutually independent, and fully collaborative' (p. xiii). A more recent example of collaboration is Marsden and Duff's work (1974) on the unemployed in England in the early 1970s, *Workless* – a study which was initiated as a photographic work to which the text was to be complementary but where the written word become more important (indeed, the photos were dropped from the second edition).

A few sociologists have taken this further through 'narrative visual theory', where the 'implicit elements of social theory are clearly acknowledged' (Wagner, 1979, p. 18). Here the photos are systematically selected through a tacit theory – Jackson looks at prison life (1977, 1978), and Harper looks at tramps (1978). They come close to being ethnographies which instead of relying upon the written word become organised through visual imagery. In this view, the task is to theorise through photography (cf. Becker, 1974).

A further way in which photos may be used by social scientists is as a resource for further explanations. Thus Thompson (1974) was able to interview respondents through photos of the My Lai massacre, and in Banish's work on *City Families* (1976) the technique was to combine interview with photography. This researcher first visited selected families in order to take photographs of them as they wished to see themselves and then returned both to talk about the photographs, to ask which was their favourite and to interview them about their hopes and aspirations in life. The study is composed of the preferred photographs on one page matched with the interviews and observations on the opposite page. Of added interest in this study is the range of families studied and the contrasts drawn between the families of two cities: London and Chicago.

From this comes one of the most apparent methods for using photographs in social science: to ask the respondent for a look at their family albums (cf. Musello, 1979). In a most striking way, all manner of details about childhood relationships, friendship, family rituals and family history are highlighted. The sociologist who opts for this kind of approach needs to be attuned to the problems of reading photography. In a general study of photography Akeret coins the term 'photoanalysis' and suggests the following useful scheme of questions to be asked:

What is your immediate impression [of the photograph]? Who

and what do you see? What is happening in the photo? Is the background against which the photo was taken of any significance, either real or symbolic? What feelings does it evoke in you? What do you notice about physical intimacy or distance? Are people touching physically? How are they touching? How do the people in the photo feel about their bodies? Are they using their bodies to show them off, to hide behind, to be seductive, are they proud of their bodies, ashamed? What do you notice about the emotional state of each person? Is he: shy, compliant, aloof, proud, fearful, mad, suspicious, introspective, superior, confused, happy, anxious, angry, weak, pained, suffering, bright, curious, sexy, distant ... Can you visualise how those emotions are expressed in facial dynamics and body movement? If there is more than one person in the photo what do you notice about the group mood? Is there harmony or chaos? How do the people relate? Are they tense or relaxed? What are their messages towards each other? Who has the power, the grace? Do you see love present? What do you notice about the various parts of each person? Look carefully at the general body posture and then the hands, the legs, the arms, the face, the eyes, the mouth. What does each part tell you? Are the parts harmonious or are there inconsistencies? Pay particular attention to the face, always the most expressive part of the person. Learn to read any photo as you would read a book from left to right then downwards. Go over it again and again, each time trying to pick out something you have missed. Ask yourself more general questions, as many as you can think of. What is obvious and what is subtle? What is the sense of movement or is there any? What memories and experiences does the photo stir in you? How do you identify with the people in the photo? How are you alike, how different? What moves you most about the photo? What do you find distasteful about it? Is there anything that disturbs you? Try to define the social and economic class of the people photographed. What is their cultural background? If it is a family, would you want to be a member of it? Would you want your children to play with theirs? If the photos are personal – of you, your family, friends or associates – try to remember the exact circumstances of the photo session. How have you changed since then? How have you remained the same? (Akeret, 1973, pp. 35–6)

The list, concludes Akeret, could be endless, but his questions are primarily geared towards psychological interpretations rather than cultural ones. A most useful tool for sociologists would be to tease family albums and photographs of respondents through a series of sociological problems.

8 Film

If social scientists have only occasionally considered the benefits of photography to their work, most have never countenanced the significance of film. Yet with improvement in film technology, the rise in videotaping and the relative drop in costs, film-making is fast becoming a hobby and interest open to many: the photograph album will probably be replaced by the video selection in many Western homes by the end of the century. Here should be the ethnographer's dream: life as it is lived accurately recorded as it happens, and constantly available for playback and analysis (see Gottdiener, 1980). There will be problems, for sure, but it is a most remarkable resource which could change the face of social science out of all recognition in the next few decades.

Documentary film makers have provided historians with much fodder for analysis but it is anthropologists who have been most adept at exploiting this medium to date. At the start of the century, ethnographers started to film various tribal peoples engaged in social rituals – Spencer, in 1901, filmed Australian aborigines in kangaroo dances and rain ceremonies, while in 1914 Curtis filmed the Kwakiutl Indians. But the birth of the documentary film is commonly agreed to be Robert Flaherty's (1922) *Nanook of the North* about Eskimo life. Flaherty, a compassionate romantic appalled by the dehumanisation of modern technology (cf. Calder-Marshall, 1963), lived in Eskimo country for eleven years, and shot his film under the most adverse conditions on the life of one specific individual – Nanook. In this film he reveals the constant struggle for life in a hostile environment. Sensitively, the power of the image is left behind:

One of Flaherty's most successful visual techniques was to follow an exotic act visually, showing it step by step as it developed, not explaining it in words. In one sequence of *Nanook* we see Nanook tugging on a line leading into a hole in the ice. We are engaged in that act, and think about it. Eventually, the suspense is broken: our questions are answered when Nanook pulls out a seal. Flaherty creates the same visual involvement when Nanook makes the igloo – especially at the end of the sequence, when Nanook cuts a slab of ice for a window, sets it in place, and fixes a snow slab reflector along one side. For a time we are puzzled and, therefore, involved. But when Nanook steps back, finished, we understand. (Heider, 1976, p. 24)

In its original form, Flaherty's film and his others – *Moana, Man of Aran, The Land* and *Louisiana Story* – were silent, and most that followed until the early 1960s lacked synchronous sound. For

Heider, *Dead Birds* (1961) about the Dani marks the watershed of ethnographic film; thereafter synchronic sound enabled people to talk about their lives as well as simply living them on film: Robert Gardner's Ethiopian film *Rivers of Sand* takes a Hamar woman relaxing before the camera and speaking about her life, with shots interspersed to illustrate her commentary. Heider concludes his review by suggesting that since 1963 ethnographic film has become 'institutionalised, bureaucratised and established' (p. 44), reviews of films being a regular feature of the *American Anthropologist* since 1965, and a special organisation, The Society for the Anthropology of Visual Communication, emerging in 1973 with its own journal. Film is now accepted as an integral part of the anthropologist's armoury of tools.

This is far from the case in sociology. There have been a few attempts, such as Morin's work with Rouch on Parisians talking about the summer of 1960 (the Algerian War dominated) in *Chronicles of a Summer*, but in the main sociologists have either ignored the medium or used the documentaries created by film makers, like those of Frederick Wiseman.

Frederick Wiseman's films perhaps come closest to embodying sociological concerns: most deal directly with the ways in which individuals throughout their hierarchies cope (or fail to) with the day-to-day pressures of social institutions. As he puts it:

> What I'm aiming at is a series on American institutions, using the word 'institutions' to cover a series of activities that take place in a limited geographical area with a more or less consistent group of people being involved. I want to use film technology to have a look at places like high schools, hospitals, prisons, and police, which seems to be very fresh material for film; I want to get away from the typical documentary where you follow one charming person or one Hollywood star around. I want to make films where the institutions will be the star but will also reflect larger issues in general society. (in Rosenthal, 1971, p. 69)

Hence his 'documents' treat not 'lives' but 'institutions' – the police in *Law and Order* (1969), hospitals for the criminally insane in *The Titicut Follies* (1969), army life in *Basic Training* (1971) as well as films on *Welfare, High School* and *Hospital*. For Wiseman, it is blindingly obvious that all such films are 'subjective' documents – how could it be otherwise? Yet they are 'fair': honest, worked at, not driven by ideological commitment, desirous of showing that people are much the same in their daily struggles and 'very suspicious of people who can make ... glib classifications, whatever that classification may be, and wherever it may fall politically' (Wiseman, 1971,

p. 325). These concerns – for disciplined subjectivity and humanistic impartiality – are the hallmarks of life documents.

9 A Miscellanea

So far I have produced a simple catalogue of life documents, but the listing could go on. Some researchers, for example, have made use of the inscriptions on tombstones (Warner, 1959 and Woltemade, 1976, cited in Curry and Clarke, 1977), while others have scrutinised suicide notes showing how they provide 'an unsolicited account of the victim's thoughts and emotions regarding his intended act, and often, what he felt was responsible for it' (Schwartz and Jacobs, 1979, pp. 156–67). Others have shown the diversity of 'Documentary Expression' (cf. Stott, 1973). To conclude this section, therefore, I would like to raise just two final sources that could prove helpful: (i) possessions and (ii) self observation.

What a person owns, or fails to own, can serve both as a useful indicator of lifestyle and, when combined with an interview especially, can act as a remarkable memory jogger. To grasp the significance of this, conduct a little experiment on yourself. Simply move around your house or room, inspecting each item you have purchased or have been given as a present. Ponder the circumstances in your life that led to you getting this 'possession' – your interests and friends, where you were at the time, what's happened to it since, your feelings towards it then and now. A bookcase or a record collection is a goldmine of biographical incidents – many items may have been acquired randomly and have little history, but many others will speak to hugely complex stories. Rummaging through attics can be particularly rewarding and, on occasions, as Hughes has shown, dustbins are not without a tale to tell (cf. Webb *et al.,* 1966, p. 41).

A classic illustration of this concern is the systematic examination of the possessions of fourteen poor families living in a Mexico City slum, by Oscar Lewis (1969). As he puts it:

The inquiry opens up a mine of interesting questions. What proportions of their income do poor people spend on furniture, on clothing, on religious objects, on luxury items, on medicines? How much of what they buy is new? How much second hand? To what extent do they depend on gifts or hand me downs? How do families in poverty finance their purchases? Where do they do their shopping? How wide are their choices? What is the physical condition of their possessions? How long do they manage to hold on to them? I was able to obtain rather detailed information on all these matters. (Lewis, 1970, p. 442)

His analysis considers thirteen categories of possession and does provide a number of interesting insights. For instance, all the poor families had at least one shelf for religious ornaments, but this was the only category of possessions where the poorer families had spent more than the better off.

Another sorely neglected source is systematic self-observation. Freud, of course, left a model for doing this in *The Interpretation of Dreams* (1976), and many linguists and child psychologists have taken their own children and families as basic units of study, creating detailed documents about them. But it is comparatively rare for sociologists to explicitly do this, even though Znaniecki argued the case for such work nearly fifty years ago (cf. 1934, ch. IV).

> When I wish to ascertain at first hand what a certain activity is . . . I try to experience it. There is only one way of experiencing an object; it is to *observe* it personally. There is only one way of experiencing an activity; it is to *perform* it personally. Practical men insist on this: they will tell you that you cannot fully realise what they are doing till you do it yourself. Scientists have come to recognise this . . . (Znaniecki, 1934. p. 49)

Somehow our scientific work is taken less seriously if it is known to be based on personal experience. Yet, given the argument of this book on the need to grasp subjective worlds, this method of self-documentation must be one of the most critical of all tools. We can never *really* know another's world, we might *just* know our own. And certainly, in the past, sociologists have used their own experiences. Anderson came from a hobo family and this informed much of his research for his monograph *The Hobo* (1961) a fact he concealed till much later (cf. Anderson, 1975, p. 170). Riemer (1977) calls it 'opportunistic research' and lists over twenty such researchers. Yet, in the main, such a strategy is concealed. As Jack Douglas says:

> I know of any number of studies in which the author's fundamental way of knowing the things he [sic] reports was through direct personal involvement, a fact that has been carefully hidden from the readers because revealing it would stigmatise him as a creep, a weirdo or maybe even a criminal. In all instances I know of, these sociologists have been unhappy that they felt it necessary to do this and in each case with which I am familiar they have not lied. They have merely evaded the issue. (Douglas, 1976, p. xiii)

Maybe the time has come to stop the evasion, and for sociologists to record and document their personal experiences systematically. If

Freud can turn his dreams into a masterpiece of understanding, why shouldn't other social scientists?

Conclusion

Imagine another research text that huddled together in one chapter an outline of surveys, questionnaires, interviews, attitude scaling, participant observation and a few other common research techniques! The result would be laughable: we know too much about these methods for them to be discussed in such brief terms – most frequently whole volumes would be devoted to each method. Yet in this chapter I have been deliberately wide-ranging: from photography and film through diaries and oral history to self-analysis and letters. My intent, therefore, was not to be comprehensive but merely suggestive. For here are a whole battery of research tools, widely ignored and neglected in both research texts and courses, which have enormous potential for exploring concrete social experience in humanistic fashion. They can be put together in various combinations – from the simple 'vox populi' transcription to the dense amalgamation of life history, letters, diaries, photography and observation. They may deal with only one 'case' (a biography like *Jane Fry*) or many (as in Banish's collection of family portraits). They may be created by the sociologist (as in 'the diary–diary interview') or simply raw materials to be used by him or her (as in Jenny's letters). They may be focused on a life, an occupation, a problem, an institution. They may be used by historians, sociologists, psychologists, anthropologists, literati, linguistic and political scientists. They are powerful yet neglected tools; and in the two chapters to follow I hope to show both their intellectual justification and their practical value.

Suggestions for Further Reading

For discussions of the approach of different disciplines to personal documents the following sources are useful. S. Paul's *Begegnungen* (1979) is a two-volume, 954-page comprehensive review which is at present untranslated into English. On **anthropology**, both C. Kluckhohn's 'Personal document in anthropological science' (1942) and L. Langness's *The Life History in Anthropological Science* (1965) provide detailed overviews and references. On **history**, see L. Gottschalk, 'The historian and the historical document' (1942), and C. Pitt, *Using Historical Sources in Anthropology and Sociology* (1972). On **psychology**, the classic text is G. Allport's, *The Use of Personal Documents in Psychological Science* (1942). On **sociology**, the early work of R. Angell, 'A critical review of the development of the personal document method in sociology 1920–1940' (1942) summarises many studies during the earlier decades of this century, while there has been a recent revival of interest in this source to be found in qualitative methods textbooks. In particular, see M. D. Shipman (1972), *The Limitations of Social Research* (ch. 8), R. Bogdan and S. J. Taylor, *Introduction to Qualitative Research Methods* (1975), N. K. Denzin, *The Research Act* (1978) and H. Schwartz and J. Jacobs, *Qualitative Sociology: A Method to the Madness* (1979).

On the **life history** method in particular, the earliest book-length study is J. Dollard's *Criteria for the Life History* (1935) which sets out criteria for the appraisal of life histories and applies them to a number of cases (see Chapter 3 for a summary of this.) Subsequent overviews and commentaries are those by H. S. Becker in his introduction to C. Shaw's, *The Jack Roller* (1966 edition) which is reprinted in his *Sociological Work* (1971); Denzin's work cited above (1978); A. Faraday and K. Plummer's 'Doing life histories' (1979) which overviews the literature briefly and has a discussion of the ethics involved in a particular study; and D. Bertaux's *Biography and Society* (1981) which contains papers dealing with epistemology, recent uses of 'life stories' and the role of life histories as historical data.

Diaries have received relatively little discussion, although Allport (1942) and Denzin (1978) both consider them. V. Palmer's early text *Field Studies in Sociology* (1928) devotes a chapter to them, and they are mentioned in M. Riley's *Sociological Research* (1963). All these treatments, however, are very brief, and only Zimmerman and Wieder's 'The diary–diary interview method' (1977) provides a sustained methodological discussion of its use (but this is related to one specific study). Of more general value, therefore, are the literary studies. The classic here is A. Ponsonby's *English Diaries* (1923), and a more recent study is R. A. Fothergill's *Private Chronicles* (1974). These studies give many illustrations of literary diary writing.

Letters get even scantier treatment, and so the reader is advised to look at the three studies mentioned in this chapter: W. I. Thomas and F. Znaniecki's *The Polish Peasant* (1958), G. Allport, *Letters from Jenny* (1965) and R. Strauss, *Escape from Custody* (1974). In addition, see the letters of William Tanner in J. Spradley, *You owe yourself a drunk* (1970).

On **'guerrilla' journalism'** and 'oral testimony', see the interviews and commentaries with practitioners in R. Grele's (1975) *Envelopes of Sound* as well as the brief comments in many of the introductions to the volumes which use the method. Tony Parker's work includes *The Courage of his Convictions* (1962), the story of Robert Allerton (tape-recorded over six months) and telling of a violent working-class recidivist who at 33 has nine convictions, spent twelve and a half years in prison, and espouses high moral principles; *The Unknown Citizen* (1963) which tells the story (partly in the form of an essay) of 'Charlie Smith' who has spent nearly all his life in institutions; *A Man of Good Abilities* (1967) which includes many letters and tells of a middle-class criminal, Norman Edwards; *Five Women* (1965) which provides the voice of five female criminals, and *The Twisting Lane* (1969) on sex offenders. His work remained prolific throughout the 1970s with studies of lighthouse keepers, unmarried mothers, prison life and so forth, and has often been adapted for television documentaries. Jeremy Seabrook's work is no less prolific, though he seems less happy about using tape-recorders and often deals with more people. He treats issues of social class and urban deprivation particularly well, and often combines his work with photography. For examples, see *The Unprivileged* (1967), *City Close Up* (1971) and *Loneliness* (1973).

The work in **oral history** is vast and I have treated it skimpily because there is now an excellent volume discussing it and providing a comprehensive bibliography of work in this field: P. Thompson's *The Voice of the Past* (1978). For updating and regular information see the two journals, *Oral History* (available from the Department of Sociology, University of Essex, UK) and the *International Journal of Oral History*. Three studies of value published as I am completing this book are T. Thompson's *Edwardian Childhoods* (1981), S. Humphries' *Hooligans or Rebels* (1981) and R. Samuel's *East End Underworld: Chapters in the Life of Arthur Harding* (1981). The latter promises a sequel which is to include a discussion of method.

'The **Literature of Fact**' on 'non-fiction novel' is an ill-defined and amorphous area, but one which could well be developed by social scientists. Literature students have recently started to analyse its form, notably M. Berger's *Real and Imagined Worlds* (1977), M. Zavarzadeh's *The Mythopoeic Reality* (1976), A. Borenstein's *Redeeming the Sin* (1978), and R. Weber's *The Literature of Fact* (1981). The latter is particularly useful in analysing some examples including the work of Capote, Mailer, Agee, Hersey and Wicker.

On **photography**, three helpful general accounts are those by J. Berger (1972), *Ways of Seeing*, S. Sontag (1978), *On Photography*, and F. Webster (1980) *The New Photography*. The central texts on photography in sociology are: J. Collier's *Visual Anthropology* (1967) which discusses the photographer as participant observer and reviews the history of its use; T. Curry and A. Clarke's *Introducing Visual Sociology* (1977) is a short introductory text with a 'workbook' attached, and a useful bibliography; J. Wagner's (1979) anthology *Images of Information* is a wide-ranging and useful set of readings showing many of the problems involved in using photos in research and teaching. Two journals are of particular value in including photographic studies: *Studies in the Anthropology of Visual Communication* and *Qualitative Sociology*. In England see also the magazine *Camerawork*. More recent methods textbooks are including sections on photography – H. Schwartz and J. Jacobs' *Qualitative Sociology* (1979, pp. 81–103) is an example. Finally, a major figure in the use of photography is Howard Becker whose key article 'Photography and sociology' (1974) discusses issues of sampling and theory while reviewing many studies. A shorter discussion by Becker is 'Do photographs tell the truth?' (1979).

The most comprehensive study of ˌfilm in anthropology is K. G. Heider's *Ethnographic Film* (1976) which provides a brief history, a catalogue of films, a discussion of both making films and using them for teaching, and a long account of the attributes of such film. Heider has also compiled the catalogue *Films for Anthropological Teaching*, through various editions, obtainable from the American Anthropological Association, 1703 New Hampshire Avenue NW, Washington DC 20009. Reviews of films are now commonplace in the *American Anthropologist*. Short's (1981) collection of essays *Feature Films as History* provides analyses of the way films may be used by historians. On this see also K. Short and R. Fidelius, *Film and History* (1980), P. Sorlin, *The Film in History: Restaging the Past*, as well as the *Historical Journal of Film, Radio and Television* (cited in K. Short, 1981, p. 36). On documentary film, see the early study by Grierson (Hardy's

Grierson on Documentary, 1946), and the more recent studies by G. Roy Levin *Documentary Explorations* (1971) and M. Barsam *Non Fiction Film: A Critical History* (1974). For a useful listing of 'realist' films and their distributors (as well as a critical analysis and good bibliography), see C. Williams, *Realism and the Cinema* (1980). On Wiseman's work, see Atkins (1976).

On the use of video, see M. Gottdiener, 'Field reseach and video tape' (1980).

On more unorthodox methods, the standard source is E. Webb *et al.*, *Unobtrusive Measures* (1966) and a more recent volume is L. Sechrest, *Unobtrusive Measurement Today* (1979). There is much too in H. Schwartz and J. Jacobs, *Qualitative Sociology* (1979). On the role of personal experience, see F. Znaniecki, *The Method of Sociology* (1934, ch. IV) for an early and neglected statement; and more recently, see D. Bakan, *On Method* (1967), A. Dawe, 'The role of experience in the construction of social theory' (1973) and J. W. Riemer's 'Varieties of opportunistic research' (1977), which lists many relevant studies.

3

The Making of a Method

The danger in any survey of the past is lest we argue in a
circle and impute lessons to history which history has
never taught and historical research has never discovered –
lessons which are really inferences from the particular
organization that we have given to our knowledge. We
may believe in some doctrine of evolution or some idea of
progress and we may use this in our interpretation of the
history of centuries; but what our history contributes is not
evolution but rather the realization of how crooked and
perverse the ways of progress are, with what wilfulness and
waste it twists and turns, and takes anything but the straight
track to its goal, and how often it seems to go astray, and to
be deflected by any conjuncture, to return to us – if it does
return – by a back-door. We may believe in some
providence that guides the destiny of men and we may if we
like read this into our history; but what our history brings
to us is not proof of providence but rather the realization of
how mysterious are its ways, how strange its caprices – the
knowledge that this providence uses any means to get to its
end and works often at cross-purposes with itself and is
curiously wayward. Our assumptions do not matter if we
are conscious that they are assumptions, but the most
fallacious thing in the world is to organize our historical
knowledge upon an assumption without realizing what
we are doing, and then to make inferences from that
organization and claim that these are the voice of history.
(H. Butterfield, 1973, pp. 24–5)

During the nineteenth century both researchers and reformers – like
Mayhew, Booth and the Webbs – took a great interest in personal
documents, oral histories and life stories. At the turn of the century
these tools were gaining ascendancy in the newly evolving social
work, psychiatric professions and criminological professions (cf.
Bennett, 1982). But it was not until the publication of the massive
Chicago project, *The Polish Peasant in Europe and America*, by
William Isaac Thomas and Florian Znaniecki in 1958 that the
method gained a full and proper recognition within sociology.
  In this chapter my aim is to look at the significance of this book and

to locate it and the method it espoused firmly in time (the 1920s and 1930s), space (Chicago) and theory (symbolic interactionism).

Enter a Polish Peasant . . .

Sociology was scarcely thirty years old in America when the Thomas and Znaniecki work was published, and as Blumer remarks 'there is no doubt that in the 1920's and 1930's *The Polish Peasant* was viewed extensively in sociological circles as the finest exhibit of advanced sociological research and theoretical analysis' (1979, p. vi). It has indeed variously been called a 'monumental work', 'a classic', 'a milestone' and a 'turning point' (e.g. Allport, 1942, p. 18; Bruyn, 1966, p. 9). Today it is rarely read, rarely even mentioned, but it is not too difficult to see how these early superlatives came to be applied to it.

In sheer size, it must rank as one of the largest of sociological products; it was originally issued in five volumes and contained no less than 2,200 pages. Its manifest problematic was a central 'public issue' of the time: between 1899 and 1910, Poles had accounted for one quarter of all immigrants to the United States and indeed by 1914 Chicago, with its 360,000 Poles, ranked as the third largest Polish centre in the world (after Warsaw and Lödz). But, like any adequate sociological study, its concern lay not just with a specific social problem but with wider issues of social theory. Considered in its pages are the problems of individualisation (what are the forms of social organisation that allow for the greatest amount of individualism?); of community (what happens to the community and the family under conditions of rapid social change?); of abnormality (how far is abnormality the unavoidable manifestation of inborn tendencies of the individual and how far is it due to social conditions?); of the relations between the sexes (how is the general social efficiency of a group affected by the various systems of relations between man and woman?); and, a problem still much neglected to this day, the issue of social happiness. (See Thomas and Znaniecki, 1958, pp. 78–86 especially.)

Of equal importance was their methodological position, most of which is found in the introductory 'Methodological notes', written largely by Znaniecki, after their empirical work was completed (see Znaniecki, 1934). Apart from their general claim that sociology should be 'an inductive, analytic, classificatory, and nomothetic science' (Blumer, 1979, p. 90), they notably took a middle position on the two debates which have dominated sociology since its inception. The first concerns the relationship between the individual and the social: unlike Durkheim's famous dictum to treat social facts as things, Thomas and Znaniecki advocated a position in which both individual and social factors must always be taken into account in any social study. Their dictum, now largely forgotten, states that '*the cause of a social or individual phenomenon is never another social or individual phenomenon alone, but always a combination of a social and an individual phenomenon*' (Thomas and Znaniecki, Vol. 1, 1958, p. 44). In the text they illustrate this with reference to two brothers who have a tyrannical father; a good son who tends to be submissive to the father and a bad son who tends to revolt against the father. The response here is a combination of two different factors: the tyranny of the father remains constant, but the interpretation that the boys have towards him varies. Thus for one boy there is a sense of family solidarity while for the other boy there is a tendency to self assertion. This leads them to the important distinction (which now runs right through sociology) between the *objective* factors of the situation and the *subjective* interpretation of that situation. For them, *both* issues must always be taken into account. Blumer, interpreting Thomas and Znaniecki, puts this well:

In any and every instance of social action . . . the acting individual or group has to deal with a set of outside circumstances, particularly a set of group rules as to how to act; these circumstances and social rules constitute the objective setting of the given line of action. At the same time, the actor approaches these objective conditions with a set of subjective dispositions such as wishes, appetites, hopes, fear, aversions, intentions and plans. Social action, or what people do, results in a combination of the objective condition and the subjective disposition; that is to say that a person acts towards something that has a group meaning (the objective factor) yet he acts towards that thing in response to how he feels about it and how he sizes it up (the subjective factor). Thomas and Znaniecki lump all the subjective factors under the central concept of 'attitudes' and the objective conditions under the central concept of 'values'. (Blumer, 1979, p. ix)

All these features amplified as they are in considerable detail, should be enough to provide interest in the study. But it is a combination of all of this with an intensive use of human documents that is its major claim to fame, for throughout the volume there is sustained the most thoroughgoing use of personal documents to be found in the social sciences. These personal documents fall roughly into five main groups: the use of letters – the greater part of one volume consists of 764 separate letters arranged into fifty series; a major life history statement by one Polish peasant, Wladek, which, while it runs into 300 pages, is abridged from a larger version, and may be only one of a number of similar life histories (both of these were introduced in

Chapter 2); a set of newspaper materials coming from the archives of a Polish peasant newspaper; a series of documents collected primarily through social agencies – both those in Poland where people wished to emigrate to America and those in America where people had arrived; and a final source of third person reports gleaned from social work agencies and court records. Whilst the last three sets of records are of interest, it is primarily for the letters and the life history that the study is famed.

Undoubtedly, then, *The Polish Peasant* is a classic and makes many central contributions to sociological debate. Yet, shamefully, it has fallen into obscurity. Indeed, even by 1948, Shils could note its neglect with alarm:

> The neglect of *The Polish Peasant in Europe and America* is another witness to the American sociologist's tendency to disregard and then re-do what was done before because of the slipshodness of the education of students and the failure of their teachers to assimilate and extend the best that has preceded them. (Shils, 1948, p. 26)

Shils's comment highlights the position that existed in America after World War II and has remained the same since then. But before it was to fall into decline, life history research was to enjoy a brief flowering period: indeed, there is much evidence that during the 1920s and 1930s it was a central approach for sociologists in America, and was gathering momentum in Europe.

The Hey-Day of the Human Document

The Polish Peasant was met with much critical acclaim, and sparked off a series of methodological disputes over the relative merits of clinical and statistical techniques. Although Thomas left Chicago in 1918 (at the age of 55) the new leaders of the Sociology Department Robert Park and Ernest Burgess (under the chairmanship of Albin Small initially) were highly instrumental in encouraging the use of such an approach. Park, especially as director of the Pacific Coast *Race Relations Survey* (1923–5), produced a number of life-history questionnaires and encouraged their use, along with that of diaries and letters: Emory S. Bogardus's research text of 1926, *The New Social Research*, not only reviews these documents, and Park's role in them, but shows just how significantly they were regarded. While a quarter of the book is explicitly devoted to their discussion (Bogardus, 1926, pp. 131–89), much of the remaining discussion is focused upon the interviewing styles for such work (for other texts, see Table 3.1). Likewise, Burgess believed that the case study was to sociology what the microscope was to biology (cf. Burgess, 1945). Both in his work on delinquency and on the family, he placed enormous value on the personal document case study, and saw no conflict with the supposedly rival statistical approach. In 1927, he remarked that 'if statistics and case study are to yield their full contribution as tools of sociological research, they should be granted equal recognition and full opportunity for each to perfect its own technique' (Burgess, in Cottrell *et al.*, 1973, p. 287). He was to hold this view for a long time, exploring both approaches fully in his study of the adjustment of 1,000 engaged couples! (cf. Burgess, 1941, 1945).

Table 3.1   *A Selection of American Research Texts and their Discussions of Personal Documents 1920–1940*

1920 F. Stuart Chapin, *Field Work and Social Research* (esp. ch. IV, pp. 73–97)	sees three major types of fieldwork (case study, sampling and census) and devotes a chapter to case study; Mary Richmond's *Social Diagnosis* evoked (social work influence).
1926 Emory S. Bogardus (with an introduction by Robert Park), *The New Social Research* (esp. chs VI–IX)	A key text on personal documents: diaries, letters and personal experience are discussed, and there are two chapters on life histories, providing discussion and a number of schedules (especially from Park's *Race Relations Survey*).
1928 Vivien M. Palmer, *Field Studies in Sociology: A Students' Manual* (esp. I, ch. 2; III, ch. 4)	An early 'Chicago' manual which sees 'case studies' as a key method and discusses it throughout the text.
1929 George A. Lundberg, *Social Research* (esp. ch. VIII, pp. 168–96)	A major positivist and critic of life documents, provides a detailed chapter and contrast with the (superior) statistical method.
1929 T. V. Smith and L. D. White (eds), *Chicago: An Experiment in Social Science Research* (esp. chs 9 and 10)	A study of the Chicago research tradition from 1923–8 with contributors on specific areas (e.g. Park on the city, Burgess on 'Basic Social Data'), and appendices listing all research publications and research officers. It is surprisingly thin on discussion of personal documents.

Table 3.1 (continued)

1929 H. Odum and K. Jocher, *An Introduction to Social Research* (esp. ch. XV)	Covers all the approaches and methods of the social sciences and is full of early examples and illustrations. Naturally, the case study is given due attention as 'one of the oldest methods as well as one of the most important' (p. 229).
1930 Charles M. Cooley, *Sociological Theory and Social Research* (esp. chs X and XII)	A self-selected posthumous collection of essays, two of which highlight 'life studies'.
1931 Stuart A. Rice (ed.), *Methods in Social Science: A Case Book* (esp. chs 4, 8, 40)	An edited volume, sponsored by the SSRC, which discusses methods used in particular studies. While personal documents are present, they constitute only a limited part of a hefty work.
1934 Florian Znaniecki, *The Method of Sociology* (esp. ch. 4)	A neglected classic. In ch. 4, he sees four main sources of sociological material (personal experience and observation by the sociologist and personal experience and observation by other people). Many 'personal documents' are highlighted but 'autobiography' is seen as the 'best kind of second hand source'.
1934 Charles L. Fry, *The Technique of Social Investigation* (pp. 69–72)	A text which takes the reader through all the stages of research from 'planning' to 'disseminating the findings'. An interesting survey but personal documents receive only scant treatment.
1939 Pauline V. Young, *Scientific Social Surveys and Research* (chs 3 and 10)	This first edition of a text which was central to the social science literature for several decades (the 4th edn was 1966), includes full recognition of the central role of Thomas and Znaniecki, and a chapter on 'The Case Study Method'.

It is of little surprise, then, that under their inspiration – and in line with the general Chicago injunction to 'get off your seats and *do* research' – this period produced a number of central studies. In the field of criminology especially the reforming Clifford Shaw discussed the case study (Shaw, 1927) and gathered numerous life histories (with Burgess) producing his celebrated trilogy *The Jack Roller* (1966), *The Natural History of a Delinquent Career* (1931), and *Brothers in Crime* (1938). Edwin Sutherland, the dean of American criminology, was at Chicago until the mid-1930s and detailed the craft of Chic Conwell, *The Professional Thief*, (1937, 1967). Many of the Chicago monographs of this period drew upon personal documents of some form – one thinks of Cavan's *Suicide* diaries (Cavan, 1928), Thrasher's photographs of *The Gang* (1926), Zorbaugh's observers' reports on *The Gold Coast and the Slum* (1965), and Mowrer's (1927) cases of family breakdown. Everywhere, it appears, case studies were encouraged: A. S. Stephan, one of Burgess's students, remarks:

> You would have to write a paper on why you were interested in the family. In fact, every course that Burgess taught you could be sure that the first paper you write [would be] why are you interested in criminology, why are you interested in the family. Then you would write a paper on 'A Day in the Life of the Family' . . . Yes, you'd remember your own family. (Carey, 1975, p. 179)

And Burgess himself remarks on some comments he made to Nels Anderson during his study of *The Hobo*:

> I recall Nels Anderson telling me he was greatly bored by his land-lady, in the rooming-house district where he was studying the homeless man, telling him her life history. I told him, 'Why it's invaluable, you must get it down on paper' . . . Out of this one document you get more insight into how life moves in a rooming-house area, and especially from the stand-point of the rooming-house keeper, than you do from a mountain of statistics that might be gathered. So what we get from the life history, of course, also enables us to pose more questions to the statistician, to get to the other answers. (Cottrell *et al.*, 1973, p. 13)

More frivolously – but surely an excellent social indicator – is Hauser's remark that when he was a graduate student at Chicago, the baseball sides on the annual faculty/student picnic were drawn from representatives of the case study and representatives of the statisticians! (cf. Platt, unpublished).

The 'case study' and the 'statistical method' generally appear to have been the two major approaches to research during the 1920s, and most sociologists – like Park, Burgess, Shaw (cf. Shaw and

McKay, 1969) and Faris (1937, pp. 102–3) – appear to have accepted their mutual benefits. Some, like Samuel A. Stouffer (in his 1930 Ph.D) drew out 'experimental comparisons' between the two methods to show that *both* were valid, that an investigation could get at the same material accurately through either method. In so doing, however, he hinted that case study material was much more arduous to collect and analyse, and hence by implication suggested that quantitative research was preferable (cf. Stouffer, 1930; Cavan, Hauser and Stouffer, 1930). Others were less compromising and more acidic in their view of case studies, the most outspoken being the positivist George Lundberg who waged war on 'cases' for nearly two decades. For him, the case study was not and could not be scientific: it was always 'the tail to the statistical kite'. It could be used as a 'first step', but for any scientific work the cases then had to be 'classified and summarised in such form as to reveal uniformities, types and patterns of behaviour' (Lundberg, 1926, p. 61; Lundberg, 1941). Likewise, prediction, so necessary for science, was only possible if a sufficient number of cases had been observed (a debate much more fully discussed in 1951 by Paul Meehl).

Despite these criticisms, case histories remained at the centre of the sociological stage during this period. Perhaps the major indication of the importance that American sociology was beginning to place on the role of human documents was the interest taken in it by the newly formed Social Science Research Council. Fifteen years after its inauguration in 1923, it set up a committee on the appraisal of research whose aim was to look at studies that had made 'the most significant contributions to knowledge in their particular discipline'. Six such studies were selected, the representative for sociology being *The Polish Peasant*.

The ensuing appraisal by Herbert Blumer must still stand not only as the most thorough review of Thomas and Znaniecki's work but also of the more general use of personal documents. Blumer's background as a Chicago sociologist and the mantle-bearer of George Herbert Mead's philosophy led him to be highly sympathetic to the report whilst nevertheless subjecting it to stringent criteria of assessment. Indeed so stringent were his criteria that in general he found the report to be a scientific failure. He argued, for instance, that the *representativeness* of each document was not established; that the *adequacy* of each document for the purpose for which they were employed was not proved; that their *reliability* was not checked by independent sources; and, finally, that the *validity of the interpretation* drawn from any single document was not demonstrated. Paradoxically, despite these severe failings, Blumer went on to claim that the report was a success and lists eight 'important contributions which have made *The Polish Peasant* meritorious and which explain the profound influence which it has had on sociology and social psychology'. These were:

(1) A demonstration of the need of studying the subjective factor in social life.
(2) The proposing of human documents as source material, particularly the life record, thus introducing what is known as the life history technique.
(3) A statement of social theory which outlines the framework of a social psychology and the features of a sociology. The view of social psychology, its subjective aspects of culture is particularly influenced.
(4) A statement of scientific methods which have stimulated and reinforced the interest in making sociology a scientific discipline.
(5) A number of important theories, such as that of personality and social control and disorganisation.
(6) A variety of concepts which have gained wide acceptance, such as attitude, value, life organisation, definition of situation and four wishes.
(7) A rich content of insights, evocative generalisations and shrewd observations.
(8) An illuminating and telling characterisation of Polish peasant society.

What is perhaps of chief importance is the marked stimulation which it has given to actual social research. (Blumer, 1939, pp. 81–2)

Following on Blumer's appraisal a one-day conference was organised by the Social Science Research Council on 10 December 1938, to consider the value of *The Polish Peasant* study and personal documents, of which the full proceedings were published (Blumer, 1939). Again, this indicates something of the importance which American sociology was attributing to this method, and it was an importance which was to be further extended when the conference decided that four of its disciplines (sociology, history, psychology and anthropology) should set up their own appraisal of the personal document method for submission to the Council. This heralded the publication of two significant volumes extending the debates further during the early 1940s.

The most prominent of these reports was written by Gordon Allport (1942), prominent because, although it was the psychology submission, he discussed in a 200-page document the general use, forms and value of the life history approach, and prominent too because Gordon Allport was to go on during his lifetime to advocate, more strongly than anybody else, the use of the idiographic case study method in psychology. His major illustrative example of this approach, *Letters from Jenny* (described in Chapter 2), was not to be published until 1965, but from the 1940s until his death in 1967, he remained the most ardent champion of the individual case study in psychology. He firmly argued that every life was unique and needed to be carefully studied for its own generalisable patterns: most psychology went in pursuit of general laws about traits abstracted from concrete individuals (the intelligence quotient, the attitude) and ignored the unique constellation of these traits in one individual. Prediction about individual behaviour was never possible on the basis of theories about universal traits which ignored unique constellations. As he put it, rather strikingly,

> Suppose we take John, a lad of 12 years, and suppose his family background is poor; his father was a criminal; his mother rejected him; his neighbourhood is marginal. Suppose that 70 per cent of the boys having a similar background become criminals. Does this mean that John has a 70 per cent chance of delinquency? Not at all. John is a unique being with a genetic inheritance of his own; his life-experience is his own. His unique world contains influences unknown to the statistician: perhaps an affectionate relation with a certain teacher . . . such factors . . . may offset all average probabilities. There is no 70 per cent chance about John. He either will or will not become delinquent. Only a complete understanding of his personality, of his present and future circumstances, will give us a basis for sure prediction. (Allport, 1962, pp. 411–12)

The second major report to emanate from the SSRC inquiry drew together what was known about personal documents in history, anthropology and sociology. The historical survey by Louis Gottschalk focused mainly on criticisms of the approach, the anthropological review by Clyde Kluckhohn focused mainly on the types of documents available and the means of gathering and analysing them, while the sociological survey of Robert C. Angell (Cooley's nephew) reviews some twenty-two studies produced between 1920 and 1940 and their bearings upon research into historical sequences, sociological theory and sociological method. It is an important review because it locates the 'state of play' of such research by the early 1940s very thoroughly, concluding that 'there has been real advance, although the gains are not startling' (Gottschalk *et al.*, 1942, p. ix). Whatever 'advance' was made by this time was to be largely ignored during the next forty years – certainly no comparable review has ever been made.

These two major SSRC reports probably only signpost the iceberg tip of concern about personal documents: 'statistics' *v* 'case studies' seems to have been *the* central sociological debate of the period.

As an adjunct to the Council's work, Dollard had been asked to review some life history research which was subsequently published in 1935 (before the two major reports) as *Criteria for the Life History*. This neglected but central study sought to establish broad principles for assessing the value of any social science life history – criteria which would set it apart from literary biography or the commonsense tales of everyman. 'The material,'·claims Dollard, 'must be worked up and mastered from some systematic viewpoint.'

Table 3.2   *Dollard's Evaluation of Six Cases*

Criterion	Adler	Taft	Freud	Thomas	Shaw	Wells
(i) Subject viewed as specimen in cultural series	–	–	+	++	++	++
(ii) Organic motivation must be socially relevant	–	+	+	+	– –	+
(iii) Role of family group in transmitting culture must be recognised	–	–	+	O	+	O
(iv) Elaboration of organic materials into social behaviour must be shown	O	–	++	–	–	–
(v) Continuous related character of experience from childhood through adulthood must be stressed	++	+	++	O	+	+
(vi) 'Social situation' must be continuously and carefully specified	O	–	+	–	++	–
(vii) Life history material must be organised and conceptualised	+	+	++	O	O	–

Key:
+ indicates fulfilment of the criterion
O indicates the criterion is not fully met
– indicates the criterion is not met
   (See A. Adler (1929), J. Taft (1933), S. Freud (1925), W. I. Thomas and F. Znaniecki (1958), C. Shaw (1966), H. G. Wells (1934)).
   Source: Allport, 1942, p. 27.

Such a viewpoint entailed seven principles, which are spelt out in some detail. In summary, Dollard argued that any life needed to be analysed through its various contexts and stages, and then adequately conceptualised. Four criteria were elaborated which analysed the life in its various contexts: (i) the organic, (ii) the familial, (iii) the situational and (iv) the historical–cultural. Thus for Dollard, life history research is interdisciplinary – we need to draw from biology, psychology, psychiatry, history and sociology in order to see how lives are embedded in four shaping and shaped contexts. But these contexts then need to be viewed developmentally: (v) 'the continuous related character of experience from childhood through adulthood must be stressed' (p. 26), and interactionally: to show (vi) how 'the organic materials' get elaborated into social behaviour. Finally, Dollard argues that the social scientist must arrange and systematise the material: he must (vii) 'play an active role over against his material; he must do the critical work of fashioning the necessary concepts, of making the required connections, and of piecing the whole life history together' (1935, p. 34).

Dollard encourages the use of these seven criteria both in the construction of future life histories, and in the teaching and appraisal of existing ones. Indeed, his own study then proceeds to assess six studies (seven, if the passing consideration of Radin's *Crashing Thunder* is included) which represent different approaches and disciplines. Allport has usefully summarised this data (see Table 3.2).

The discussion by Dollard may be due for resuscitation but it has been largely ignored, perhaps because the criteria are regarded by some as merely reflecting Dollard's own 'personal' preferences (especially for psycho-dynamic theory), but more probably simply because the publication came at the end of the hey-day of life history research. For, since the early 1940s, there has been a manifest decline in discussion and interest in the kind of research that Dollard favoured (cf. Zetterberg, 1956).

The Chicago Vision

If there was a time when life documents were given their due attention, there was also a place: Chicago – a spectacular new city that had grown from a small log port on a swampy lake in 1833 to one of the world's greatest cities by the end of the nineteenth century. A city with seething social problems, rapid social change, high immigration: a city that was, in the words of Park, to become a 'social laboratory'. The new university that was established there with the finance of John Rockefeller and the leadership of William Harper was full of innovations. It was the first university to be established 'full blown and ready to take its place at once in the first ranks of institutions of higher education (Faris, 1967, p. 22). It was the first American university to establish an original collective school of thought: pragmatism. As James proclaimed: 'The result is wonderful – *a real school*, and *real thought*. Important thought, too. Did you ever hear of such a city or such a university? Here (at Harvard) we have thought, but no school. At Yale a school but not thought. Chicago has both.' (Rucker, 1969, p. 3)

Most important, it was the first American university to establish a department of sociology. Out of it came the American Sociological Society in 1905, the *American Journal of Sociology*, the 'Green Bible' of Park and Burgess which was the central sociology text and commonly agreed to be 'one of the most influential works ever written in sociology' (Faris, 1967, p. 37), the largest post-graduate school existing in America at that time, the growth of the Society for Social Research (Bulmer, 1983), the propagation of a massive research programme (often published in the Chicago Monograph series), and an array of key sociology figures – Burgess, Park, Ogburn, Shaw, Faris, Cavan, Wirth, Thrasher – and, up to 1918, Thomas. 'It was,' as Faris observed, '*the* place to go' (Faris, 1967, p. 32). More recently, Hawthorn remarked that 'The history of sociology in America in the 1920's [was] the history of the department of Chicago' (Hawthorn, 1976, p. 209). From the publication of *The Polish Peasant* in 1918 until the mid-1930s, then, American sociology was almost synonymous with the Chicago Department.

It was in this new city, new university and new department that the personal document was to be given a proper symbolic birth. These developments cannot be seen as random or marginal excrescences from the sociology department: they were bound up with the philosophy of the whole university (Rucker, 1969). What united the university primarily was excitement and involvement with the emerging philosophy of pragmatism. Like all philosophical schools it was not unified, but contained within its ranks wide discrepancies. The founder C. S. Pierce, for example, ultimately held a position of absolutism which was antithetical to the ideas of William James and John Dewey (Scheffler, 1974; Lewis and Smith, 1980). Nevertheless all pragmatists held in common the importance of experience as the mediator of truth, and saw pragmatism as a fundamentally mediating philosophy. As Rucker succinctly comments:

The Chicago group represented an important shift in thinking away from belief in a world as a given external reality and mind as a different internal reality. What had long been viewed as disparate ultimate entities, mind and world, became two factors in a process, necessarily related through the process, neither having any existence independent of the other. Not only does the environment determine the organism, but the organism, in turn, introduces new objects into the environment. (Rucker, 1969, p. 28)

Central as pragmatism was to the whole Chicago school, the socio-logical variant, symbolised by its leader Robert Park (1864–1944), was altogether wider. Park's background and concerns have been vividly brought to life in his biographies (Matthews, 1977; Raushenbush, 1979). For sure, the pragmatist influence is there: as an under-graduate Dewey taught Park at Michigan, and a sustained friendship emerged; while as a graduate at Harvard he encountered both William James and the argument of 'A certain blindness' (cited at the start of the book) which was later to become one of Park's 'habitual weapons' (Matthews, 1977, p. 32). But equally important seems to be Park's flirtations with European, and especially Germanic, thought. In 1899 Simmel provided the only formal instruction in sociology that Park was ever to receive, and henceforth Simmel's subtle distinctions of 'form' and 'content' became central to the Chicago heritage (cf. Levine, 1971). In 1903, Park encountered the neo-Kantian philosopher Windelband and from him the methodological distinctions between 'nomothetic science' and 'idiographic history' probably set the scene for the ongoing debate in Chicago during the 1920s between statistical generalisation and case study research. Less tangible, but strikingly present, was Park's naturalism and romanticism; it is likely that Dilthey's overarching concern with 'life and lived experience' (cf. Ermarth, 1978, ch. 2) played a role here, for Park had a profound reverence for the common man and his common struggles along with an abhorrence for 'the pretentious . . . the self-conscious intellectuals and social climbers who deliberately separated themselves from the majority' (Matthews, 1977, p. 17). Central in this last group were the do-gooders and reformists who arrogantly presumed to judge and manipulate others. It was ordinary 'earthiness' he admired and human hypocrisy he despised; the sympathies of the anarchist came to him naturally (cf. Raushenbush, 1979, p. 23).

All these strands of thought – pragmatism, formalism, humanism, mild anarchism and romanticism – played their part in giving rise to that curiously American sociological theory now known as symbolic interactionism. The term was coined in 1937 (by Blumer), and the theory became codified in texts, readers, journals and associations from the early 1960s onwards (e.g. Manis and Meltzer, 1978; Hewitt, 1979; Denzin, 1978a), but its central ideas were in effect being worked out in Chicago during the 1920s – and *The Polish Peasant* with its key idea of the *subjective interpretation of the situation* must have played an influential role.

The cornerstones of interactionist thought embody a profound distaste for abstraction, reification and absolutes; the humanly constructed, and hence ambiguous and emergent, meaning is their root concern. That humans inhabit dual worlds, material and symbolic; that their interactions are predicated upon the emergences of *selves* through which they are able to be self-reflexive, communicate and take the roles of others; that meaning has to be worked out in encounters and whilst tentatively agreed upon, is ever flowing and never fixed; that lives, and indeed the social order, themselves are constantly 'open' and 'negotiable': these are some of the themes that interactionists explore. They flow from the Chicago philosophy and they will re-occur throughout this book. The key feature, though, is their unrelenting focus on the importance of the subjective viewpoint: it is this which the life document critically embodies and why there is such a strong affinity between interactionist theory and personal document method.

It will be helpful to clarify some of the links between the Chicago sociologists, the symbolic interactionists and personal documents. This is an intellectual reconstruction and it is likely that for those working in the Department of Sociology during the 1920s and 1930s there was no similar understanding of the affinity between these strands of thought: life histories were not systematically connected with symbolic interactionism (it did not even formally exist at the time!) and symbolic interactionism was not systematically linked to Chicago pragmatism. While therefore an artificial construction, it should nevertheless serve to clarify certain common strands of thought.

Briefly I want to consider three images left by the Chicago inheritance and firmly embedded in life history research. The first image highlights life as a concrete experience (notice the affinity with humanism discussed in the first chapter); the second views life as an ever-emerging relativistic perspective; the third captures the inherent marginality and ambiguity of life. I will discuss each of these in turn.

LIFE AS CONCRETE EXPERIENCE

The approach of the Chicagoans shunned analytic abstractions, deductive logic, philosophical dualisms or truths ripped from their very contexts: in place of the philosophical games which philosophers play (and which may or may not be true, we have no way of telling) the Chicagoans substituted a concern with concrete experience embedded in problem-solving. Further, in the place of abstract notions like 'society' or 'individuals' the Chicagoans brought home the importance of dealing with particulars rather than abstractions. Thus James complains in *Pragmatism*, 'Damn great empires including that of the absolute ... give me individuals and their spheres of activity', while Cooley (1956) announces in *Human Nature and the Social Order*, 'A separate individual is an abstraction unknown to experience, and so likewise is society when regarded as something apart from individuals. The real thing is human life . . .'. In these exclamations, they echoed the thought of Dilthey, who had made 'lived life' the cornerstone of his entire philosophy.

A consequence of this concrete image of life was a firm belief in the dialectical compound of self and society and the organic matrix of body and mind: in every case of study we must acknowledge that experiencing individuals can never be isolated from their functioning bodies and their constraining social worlds – there is no room for a bodiless idealism or a mindless materialism. Body, mind, context, society – *all* are in constant engagement with each other, and *all* need to be taken into account. A sociology that gravitates to social structure alone will most likely lead to an unwarranted abstraction and reification; a sociology that totters towards 'mind' alone will be guilty of an unwarranted solipsism. A dialectical compound of inter-acting bodies and structures, meanings and motives must be the proper concern. Thomas and Znaniecki had recognised this in their *Polish Peasant* by stressing the need to consider both 'the combina-tion of a social *and* an individual phenomenon' and the need to take into account both the subjective *and* objective definition of the situation. (Thomas and Znaniecki, 1958, esp. pp. 44 and 68). Con-crete life cannot separate out bodies from people, minds from activities, individuals from groups: adequate conceptualisation demands recognising their interpenetrations. Over and over again this is to be found: 'a society is a structure which consists of beings who stand inside and outside of it at the same time' (Simmel, in Levine, 1971, p. 15). Likewise the Meadian concept of self is one strategy designed specifically to get round the classic philosophical problems of individualism and collectivism. The individual self is a dialectical process between two phases, the 'I' and the 'me', whereby the 'I' allows for individuality and spontaneity and the 'me' allows for the objective constraints of the wider society. The images and ideas then of interactionism constantly harp back to the idea of the concrete experience bringing together potential conflicts and opposites into an amalgam, an organic unit.

There is a clear affinity between these sociological premises and the methodological directive to study life histories and personal documents. Here are real concrete experiences. Abstractions, logical systems, philosophical meanderings are bypassed and one is con-fronted through the personal document with the very substance of experience. But note what this brings with it. It does not bring with it the isolated individual; rather it brings with it an immediate aware-ness of the relationship of the individual's body, the individual's definition of a situation, and the groups with which the individual is persistently engaging throughout life. 'The isolated individual was an abstraction; in reality the irreducible unit was the individual embedded in a network of relationships and statuses – fathers, sons, masters, workers, burgers, peasants' (Matthews, 1977, p. 37). Through the letters in *The Polish Peasant*, for example, a reader cannot fail to be aware of the importance of looking at both the person's subjective definition of a situation and the objective constraints which impinge upon them; one cannot fail to be aware that the individuals have bodies which bring them pain and that they live in groups which sometimes coerce and frustrate and sometimes give them joy. The focus upon the concrete experience permits one to see the reconciliation of these supposed interminable opposites and dualisms. Furthermore, grounded in all these documents and life histories is an individual engaging in concrete problem-solving. Indeed, for the life historian there are no simpler or better questions to generally pose than 'What is this person worrying about here? What is this person trying to do? What is it that is motivating this person? What is it that forces them on?'. The answers to such questions will never be reducible to a simple-minded biologism, psychologism or sociologism alone.

LIFE AS AN EMERGENT PERSPECTIVE

Closely linked to the rejection of abstractions and analytic truth is the rejection of all absolutes, all closed systems of thought and all statics. Experience is a stream, a flow; social structures are seamless webs of criss-crossing negotiations; biographies are in a constant state of becoming and as they evolve so their subjective accounts of themselves evolve. There is no static conception of the world in interactionist thought but one in which flux, emergence, precariousness and change are persistent facts at all levels of analysis.

In John Dewey's famous example, 'Things . . . are what they are experienced as': a sudden bump in the night may evoke fear and terror in a listener lying in bed who believes it is a burglar thence a fearsome noise, or it may evoke only mild irritation as it is discovered to be simply a flapping window curtain. Either interpretation will be real for the person who apprehends the noise in that way. If the noise is believed to be fearsome then a person will start to sweat, feel anxious, lie in bed incapacitated, petrified and afraid to rise. The reality of the situation for the individual participant says that the 'bump in the night' *is* a fearsome sound. Yet if the person believes it is only a flapping curtain, then the response will be very different and unfearsome. Nevertheless, to suggest that the first experience is any less real subjectively than the second experience is to do a great disservice to understanding a person's behaviour. The reality shifts with a person's life and people act towards things on the basis of their understandings, irrespective of the 'objective' nature of those things. It is important to notice, though, that from a different perspective an 'objective nature' of things can be seen. Yet this too is the product of a perspective and will always need to be linked to it. An objective world independent of subjective interpretations which surround it cannot be apprehended and these subjective interpretations are themselves shifting around. Ellsworth Faris, a noted student of Mead, could remark in an essay on 'The standpoint and method of sociology' (1937, p. 99):

> . . . Things exist because they are experienced. If Buddha exists for the Buddhist, and if the horned devil existed for the medieval Christian we can only say that the cultural reality must be dealt with and we can only discuss the world we live in and not the world that we might have lived in. And in a world where men recognise groups, where they love groups, fight groups, give money to groups, lay down their lives for groups – in such a world it is not possible to deny their existence.

Closely related to this is the idea that totalities can never be grasped: there are only limited selected truths or perspectives. The Chicago tradition here stems back to Kant through Simmel and Weber – a clear line of reasoning that suggests the phenomenal forms of knowledge may be grasped and apprehended while the noumenal realm is in principle a dark void which can never be known. Simmel puts this forcefully in *The Problems of the Philosophy of History*:

> It is impossible to describe the single event as it really was because it is impossible to describe the event as a whole. A science of a total event is not only impossible for reasons of unmanageable quantity: it is impossible because it would also lack *a point of view* or *problematic*. Such a problematic is necessary in order to produce a construct that would satisfy our criteria for knowledge. A science of a total event would lack the category that is necessary for the identification and coherence of the elements of the event. There is no knowledge as such: knowledge is possible only in so far as it is produced and structured by constitutive concepts that are qualitatively determined. Because these concepts are qualitatively determined, they are inevitably partial and biased. Given a criterion for knowledge that is perfectly general, it would be impossible to identify or distinguish any element of reality. This is the deeper reason why there are only histories, but no history as such. What we call universal history or world history can at best be

the simultaneous application of a variety of these differential problematics. Or, on the other hand, it may be the sort of history which throws into relief the aspects of the event which are most *significant* or important from the perspective of our sense of value. (G. Simmel, 1977, pp. 82–3)

Now it is precisely these different perspectives and the awareness of the changing subjective definitions of the real that lead us back to the need to specify the concrete individual whose truth we are considering. All perspectives dangle from some person's problematic. Views, truths and conceptions of the real can never be wholly ripped away from the people who experience them. Hence one fundamental source of knowledge again is the biography and the life history which grasps the sense of reality that people have about their own world.

But there are immediate problems with such a position. If perspectives shift across time and across people, how are we to have anything other than momentary fragmented glimpses of people's definitions? To simply take a biography at face value is to obtain an account of a person's life as seen by them at that moment; it will of course tell a great deal about their subjective definitions of the reality of that moment but it will not necessarily tell their definitions of reality in the past, how their definitions of reality shift from group to group in the present or how their definitions of reality differ from other people's definitions of reality. These points most certainly become important areas of caution in looking at a biography, but they do not impede its validity. As W. I. Thomas said in his classic answer to this problem:

... It must be recognised that even the most highly subjective record has a value for behaviour analysis and interpretation. A document, for example, prepared by one compensating for a feeling of inferiority or elaborating a delusion of persecution is as far as possible from objective reality, but the subject's view of the situation, how he regards it, may be the most important element for interpretation for his immediate behaviour is closely related to his definition of a situation, which may be in terms of objective reality or in terms of subjective appreciation – 'as if' it was so. Very often it is the wide discrepancy between the situation as it seems to others and the situation as it seems to the individual that brings about the overt behaviour difficulty. A paranoic person, at present in one of the New York institutions, has killed several persons who had the unfortunate habit of talking to themselves in the street. From the movement of their lips he imagined that they were calling him vile names and he behaved as if this were true. *If men define those situations as real, they are real in their consequences.* The total situation would always contain more or less subjective factors, and the behaviour reactions can be studied only in connection with the whole context, that is, the situation as it exists in verifiable, objective terms, and as it has seemed to exist in terms of the interested person. (Thomas, in Janowitz, 1966, pp. 300–01, my italics)

Thomas was certainly never espousing the view that only the subjective needs looking at, but he was certainly highlighting its value.

LIFE AS AMBIGUOUS AND MARGINAL

Alvin Gouldner, in *For Sociology* (1973), has suggested two master motifs as underpinning the whole of Western thought: the classical (which pursues pattern, regularity, and generalisation) and the romantic (which finds disarray, eccentricity and uniqueness). A linear world of laws and order is juxtaposed against the booming confusion of fragile subjectivity. The contrasts are starkly drawn by Gouldner, acknowledging that both traditions have a place, and Chicago is firmly located within romanticism. This is not wholly fair as there are certainly major strands of statistical science and formalism to be found in their work; but in the main, the point is well taken. Much of their work – to use their favourite phrases – is 'interstitial' and 'marginal': they studied the 'interstitial zone', the 'marginal man', the immigrant and, of course, the stranger. A 'perspective of incongruity' informs their work by which the known is placed side by side with the unknown, the familiar is rendered unfamiliar, and a curious distancing from everyday reality occurs. Taking one person's subjective reality in a document, seriously on its own terms, but then placing it against another person's serious reality soon leads to a sense of contradiction, ambiguity – even absurdity. And as the mosaic grows, so the sense of ambiguity ascends.

Politically, too, marginality is important as the sociologist appreciates that different perspectives are accorded different credibility by other groupings: a hierarchy of perspectives becomes graspable. Some of these 'underdog' perspectives may persistently be denied voice or simply liquidated through more acceptable rhetoric; other 'overdog' perspectives seem to be proclaimed as *the* truth. But the sense of *the* truth has been already dismantled sociologically, so the researcher is left with a brooding sense of injustice: who are these to be believed, and who are these to be negated? Oscar Lewis, reviewing his own work, can remark that 'One of the major objectives of my recent work has been to give a voice to people who are rarely heard and to provide readers with an inside view of a style of life which is common in many of the deprived and marginal groups in our society' (Lewis, 1970b, p. xiv). Later, he comments, 'Concern with what people suffer from is much more important than the study of enjoyment because it lends itself to more productive insight into the human condition, the dynamics of conflict and the forces of change' (Lewis, 1970b, p. 252).

Although a concern with marginality is to be found both theoretically and politically, in practice it has also had a personal base. Not only was there a marginality, given its newness, about sociological work, about Chicago as a city, and about the topics that sociologists study, there was frequently a marginality about the sociologists themselves. W. I. Thomas, for example, was undoubtedly a controversial figure – he was dismissed in 1918 from the university after an arrest by the FBI and he was renowned for his tolerant views towards deviant behaviour and flamboyant personal manner; his wife, too, was involved in the Henry Ford peace movement (Janowitz, 1966, p. xiv). Likewise, Burgess maintained contacts with Soviet Russia and was ultimately brought before the McCarthy Committee (Cottrell, 1973, pp. 263 and 326). Park 'appeared almost bohemian to provincial students' (Matthews, 1977, p. 106) and came to sociology after a long career as a journalist, covering 'more ground tramping about in cities in different parts of the world, than any other living man' (Park, in Faris, 1970, p. 29) and spending ten years as publicity man to Booker T. Washington, the 'negro' reformer. Their students too had marginal roles: Anderson, for example, studied the hobo, but had himself been involved in hobohemia (Anderson, 1975).

I do not want to overstate this case, but it does seem that the tradition of Chicago sociology was grounded in a sense of marginality and it may well have been this which permitted them to experiment with a most unorthodox method – the personal document and the life history. How, for example, could one superficially justify the use of such a seemingly individualist method in a discipline that was fundamentally collectivist?

In many ways the approach of the personal document and life historian student – lodged with the unique concrete experience and aware of the relativity of different perspectives – leads them to study the marginal and downtrodden groups whose voices may not be so readily heard. This, of course, was an argument to be voiced many years later by the contemporary interactionist Howard Becker in his famous article, 'Whose side are we on?' (Becker, 1971, ch. 8), and it is a concern I will return to in Chapter 4 (pp. 64–83).

Conclusion

It would be quite wrong to infer from the above that the Chicago perspective actually *created* 'documents of life' as a distinctive, humanistic approach: clearly, there were many examples of it prior to the 1920s (in the work of Mayhew in England, for example); many of its forms (such as documentary films) have their own distinctive developmental roots, and amongst some contemporary exponents there is little reason to believe that they have ever studied James or Mead (cf. Bertaux, 1981, p. 10). It would be pretentious, therefore, to suggest such a monolithic foundation for such a diffuse enterprise.

And yet, I have tried to show that the approach came most into its own at a time when there were intellectual arguments developing that could lend weight to its strategies. For the documentary approach to become academically acceptable, it required institutional and intellectual legitimation; and this is what Chicago accomplished. Of course, from the mid 1930s onwards, the arguments subsequently tottered as the more 'scientific', less subjective approaches of Lazarsfeld and Parsons came to ascendancy. The approach remained but the legitimations got lost; and hence it was slowly relegated to the subterranean margins of proper research.

Chicago sociology was an amalgam of philosophies – pragmatism, formalism, humanism, romanticism – and although it embodied a number of contradictions and fostered dissenting traditions (it was also renowned via Ogburn for its quantitative work and its Community Fact Book), it assembled arguments that made it lastingly clear just how important 'human documents' should be for social science.

In the first place, it urged the researcher to shun abstractions and to go instead in pursuit of the detailed, the particular and the experiential. Life documents were always manifestations of such concreteness; and within them, the researcher would find the multiple dichotomies that philosophers debate to be only so much intellectual nicety. The organic compound revealed in the human document blends mind with body, individual with group, subjective with objective, freedom with constraint. Philosophers have spent millenia debating such ideas, and whilst small advances have been made, the actual debates still exist. Look at lived life, said the Chicagoans, and there you will find the contradictory antimonies being worked out. A naturalistic fidelity to the world was thus encouraged – a naturalism which invariably shows that concrete humans cannot be grasped in abstraction (cf. Matza, 1969; Blumer, 1979).

A second strong claim to emerge from Chicago highlighted the need for a dual concern with the subjective and the objective: 'values' and 'attitudes', 'subjective and objective definitions of the situation', 'natural and cultural sciences', 'humanistic coefficients' – throughout all the writing, the necessity to look at how people grasp their own worlds was persistently stressed as one crucial component of the account. It is hard to imagine a single better tool for getting at this than the human document.

Another claim to emerge from this tradition was the inevitability of perspective: all tales, even scientific ones, are told from a point of view. A modesty, a scepticism and a disdain for the Grand Absolute followed in its wake, leaving, once again, the life document as the exemplary case of the more tentative perspective. They could never be the whole truth, since that was inaccessible anyway; but used carefully, they could throw out a limited truth and challenge that 'certain blindness' common to most people.

And, finally, its stake was with the marginal and the underdog. Spawned on romanticism and libertarianism, it believed humans were equal but mutilated by power. Its politics were naïve, and its practice straightforward: no grand claims, just repeatedly show little groups of humans what they do to each other – especially 'give voice' to those who may not be heard – and then trust for a quiet catharsis of comprehension with a re-alignment of action. All wider dreams of change are utopian.

None of the claims of Chicagoans are grand ones: by the logic of their thought they cannot be. Nor, today, in the 1980s are they popular views: they could be dubbed with some justification 'anti-intellectual', 'liberal' and 'reformist'. It is unlikely that they will gain much support in the future.

But the history, the examples and the arguments are there for those who would wish to take them seriously.

Suggestions for Further Reading

For brief historical reviews of research traditions see M. Abrams, *Social Surveys and Social Action* (1951), M. Jahoda *et al.*, *Marienthal* (1972; appendix), and G. Easthope, *History of Social Research Methods* (1974). A helpful discussion of American documentary research in the 1930s may be found in W. Stott, *Documentary Experience and Thirties America* (1977).

The Polish Peasant in Europe and America was first published between 1918 and 1920 in five volumes but republished in a two-volume edition in 1927. I have been using the 1958 Dover reprint. Since it is a very long study, a clear introduction to it is C. Madge's excellent *The Origin of Scientific Sociology* (1963, ch. 3). The most helpful general appraisal is H. Blumer's *Critiques of Research*, originally presented to the SSRC in 1939 but reprinted in 1979 with a new introduction and re-appraisal by Blumer.

An early commentary on life history research is R. S. Cavan (1929), 'Topical summaries of current literature', but the key texts of the 'hey-day' period which are absolutely central reading for anyone interested in this area are J. Dollard's *Criteria for the Life History* (1935), L. Gottschalk *et al.*, *The Use of Personal Documents in History, Anthropology and Sociology* (1942) and G. Allport's *The Use of Personal Documents in Psychological Science* (1942). Since this period there has been little development. In 1965 L. Langness published *The Life History in Anthropological Science* – a slender volume that outlines the uses of the life history in three eras (to 1925,

1925–44, 1944–), discusses its value to anthropologists, and provides some remarks on technicalities; a year later Howard S. Becker provided a good overview of the field in his (1966) introduction to Shaw's *Jack Roller*. Three textbooks published during the 1970s treated the method in a detailed chapter – N. K. Denzin's *The Research Act* (1978a), R. Bogdan and S. Taylor's *Introduction to Qualitative Research Methods* (1975), and H. Schwartz and J. Jacobs, *Qualitative Sociology* (1979). At the turn of the decade there were signs of renewed interest: Thompson's (1978) *The Voice of the Past* signposts the interest in oral history, and D. Bertaux's *Biography and Society* (1981) indicates a renewal of interest in the life story.

The history of Chicago sociology is well documented. The stages leading to its hey-day in the 1920s and 1930s are detailed in R. C. Hinkle's *Founding Theory of American Sociology* (1980), its relation to other departments of sociology is considered in A. Oberschall *The Establishment of Empirical Sociology* (1972) and to American sociology in general in L. Bramson's *The Political Context of Sociology* (1961) and E. Shils's *The Calling of Sociology* (1980). The wider tradition of Chicago and pragmatism is spelt out in D. Rucker, *The Chicago Pragmatists* (1969) where chapters are devoted to departments at Chicago University other than sociology and the common concern with pragmatism is identified. The history of the Chicago sociologists is well discussed in both E. Faris, *Chicago Sociology* (1970), and J. Carey, *Sociology and Public Affairs* (1975) and reminisced in H. Blumer and E. Hughes 'Reminiscences of Classic Chicago' (1980). Of more specific value are the biographies of Robert Park by F. Matthews, *Quest for an American Sociology* (1977) and W. Raushenbush, *Robert E. Park* (1979) – the former giving a great deal of background Chicago history through the personal details of Park's life. There are many accounts which focus on particular areas of substantive interest: two examples are D. Matza's *Becoming Deviant* (1969), on deviance and H. A. Farberman, 'The Chicago School: continuities in urban sociology' (1979) on urban sociology.

Some of the philosophical inspirations to the personal document tradition and symbolic interactionism may be found in the work of Dilthey (for an introduction to his work see M. Ermarth, *William Dilthey*, 1978), and the pragmatists (see I. Scheffler, *Four Pragmatists* (1974) for an introduction). P. Rock's study, *The Making of Symbolic Interactionism* (1979) traces symbolic interactionism back to Hegel and Kant and provides a sturdy epistemological defence of it in the wake of critiques from 'realist' theoreticians. Contrasting accounts about the interactionist intellectual heritage may be found in B. Fisher and A. Strauss, 'Interactionism' (1978), C. McPhail and C. Rexroat's 'Mead *vs.* Blumer' (1979), and D. J. Lewis and R. L. Smith, *American Sociology and Pragmatism* (1980).

All the key sociologists at Chicago are to be found in the *Heritage of Sociology* series. These studies include W. I. Thomas (by M. Janowitz, 1966), F. Znaniecki (by R. Bierstedt, 1969), R. Park (by R. Turner, 1967), E. Burgess (by L. S. Cottrell *et al.*, 1973), E. Sutherland (by K. Schuessler, 1973), and G. H. Mead (by A. Strauss, 1964). The influential G. Simmel is also considered in this series (by D. Levine, 1971).

The theory of symbolic interactionism is outlined in H. Blumer's *Symbolic Interactionism* (1969), given a textbook treatment in J. P. Hewitt's *Self and Society* (2nd edn, 1979), and a reader in J. G. Manis and B. N. Meltzer,

Symbolic Interactionism: A Reader (3rd edn, 1978). Its position in relation to method is most helpfully discussed in N. K. Denzin, *The Research Act* (1978, 2nd edn). The Society for the Study of Symbolic Interactionism can be contacted via Regan Smith, Department of Sociology and Anthropology, Sangaman State University, Springfield, Illinois, USA. It produces its own journal *Symbolic Interaction* and an annual volume of *Studies in Symbolic Interaction* (vol. 1, 1978), edited by Norman K. Denzin.

4

Some Uses of Life Documents

During the sixties thousands of students in many countries came to sociology because they wanted to find out how people live, and what social life is like concretely. But instead of finding what they were hoping for, they found academic sociology. Is it necessary to make any further comment? The disillusion was as great as the expectations had been. (Bertaux and Wiame, 1981, p. 173)

Writing in the first major sociological life history, that of Wladek in *The Polish Peasant in Europe and America*, Thomas and Znaniecki observed:

In analysing the experiences and attitudes of an individual, we always reach data and elementary facts which are not exclusively limited to this individual's personality, but can be treated as mere instances of more or less general classes of data or facts, and can thus be used for the determination of social becoming. Whether we draw our materials for sociological analysis from detailed life records of concrete individuals or from the observation of mass phenomena, the problems of sociological analysis are the same. We are safe in saying that personal life records, as complete as possible, constitute the *perfect* type of sociological material, and that if social science has to use other materials at all it is only because of the practical difficulty of obtaining at the moment a sufficient number of such records to cover the totality of sociological problems, and of the enormous amount of work demanded for an adequate analysis of all the personal material necessary to characterise the life of a social group. If we are forced to use mass phenomena as material, or any kind of happenings taken without regard to the life histories of the individuals who participate in them, it is a defect, not an advantage, of our present sociological method. (Thomas and Znaniecki, 1958, pp. 1832–3)

For Thomas and Znaniecki then, life histories are not merely useful for sociology, they are 'the *perfect* type of sociological material'. Given such a bold claim – and such a powerful entrée to the sociological community over sixty years ago – it is remarkable how, in recent times, the approach is persistently ignored, minimised or critically extinguished. In the previous chapters I have shown a small steady stream of such studies during this century but they have, with the exception of the brief hey-day of Chicago sociology, always been the soft underbelly to mainstream social science.

The attacks mounted against such studies look formidable. Superficially life history research particularly can be accused of substantive and theoretical neglect; of ignoring the proper theoretical and structural concerns that an adequate sociology must focus upon. In this view, a focus on individual lives distorts and maligns the sociological enterprise. More accurately, and more technically, life history research can be accused of technical inadequacy; of a failure to pay proper attention to issues of representativeness, validity and objectivity. In this view, life histories certainly have a value but they have been inadequately developed as a scientific tool. Such is the nature of Blumer's classic (1939) critique of *The Polish Peasant*. I will examine these latter serious criticisms in Chapter 6 where I will discuss the technical skills involved in life history research. In this Chapter I propose to consider the more general attacks through a focus on the substantive, research, teaching and practical contributions of life history research.

The Substantive Contribution: Getting at Human Phenomena

At the very core of life documents is their subject matter: the continuous, lived flow of historically-situated phenomenal experience, with all the ambiguity, variability, malleability and even uniqueness that such experience usually implies. Whether this be the experience of coalmining or prostitution (Bulmer, 1978; Heyl, 1979); of political machination or trade union activity (Lynd, 1973); of slavery or revolution (Rawick, 1978; Lewis, 1977); of religious life or family life (James, 1952; Henry, 1973); of race or old age (Rosenblatt, 1980; Blythe, 1979); of drinking or dying (Strauss, 1974; Hanlan, 1979) – whatever may be of interest to the sociologist, one pivotal perspective which should always be entertained is that of the participant's experience itself. This is not to say that social scientists should always rest content with such a perspective; it is to assert that if they fail to seriously consider peoples' concrete experience and have 'intimate familiarity' with them then they will invariably run the extreme risks of simply being wrong – of speculation and abstracting about a phenomenon which does not really exist (cf. Lofland, 1976), or of committing the fallacy of objectivism (Denzin, 1978a, p. 10) – of substituting your own research perspective for that of your subjects. How can one possibly theorise or interpret coalmining or car production if

one does not have familiarity with what that means to the participants themselves?

Such a position has a long and respectable pedigree; all the way at
least from Weber's notion of *verstehen* to the more contemporary
phenomenological and hermeneutic sociologists. One central, but
today largely neglected, figure in clarifying this position was Florian
Znaniecki. Both in his 'methodological note' to *The Polish Peasant*
(with Thomas) and in his *The Method of Sociology* (1934), he
presents a strong concern with the neo-Kantian distinction between
two systems, natural and cultural. Natural systems are given
objectively and exist independently of the experience and activity of
people, while cultural systems are intrinsically bound up with the
conscious experiences of human agents in interaction with each
other. As he puts it:

> Natural systems are objectively given to the scientist as if they
> existed absolute independently of the experience and activity of
> men. The planetary system, the geological composition and
> structure of the rind of the earth, the chemical compound, the
> magnetic field, the plant and the animal, are such as they appear to
> the student, without any participation of human consciousness;
> scientifically speaking, they would be exactly the same if no men
> existed. The essential characters of their elements . . . are such that
> they are apart from the question whether and how anybody
> experiences them; they are bound together by forces which have
> nothing to do with human activity . . . Very different appears such
> indubitably cultural systems as those dealt with by students of
> language and literature, art, religion, science, economics, indus-
> trial technique and social organisation. Generally speaking, every
> cultural system is found by the investigator to exist for certain
> conscious and active historical subjects, i.e. within the sphere of
> experience and activity of some particular people, individuals and
> collectivities, living in a certain part of the human world during a
> certain historical period. Consequently, for the scientist this cul-
> tural system is really and objectively as it was (or is) given to those
> historical subjects themselves when they were (or are) experiencing
> it and actively dealing with it. In a word the data of the cultural
> student are always 'somebody's', never 'nobody's' data. This essen-
> tial character of cultural data we call the humanistic coefficient,
> because such data, as objects of the student's theoretical reflection,
> already belong to someone else's active experience and are such as
> this active experience makes them. If the humanistic coefficient
> were withdrawn and the scientist attempted to study the cultural
> system as he studies a natural system . . . the system would dis-
> appear and in its stead he would find a disjointed mass of natural

things and processes, without any similarity to the reality he started to investigate. (Znaniecki, 1934, pp. 136–7)

One major tradition of sociology has always stressed the importance of studying this 'humanistic coefficient'; of getting at the ways in which participants of social life construct and make sense of their particular world – their 'definitions of the situation', their 'first level constructs'. Many research methods have been identified with this particular tradition, for example Bruyn has shown the strong connection between this phenomenological approach and participant observation (see Bruyn, 1966). In this section, however, I wish to suggest a number of areas by which personal documents are bound to this broad tradition.

THE SUBJECTIVE REALITY OF THE INDIVIDUAL

Life history research advocates, first and foremost, a concern with the phenomenal role of lived experience, with the ways in which members interpret their own lives and the world around them. Indeed for Watson this is the central justification:

> When all is said and done, the only purpose to which the life history lends itself directly, that is where it is not used as a basis for inferences tied heavily to external constructs, theories or measures, is as a commentary of the individual's very personal view of his [sic] own experience as he [sic] understands it. (Watson, 1976, p. 97)

Likewise Ernest Burgess comments:

> In the life history is revealed, as in no other way, the inner life of the person, his moral struggles, his successes and failures in securing his destiny in a world too often at variance with his hopes and ideals. (As quoted by Shaw, 1966, p. 4)

There are many ways of getting at the phenomenology of experience, but in the end there is probably no substitute for spending many hours talking with the subject, gathering up his or her perceptions of the world, encouraging these to be written down, reading through letters and diaries, and developing an intensive intimate familiarity with one concrete life. Consider for example the case of Don the Sun Chief, presented by Simmons (1942). His life can only be adequately understood once the realness to him of an environment peopled with imaginary spirits is grasped: the sun god – a 'strong, middle aged man who makes daily journeys across the sky, lights and heats the world and sustains all life'; the moon and star gods, the eagle and the hawk deities who live in the sky and look after people; the lesser gods like the wind, the lightning, the thunder and the rain; and the snakes – gods who live in the water springs who must be protected. If you kill them you will bring shame to yourself. Without getting close to Don's life this fundamentally different way of organising his world would not be grasped. His cultural system may differ greatly from the researcher's cultural system but it has to be intimately entered if sense is to be made of his social world. This, then, is the paramount justification of life documents.

PROCESS, AMBIGUITY AND CHANGE

Most social science in its quest for generalisability imposes order and rationality upon experiences and worlds that are more ambiguous, more problematic and more chaotic in reality. If we check our own experiences, for example, we know that our lives are often flooded with moments of indecision, turning points, confusions, contradictions and ironies. A lot of social science glosses over this interstitial but central region of life. Questionnaires, experiments, attitude scales and even the perusal of existing social science literature and historical documents can often give a form and order to the world which it frequently does not have. Researchers seek consistency in subjects' responses when subjects' lives are often inconsistent. The life history technique is peculiarly suited to discovering the confusions, ambiguities and contradictions that are played in everyday experiences. When Wladek is giving his story to Thomas and Znaniecki, 'there is little consistency of standpoint. He changes his standpoints during the description, as he changed them during his life; for example his momentary attitude towards any member of his family is dependent on just the phase of relation with him that he happens to recall' (Thomas and Znaniecki, p. 1913). As Howard Becker comments:

> The life history, more than any other technique except perhaps participant observation, can give meaning to the overworked notion of process. Sociologists like to speak of ongoing processes and the like but their methods usually prevent them from seeing the processes they talk about so glibly. (Becker, 1966, p. xiii)

PERSPECTIVE ON TOTALITY

Most social science is involved in a process of amputation – qualitative research and life history research in particular make no claims to grasp wholes. Psychologists will amputate a 'personality', the 'attitude', the 'intelligence quotient' from the totality of the life experience while sociologists will amputate the 'structure' and the 'culture' from the totality of daily lived experience. All social science invariably has to amputate, select and organise materials from a point of view. The perspective (or point of view) of life history research, however, is the totality of the biographical experience – a totality which necessarily weaves between biological bodily needs, immediate social groups, personal definitions of the situation, and historical change both in one's own life and in the outside world. It is quite mistaken to see life histories as thoroughly individualistic – lives move persistently through history and structure. As such more than almost any other method it allows one to grasp a sense of the totality of a life. As Bogdan says:

> The autobiography is unique in allowing us to view an individual in the context of his whole life, from birth to the point at which we encounter him. Because of this it can lead us to a fuller understanding of the stages and critical periods in the processes of his development. It enables us to look at subjects as if they have a past with successes as well as failures, and a future with hopes and fears. It also allows us to see an individual in relation to the history of his time, and how he is influenced by the various religious, social, psychological and economic currents present in his world. It permits us to view the intersection of the life history of men with the history of their society, thereby enabling us to understand better the choices, contingencies and options open to the individual. (Bogdan, 1974, p. 4)

This is a particularly useful contribution in the field of deviancy study, where so much work has disconnected the deviant from his or her total life experience and the wider social formations. Through the use of the life history, the deviant is seen to be much more than a deviant; following him or her over their different life experiences generally shows that deviancy constitutes only a small fragment of any one individual's life. It can help put the deviance in its wider place.

A TOOL FOR HISTORY

Although it is a well trodden critique of both qualitative research and symbolic interactionism that they harbour a neglect of history, it is in fact an empty criticism. For while it is true that interactionists acknowledge the difficulties of producing history (cf. Rock, 1976), they firmly highlight the fact that 'a social psychology without a full attention to history is a blind psychology' (Strauss, 1969). Likewise in an earlier appraisal of life history research in sociology, Angell (1945) saw the explanation of historical sequences as one of three major interests underpinning research with personal documents (the other two being a concern with analysis and a concern with methods), and he praised eight studies for the arduous task of collecting such materials. Each of these studies documented the life problems of particular groups – college women, black youth, prostitutes, delinquents, broken marriages – and traced their subsequent life course. A sense of personal history was thus firmly present in these earlier works. The accusation, therefore, that history is neglected in both symbolic interactionist theory and life history qualitative research is misconceived.

Indeed it is in life history research, as the very name implies, that a proper focus on historical change can be attained in a way that is lacking in many other methods. Such a focus is a dual one, moving between the changing biographical history of the person and the social history of his or her life-span. Invariably the gathering of a life history will entail the subject moving to and fro between the developments of their own life cycle and the ways in which external crises and situations (wars, political and religious changes, employment and unemployment situations, economic change, the media and so forth) have impinged on this. A life history cannot be told without a constant reference to historical change, and this central focus on change must be seen as one of life history's great values (Thompson, in Bertaux, 1981).

In some of my work and that of Jeffrey Weeks, for instance, we have gathered the life histories of elderly and young homosexuals. Although they have faced broadly common problems – stigma, oppression, discrimination – the experience of a 21-year-old gay man John, and a 70-year-old gay man William, are hugely different, largely as a result of different historical circumstances each confronted. The older homosexual was brought up in a period of economic depression, two world wars, a 'denial' (legally and socially) of most forms of sexual experience: it led him to marry against his desires – 'from the word go it was a mistake' – to undergo psychiatric treatment and to keep his sexuality a secret. Only in the climate of the mid-1970s and the rise of gay liberation could he come out publicly and accept his sexuality. As he said:

> I think it's incredibly changed . . . I suppose that Act was the big thing that did the turn over, and now Gay News and all the published books there are . . . and films all on radio and television. I said that before it was concealed and sinful and now it's revealed and joyful . . . (from interview transcript, p. 40, cf. Plummer, 1981)

Through William's account we can glimpse not only the social life of England (and America) between 1920 and 1975, we can also begin to grasp how the very experience of homosexuality has shifted. John's life history, for instance, shows him reaching the stage of 'coming out' and positively accepting his gayness by the age of 21 – fifty years biographically ahead of William's experience! And it is not hard to see why when his historical environment is considered. For a while John, like William, certainly faced problems of stigma, yet he did so in a context where homosexuality was no longer illegal for men over 21 in England and Wales, where organisations existed for gay befriending and gay politics, and where public figures such as the superstar of the late 1970s Tom Robinson have spoken publicly about their gayness. Through these two life histories a great deal can be learned about the impact of historical change on sexual experience (cf. Open University, 1981).

This is only a brief illustration; there are at least three major modes of approaching history through life histories. The most apparent is oral history (discussed in Chapter 2) where the biographical account may recede somewhat and the issue of history becomes the key focus. A second mode – derived largely from interactionist writings – places a great emphasis upon the changing meaning of an individual's life course as he or she moves through personal crises ('careers') side by side with a given age cohort in an evolving historical culture: the personal, the interactional and the cultural are all given attention. Through a 'life' all three may be charted together (cf. Kimmel, 1980), and sometimes – as in Elder's *Children of the Great Depression* (1974) – many life histories can be gathered in a longitudinal study (cf. Elder, in Bertaux, 1981).

A third mode of approaching history derives less from symbolic interactionist theorising and more from pscyhodynamic writings. It is commonly referred to as psychohistory and also like oral history has its own journals and a proliferation of writings. Two broad traditions can be distinguished here. One which is identified with Erikson focuses upon great men like Gandhi and Luther in order to show how the crises of particular historical periods can be mirrored in the crises of particular great men – how these great men have 'a grim willingness to do the dirty work of their ages' (Lifton, 1974, p. 28). The other tradition is often referred to as the 'shared psychohistorical themes approach' and focuses particularly upon the collective symbols of an era. In this tradition the work of Coles on deprived *Children of Crises* but most especially Lifton on collective trauma such as Hiroshima (*Death in Life*) and the Vietnam War (*Home from the War*) are particularly significant.

The Research Contribution: Getting into Different Stages

Life histories not only have considerable value for the researcher who wishes to focus upon subjective realities, ambiguity, totalities and history, they can also be extremely useful at certain stages of the research. Below I will discuss three critical stages – the exploratory stage, complementary stage and the concluding stage. The discussion, however, must not be taken to indicate that life history research only has use as an adjunct to other methods; all methods are enhanced when used with other methods, but the life history research, like all other forms of research, can, under some circumstances, be used on its own.

EXPLORING

In areas of inquiry about which little is known, the life history technique can become a sensitising tool to the kinds of issues and problems involved in that field. It is especially useful in areas in which the conceptualisation of problems has been ill worked out. For instance in the field of sex research many crucial notions – of love, of orgasm, of sexual meaning, of drive, of turn-on – are poorly articulated. In order to build up a theoretical understanding that is grounded upon the empirical world, a first-hand acquaintance of that world becomes necessary. Through the life history technique one is able to build up miniature sensitising concepts and small-scale hypotheses which can be subsequently transferred to a statistical deductive method should one choose. It is this contribution of course which is highlighted in the writings of Glaser and Strauss, Blumer, Lofland, and Denzin. As Angell and Freedman say:

> Expressive documents [life histories] have generally been used in the exploratory rather than the final stages of the research process. Their greatest value perhaps has been in giving investigators a feel for the data and thus producing hunches with respect to the most fruitful ways of conceptualising the problem. The research scientist must become intimately familiar with the situation under study, and one of the best ways to do this is with careful readings of insightful expressive documents. (Angell and Freedman, 1953, pp. 305–6)

COMPLEMENTING

If the first value highlights the use of life history methods at the outset of the research, a second value highlights its use throughout the research process – to complement other methods and 'to balance the objectivism of the experiment, the survey and participant observation with the internal, covert and reflective elements of social behaviour and experience' (Denzin, 1978a, p. 252). Life history complements the tools of objectivism with the tools of subjectivism.

This complementary function can be seen most clearly in the early Chicago studies. The three life history books produced by Shaw on delinquents should be located within the overall analysis by Chicago sociologists of delinquency. Indeed Burgess himself was very keen to combine life history documents of delinquents with a full-scale statistical survey treatment at a later stage (cf. Burgess, 1945; Bogue, 1974 and introduction to Shaw, 1966). As Becker in the introduction to *The Jack Roller* says:

Much of the background any single study would either have to provide in itself, or even worse, about which it would have to make unchecked assumptions, was already at hand for the reader of *The Jack Roller*. When Stanley speaks of the boyish games of stealing he and his pals engaged in, we know that we can find an extensive and penetrating description of that phenomena in Thrasher's *The Gang* [a participant observation study] and when he speaks of a time he spent on West Madison Street, we know we can turn to Nels Anderson's *The Hobo* [another life history] for the understanding of the milieu Stanley then found himself in. If we are concerned about the representativeness of Stanley's case, we have only to turn to the ecological studies carried on by Shaw and McKay to see the same story told on a grand scale in mass statistics. And similarly if one wanted to understand the maps and correlations contained in ecological studies of delinquency, one could then turn to *The Jack Roller* and similar documents for that understanding. (Becker, 1966, pp. ix–x)

CONSOLIDATING, CLARIFYING AND CONCLUDING

Sociology is notoriously full of dense jargon and grand theory which remains inaccessible not only to the general public but also to many sociology students! The life history can be a major tool in overcoming their theoretical fog which obfuscates so many studies: its rich detail exemplifies the theory.

An excellent example of such a benefit can be found in Glaser and Strauss's case history of a 54-year-old dying cancer patient, Mrs Abel. It represents the culmination of a five-year research project which examined the organisation of dying in contrasting hospital wards focusing particularly on the temporal ordering of the dying process (the stages through which patient and medical personnel moved in confronting pain and finally death), and the structuring of knowledge surrounding death (the awareness and non-awareness, suspicions and pretences by participants and patients of incipient death). A number of reports have resulted from this research, but the two major contributions produce substantive (or grounded) theories of 'awareness contexts' and 'status passages' connected with dying cancer patients (Glaser and Strauss, 1967b, 1968). In these studies, many different forms of 'awareness' and 'dying trajectories' are discussed, illustrated from fieldwork and theoretically clarified. For anyone interested in the area of nursing care and dying, they are instructive and insightful volumes.

But something is missing. Death is the omnipresent, overwhelming experience of the human condition; extreme emotions of grief, despair, fear and anguish become entrapped with it. All of us who have experienced the death of loved ones know the emotional upheavals it generates. And somehow to talk of this in terms of 'dying trajectories' and 'awareness contexts' invites us to be appalled at sociological aridity. The case of Mrs Abel stops all this for here is the unfolding story of two research nurses recording the lingering death of an increasingly isolated and rejected woman experiencing ever growing pain from terminal cancer, whose last words before an operation from which she never recovered were 'I hope I die' (Strauss and Glaser, 1977, p. 21). Charting her pain, her last days and her final ill-prepared and lonely death over 150 pages leaves no room for insensitivity. Yet at the same time the authors draw us back to their more theoretical volumes – a bridge is made between experience and general theory. They show 'how well a theory or theories may usefully and relevantly explain and interpret a single case history from a sociological perspective ... [and] in showing how well the theory works, the sociologist shows how well it can be used on other simple cases for understanding and possibly controlling them' (Strauss and Glaser, 1977, p. 177).

The Teaching Contribution: Breaking with Routine

The life history approach is peculiarly ignored in teaching contexts. During a three-year sociology degree, for instance, it might (but usually won't) be given very brief (usually dismissive) attention on a research methods course; hardly ever will the kind of data it produces be taken seriously on other courses. Asked to read *The Polish Peasant*, *The Jack Roller* or *Letters from Jenny*, students may feel that they have left the world of significant social theory for the world of idiosyncratic description; asked to watch *Kes*, *Family Life* or *The Naked Civil Servant*, they may feel they are simply being entertained; asked to read *Ruby Fruit Jungle*, *Akenfield* or *Invisible Man*, they may feel they have left sociology altogether and entered the world of imagination and literature. Little time can be allowed for such eccentric pursuits.

Yet the dividing lines between art and science are in reality very thin indeed – creativity and imagination tie them together closely, and the root issues of sociological substance described above can, therefore, be greatly enhanced through a focus on the life history. 'The universal is found,' says Nisbet (1976, p. 213) 'as it should be, in the concrete.' 'The particular,' says Lifton, 'is the only path to the general, but cannot itself be comprehended outside of the general' (Lifton, 1973, p. 19). The life history provides an ideal vehicle for the social scientist to sway to and fro between life's specifics and theory's generalities.

Apart from the obvious incorporation of such studies in the reading materials of each and every stage of all courses (if they don't exist, it says a lot about the meagreness of that area of inquiry!), there are four ways at least in which it can become a more central focus.

First it is one of the simpler and most suitable of approaches to adopt in student projects. Student projects in sociology generally have to be produced within a year, have to be produced by a solitary researcher, aspire towards some kind of originality and should pragmatically entail minimal disruption in the lives of other people. The life history technique fulfils all these criteria splendidly. It is suitable for the lone researcher who has access to one relevant person in the outside world who can furnish his or her account usually with a six-month span. It involves the student in 'doing' sociology, but without bringing too much disruption to the outside world (as social survey techniques employed by students can sometimes do). It should produce new and interesting findings, since the idiosyncrasies of a particular life will be tapped. And it should enable the student to appreciate the myriad difficulties in moving between the concrete and the abstract, the unique and the general, the personal and the social, the descriptive and the theoretical – problems that any adequate sociology should persistently address.

Another lively way of teaching is to introduce the life history subject into the classroom situation to tell his or her own story. This is of course a much flimsier approach than a dense life history study and the problem of situated accounts will loom large in all such classroom discussions; the students will nevertheless become sensitised to the concrete issues involved. A model of such an approach is contained in Winslow's *Deviant Reality: Alternative World Views* where a series of seminars were arranged which entailed the presentation of 'live, first hand, own story accounts from the point of view of deviant actors themselves', presentations which were then followed by question and answer sessions and which teased the account back to the theoretical concerns of sociology. Delinquents, heroin addicts, nudists, homosexuals, lesbians, transsexuals, prostitutes, embezzlers, robbers, murderers, rapists and organised criminals all present their stories in the verbatim recordings to be found in the book, alongside the theoretical discussion and commentary. It is a useful model for teaching, and it is not surprising that the focus here should be deviance since it is within this tradition particularly that a serious commitment to understanding the world from the point of view of the actor has developed.

Theoretically the deviant's perspective perceives the social world as structured in part through a 'hierarchy of credibility' by which only the more powerful groups in society can routinely have their voices heard and taken seriously – devalued underdogs find their views to be largely discredited. Deviancy theory thus seeks to give them a voice (cf. Becker, 1971). Yet while such an approach has particular relevance to deviancy theory, it can also be seen as relevant to all those courses that acknowledge the importance of *verstehen* and consciousness: the trade unionist, the religious convert, the housewife, the old person, the cancer patient, the farm worker, the journalist, the Chilean refugee, the unemployed man, the local politician, the student and the social security official all have their account to tell. Indeed a nightmarish short story has been written by Cohen (1979) which dramatically displays how the worlds of the sociological experts are far removed from the worlds of the people they study. Bringing 'people' into the teaching situation could be accused of a patronising paternalism – but so could all of sociology – and at least through direct contact with peoples' lives and their problems, the student will lose the temptation to impose wild theorising and abstract conceptualisations upon phenomena with which they have not first hand acquaintance (cf. Lofland, 1976, ch. 1).

A third way in which life histories can be given a central focus in teaching sociology is to use written biographies as organising points in a course. In my own social psychology teaching, for instance, I have used the life of Quentin Crisp (in *The Naked Civil Servant*) as a stimulant for discussion on Freudian theory in explaining homosexuality and gender development and on interactionist theory in dealing with the presentation of self in everyday life. The life of Hitler (in the studies by Bullock, Fest and Erikson (1977)) can be used as a tool for continuing the debate between Freudian and interactionist thought, along with raising new issues about conformity and authoritarianism, social and psychological explanations of fascism and of the dire need to incorporate historical analysis into generally 'timeless' social psychological theories. Ultimately the students are asked to produce a life history case themselves and to see what sense some parts of social psychological theory can make of it. Such a technique has difficulties, not least of which being that students often find it difficult to make a bridge across an academic theory on the one hand and a good read on the other. But on balance, like all the strategies outlined above, it does serve to keep the students' feet on the empirical ground of specifics whilst searching the less accessible heavens of theories.

A fourth strategy, closely related to the above, is to return to John Dollard's classic criteria for a life history produced in the 1930s. I have discussed this study previously; it provides seven unifying criteria for the appraisal of any particular life history. Dollard's work was not just concerned with social science biographies – he devotes significant analysis to the *Experiment in Autobiography* of H. G. Wells. At the end of the book he suggests that students could profitably take any biography and use the criteria as a basis for appraising its validity.

He suggests the following seven-point manual of how to go about it: (i) the student should read and remember the criteria, and then (ii) select a life history, be it an autobiography, a biography or a psychiatric history. The document should then be read and (iii) marked in the margin with a number one if the passage read is relevant to criterion number one, a two if the passage read is relevant to criterion two and so forth. These passages should then be (iv) copied out and put in chronological order according to which criteria they relate to. This should be followed by (v) a discussion from the standpoint of each given criterion, and a (vi) summary of how the life history shapes up in view of these criteria. Finally, (vii) the analysis should always give full credit where it is due. Life history material does not have to show evidence of every criterion; a document could be quite valuable even though it did not meet all of them. The problem with Dollard's approach is the validity of the criteria themselves – Allport, for example, has criticised him as being too psychoanalytically oriented and rather arbitrary. But again it could serve as a useful point of discussion in teaching (see Dollard, 1935, pp. 265–7 and my earlier discussion of this in Chapter 3).

There are many others ways in which personal documents could enhance teaching and learning: video can be made use of in fieldwork and life history interviews can be brought to the class for dissection; photographs can be taken and the images discussed (cf. Wagner, 1979); diaries can be kept and analysed (cf. Miller and Miller, 1976). Once the trail of thought is started the examples multiply and one is left wondering why so much sociology teaching has remained moribundly fixated on the book, the paper and the lecture!

The Practical Contribution

Many sociologists start out with a view of the person as an active, creative, world builder but before they have completed their theoretical endeavours they have enchained, dehumanised, rendered passive and lost that same person. The subject has become the object, the person has become the statistic, the creative has become the constrained, the human being has become the abstraction. Durkheim, Marx, Weber and Parsons can all be read in this fashion, their 'people' becoming their 'systems'. In this they replicate with theoretical practices the very theory they usually describe – how man's creativity becomes institutionalised, habitualised, structured into a system through which he or she is controlled and alienated. It is the paradigm problem of sociology, maybe even the paradigm problem of modern existence. Indeed Alan Dawe has argued that there is a direct link between the moral experience of the sociologist (and everybody else) and the kind of theories that they try to produce. The whole of sociology in one sense has been a massive attempt to grasp and reconcile the problem of individuality and collectively, of human agency and creativity matched up with collective constraint and control. All these sociologies, says Dawe, have ultimately tottered towards a sociology of collectivity, of system, of constraint and have ultimately lost the position of the human individual as a social person with worries, anxieties, but most central of all, dignity and creativity (Dawe, 1978).

There is, as I suggested in Chapter 1, a very strong affinity between life history research and a brand of humanism – 'thought or action in which human interest, values and dignity are taken to be of primary importance' (cf. Lee, 1978, p. 45). Humanism has a long and chequered history (going back at least to the fifth century BC when Protagoras of Abdara could proclaim that 'Man is the measure of all things, of the existence of things that are, of the non-existence of things that are not') and it has an enormous variety of positions within it (the liberal, the Marxist and the religious, along with 'humanistic psychology' and 'humanistic social science' (cf. Lee, 1978, p. 50). What, however, humanism always does is constantly assert the value of human creativity, human uniqueness and human value within the context of a vast planet of life and an infinite universe; the very values in fact which are frequently lost in much sociology, and which champions of structuralism would argue are a valuable loss! (cf. Althusser, 1969). The kinds of materials being discussed in this book never lose sight of the person in intimate contact with other people.

The affinity is clearly to humanism, but a humanism that persistently acknowledges the fundamental ambiguity of privatisation and collective living. Peoples' lives are the concrete details we have to study; but those lives will inevitably be trapped within the contradictions of constraint and choice, diversity and similarity. The life history's humanistic commitment leads to a humanistic praxis. There is nothing drastically practical or ravishingly radical about this style of work: tales are sifted, culled and presented of people's lives –

that alone, if done well, is enough to provide care, caution and change. There is no evidence that grander sociologies have played any accurate role in social policy, though they have certainly been symbolically referred to a great deal (cf. Scott and Shore, 1979). But from Chicago onwards – and they certainly had grander goals too – life documents have been enlisted in the service of modest practical change.

A CATHARSIS OF COMPREHENSION

Perhaps Park had the clearest view of both their *limits*, yet their *centrality*. For Park, 'the life history method should work a quiet catharsis of comprehension' (Matthews, 1977, p. 163). Park's main area of practical activity, race relations, convinced him that the best source of change was 'intimate acquaintaince with the problem itself' through the personal document; 'there was,' he asserted, 'no other technique for improvement of race relations in which I have any confidence whatsoever' (p. 163). He continues:

> My own experiences prove that there is nothing which has so com-
> pletely transformed the attitudes of people towards each other as
> these intimate life histories, of which Booker Washington's *Up
> From Slavery* is the most striking example. For this reason, we have
> put more emphasis on the collection of materials of this kind, than
> we have put on formal statistics . . . Such a study . . . will achieve
> the ends for which this investigation was undertaken without the
> necessity of making any appeal, argument or special pleas for any-
> one. (Park, quoted in Matthews, 1977, p. 163)

Park is arguing for a painstaking grasping of the other person's viewpoint and seems to believe that once people of good will are exposed to such concrete details (and they must be details) of individual human predicaments, they will come in their good will to grasp what needs to be done about the situation and bring about change within it. This view talks of a mode of approaching problems, but does not of itself take a clearly political stance. The affinity seems to lie with libertarianism, but this approach can, notoriously, be allied to the right or the left. There can be documentaries of celebra-tion as well as documentaries of critique – as has been well demonstrated in studies of American documentaries in the 1930s (see Stott, 1973, chs 10 and 13). Nevertheless, in the hand of so many practitioners it is undoubtedly a tool of critical attack (Kriseberg, 1975, ch. 3; Denfield, 1974).

Over and over again then in life history research we find the strain-ing towards 'a catharsis of comprehension', to overcome that 'certain blindness' of which all human beings are victim. Robert Bogdan's (1974) depiction of Jane Fry, the transsexual, affords once again a good illustration.

Traditionally, transsexualism has been viewed as a sickness; what the 200 pages of Jane Fry's own story allows us to see is that it is an intelligible, even reasonable, experience for her: a credence is accorded her which challenges the words and worlds of the clinical practitioner. 'Jane accepts her gender feelings for what they are, that is, she takes them for granted. The professionals, however, see them as immature verbalisations of character disorder, a castration anxiety, a psychotic profile and part of the repertoire for the resolution of core conflicts' (Bogdan, 1974, p. 215). Bogdan continues:

> We see glaring contradictions between Jane's definitions and those of the professionals. The many pages of Jane's story that have preceded this discussion have acquainted us with Jane's vocabulary and views before confronting those of the experts. Having spent more time with her and having more first hand information about her than all the professionals whose comments had been presented here we are in a position to look at them more sceptically and to give the patient's perspective more credence. Seldom are we given an opportunity to see in such detail the position of the client juxtaposed with that of the professional – be the client a juvenile delinquent, a retardate, a welfare recipient or a transsexual.

He continues further:

> The professional is seldom effectively challenged, and more rarely are the assumptions based on his training and experience publicly examined or questioned. Jane's perspective enables us to question inductively diagnostic labels, psychological constructs and the way mental illness and various forms of so-called deviant behaviour are conceptualised. (Bogdan, 1974, p. 217)

Jane Fry's story is not an isolated example of this 'catharsis of comprehension' or more strongly what Bogdan refers to as 'the politics of perspective'. Thus Chic Conwell, Sutherland's thief, shows how the whole criminal justice system is open to bribery and corruption – and how the thief would 'have to have a very beautiful imagination to believe he will get justice in a court where at other times he has his cases fixed and where perhaps at the moment the other side has the fix in' (Sutherland, 1967, p. 199). Harry King, Chambliss's *Box Man*, finds the 'square john' straight world much less honest than his criminal world – 'there was more thieves, cheaters, racketers on society's side of the fence than there was on the criminal side', (Chambliss, 1972, p. 132). William Tanner, Spradley's Drunk, describes how he was robbed by the police (Spradley, 1970, p. 14). And a dying man, Archie, writes:

> I had finished playing games with others on the subject of my illness and my dying. In refusing, I may come across as hostile; in fact, I probably did recently with the neurologist; but I will not forfeit my own well being while her or anybody else plays out a role. Virtually nothing is known medically about my disease; there is no treatment for it; my body tells me more accurately about my symptoms than any physician can tell at this point. I do not deny that the skill and technical knowledge of the physicians are invaluable in many situations, but in some, in my own, his role is a very limited one and I do not intend to aggrandise it; our society rewards medical practitioners entirely out of proportion to their specific value in society . . . (Hanlan, 1979, p. 37)

And so the stories could continue, giving flesh and bones to the injustices and indignities of the world where so frequently in social science there is only bland and horrible jargon that serves to over-distance from the issues, to conceal and mystify what is actually occurring in the social world.

It is clear then from the above, and from many of the arguments in this book, that a central thrust of personal document research is to enable voices to be heard that are usually silenced: the victims of what Becker calls a 'hierarchy of credibility' can come through to others on their own terms, slowly puncturing the 'certain blindness' that enshrouds all human beings. Not of course that it is only the underdogs whose voices can be heard in personal documents. For such research has a fundamentally democratising thrust to it: each person has a life and a story to tell. Before the tape recorder or the camera all, however momentarily, are equal. Thus, when Wiseman is accused of presenting a sympathetic view of the oppressive police in his film *Law and Order*, he can retort:

> I would certainly never agree that the only view that the film presents is of the cop as a nice guy. What I really object to is the view that the cop, as a human being, is really any different from anybody else. I don't believe it's true; I may have believed it was true before I spent six weeks with them, but I certainly don't believe it now. The ease with which some people can classify large groups of people as either being groovy or just pigs escapes me . . . (Wiseman, 1971, p. 325)

All voices need hearing: it is just that some are heard less often than others. The social scientist can, through personal documents, play a minor role of advocacy (cf. Lifton, 1972; Weber and McCall, 1978).

A final practical contribution of life history research can be found in the broad appraisal of lives. Daly has written a scathing attack on the numerous round of assessment situations found in American society (and all Western capitalist societies), each of which is blinded to a narrow conception of people's abilities 'in psychiatric hospitals, where one can observe patients put down by the medical model, in industry where one can see employees and managers put down by the personnel model, and in the study of bureaucratic operations, where one can watch students or employees being processed' (Daly, 1971, p. xiii). In each case a narrow look prohibits a concern with a life as a whole – people are 'viewed through a filter of assumptions denying much of their potential, dignity and individuality' and an overall sense of where they have come from, where they are going to, what matters to them, is amputated, ignored or denied. Drawing from the psychological models of Allport and Maslow, Daly argues that 'The ultimate criterion of truth about an individual' can only be gleaned from a life history:

A man's life is to him the most obvious and overwhelming of all realities. Traces of his past are his constant companions; as for his future do not most people act as if they will live indefinitely? It is therefore most surprising that there should be any question whether life is a substantial enough form of fact to provide data for an assessment system. Perhaps what has so long delayed the evolution of a life history assessment system, has been the undeniable problems of a person's life as an awesome, intricate, beautifully complex phenomena, much too complex for the simple descriptive procedures preferred by assessment psychologists in the past. (Daly, 1971, p. 28)

Conclusion

The central value of life documents – and the job they can best do – lies in the tapping of ordinary, ambiguous personal meanings. It is a point constantly returned to in this book. With this goal in mind, life documents become important tools in research, in teaching and in political change. Each of these has been raised in this Chapter in the hope that their further implications will be explored in the future and not ignored as they have been in the recent past.

Suggestions for Further Reading

The central value of life histories as an adjunct to phenomenological work is discussed in an article by L. C. Watson, 'Understanding a life history as a subjective document' (1976): it argues the central link to hermeneutics (not discussed in this text), outlines eleven descriptive categories 'for a framework of understanding' and then applies them to the life of a 32-year-old Guajiro woman, Blanca Gonzalez. Wider discussions of the value of documents may be found in Allport's (1942) *The Use of Personal Documents* (especially part 1, pp. 18–66). Gottschalk *et al.* (1945) *The Use of Personal Documents* (especially Robert Angell's contribution); E. W. Burgess's 'Research methods in sociology' (1945); Becker's introduction to C. Shaw's (1966) *The Jack Roller*; Bogdan's introduction to his book (1974) *Being Different*; and A. Faraday and K. Plummer's, 'Doing life histories' (1979).

Psychohistory has spawned a large literature, much of which is described in the *Journal of Psychohistory*. A useful general collection is R. J. Lifton's (1974) *Explorations in Psychohistory* and a recent critique is D. Stannard (1980), *Shrinking History*. Classic illustrations of the approach would include E. Erikson's (1959) *Young Man Luther*, R. Coles (1968) *Children of Crisis*, and R. J. Lifton's (1968) *Death in Life*, which deals with Hiroshima victims. On the general significance of history, see Part 3 of D. Bertaux's (1981) *Biography and Society*.

Very little has been written about the teaching of sociology. There are a few scattered discussions which I refer to in the text but it is an area ripe for fuller exploration.

On the practical relevance of sociology, R. Scott and A. Shore (1979) *Why Sociology does not Apply*, provides little room for optimism, while B. Glassner and J. Freedman's (1979) *Clinical Sociology* and T. Cook and C. Reichardt's (1979) *Qualitative and Quantitative Methods in Evaluation Research* purportedly leave more room for hope! But there is little discussion of the practical value of personal documents to be found.

5

The Doing of Life Histories

One of the principles of my work is to allow people to speak for themselves, to whatever extent this is possible, and in return to communicate to them, in our conversations as well as in my writing, that it is their words I seek, and not material for the generation of something that ultimately transcends their words and hence their lives. (T. Cottle, 1978, p. xii)

All research raises four basic sets of problems which have to be confronted at every stage of work. The four problems, which I call the paradigm of methodological problems, are:

(1) The social science questions. This deals largely with the justification for doing research at all, essentially with the 'Why?' questions of social research. Much of this discussion centres around epistemological arguments.
(2) The technical questions: these deal largely with the nuts and bolts, nitty-gritty of doing the actual research – of getting the samples, of interviewing adequately, of assessing validity. In essence this question deals with the 'How?' of social research.
(3) The ethical and political questions: these questions deal with the extra-technical and extra-social scientific problems – with the political justification of doing this kind of work, and with the ethical dilemmas that occur during its progress.
(4) The personal questions: these deal with the dual impact of the research on the researcher's personal life, and of the researcher's personal life upon the research.

Each of these four problems should be conceived dynamically: at the *beginning* of the research, *during* it, and at the *end* they will constantly have to be confronted. Any full account of the methodology of any project should hence involve an analysis which simply tabulated looks as in Table 5.1.

Much of the earlier part of this book has been dealing with the 'social scientific' questions – showing the intellectual foundation of life history research and its distinctive contributions. In the chapters to follow, I am turning to the last three questions – to the actual doing of life history research and with the ethical, political and personal problems that this brings in its wake.

Table 5.1   *Paradigm for the Analysis of Methodological Problems*

Kind of Problem	Stages of the Research		
	Prior to the research	During the research	At the end of the research
(1) Social scientific			
(2) Technical/Practical			
(3) Ethical/Political			
(4) Personal			

Some cautions are in order. First in this chapter I am dealing only with life history research: the work involved in the use of letters, photographs or diaries may be similar but the content would certainly be different. For convenience, therefore, this chapter is restricted to only one personal document form, the 'created' life history. Further the chapter deals only with the technical problems of doing such work; the issues of a more personal and ethical nature will be discussed in Chapter 7. It is also important to see that although I will be discussing five processes which would be viewed as moving in chronological progression (thereby constituting major phases of a research programme) this is not in fact how it actually happens. Some researchers propose that qualitative research is most usefully con-ceived as a series of stages: thus Spradley (1970) suggests 'some tasks are best accomplished before other tasks', and hence a series of steps (which he develops into a twelve-point Developmental Research Sequence (DRS)) can be spelt out. In many ways, such statements bring to qualitative research what Stan Cohen and Laurie Taylor have referred to as the lie of chronological research (Cohen and Taylor, 1972). In quantitative research it is common to see a series of well planned steps which must be engaged in from the inception of the project to its final publication; in attempts to make qualitative research more rigorous, some researchers – like Denzin (1978a) – have seen such phases as likewise necessary. It is certainly true that for analytic convenience the five processes in this chapter could be seen as following from each other; but this temptation should be resisted in practice. For every stage can be executed side by side with the next stage. Thus, although difficult, analysis of data should *always* accompany the research interviewing since accumulated data should shape the problems to follow; writing up data will not necessarily come at the end but may sometimes come during the course of the research as it can be a way of sharpening the analysis; and planning – and preparations – will inevitably be taking place constantly.

Nevertheless, for convenience alone, five broad processes can be depicted. These are:

(1) *Preparation.* This involves choosing an appropriate problem, locating a broad theoretical orientation, choosing the kinds of research strategies to be used, working out the funding arrangements and staffing arrangements in some cases, pondering the kind of subject that is required for the investigation and the ways to approach him or her, and clarifying the logistics of the interview, the mode of storing data and the final form of presentation.

(2) *Data gathering.* This is concerned with the actual strategies of gaining the life history materials. Primarily this will involve the crafts of interview technique, but it might also involve triangulation by which other strategies will be brought into play, strategies such as participant observation and letter analysis. It will also involve such issues as the way of recording the data.

(3) *Data storing.* Qualitative materials are not usually susceptible to computerisation, but they nevertheless have to be rendered 'hard' – at least hard enough to be available for longish periods of time. Hence this process is concerned largely with issues of transcription, coding and filing.

(4) *Data analysis.* This at root is concerned with three major problems: the issues of internal and external validity, of representativeness, and of theorising and conceptualisation. In the most general terms it entails making good service of the data.

(5) *Data presentation.* This is concerned with issues relating to the ways in which the material is finally written up and presented to an audience.

It will be seen that these five pages could be taken as a sequential model; this is not my view. Each stage may well proceed simultaneously with the other stages. In this chapter they will, however, be discussed in turn.

1 Preparation

(A) WHO SHALL BE STUDIED?

Erikson has remarked that 'Sampling is the strategy of persons who work with vast universes of data; it is a strategy of plenty' (Erikson, 1973, p. 15). Conversely, life history research is usually the strategy of the poor – of the researcher who has little hope of gaining a large and representative sample from which bold generalisation may be made. The issue of traditional sampling strategies is hence not usually at stake; rather the problem becomes this: who from the teeming millions of world population is to be selected for such intensive study and sociological immortality? The great person, the common person, the marginal person? The volunteer, the selected, the coerced?

There seem to be two ways researchers have approached this problem – the pragmatic and the formal. One is largely dependent upon chance, whereby the subject is not selected but slowly emerges from some wider worry, while another, more formal, tries to establish theoretical or methodological criteria for selection.

Pragmatism and Chance
Many life history studies do not appear to have been planned; a chance encounter, a subject of interest emerging from a wider study, an interesting volunteer – these seem common ways of finding a subject. Thus, Bogdan met Jane Fry in a chance encounter when she was a speaker for a gay group at a social problems seminar (Bogdan, 1974, p. 6); Sutherland met Chic Conwell in 1932 through *Reitman* – 'The King of the Hoboes' – who was both literary and keen 'to learn an honest, useful life' (Snodgrass, 1973, p. 7 and cf. Blumer and Hughes, 1980); Frank Moore was the 'thirteenth of two hundred and three' men interviewed by Straus in 1945 for a study of alcohol and homeless men (Straus, 1974, p. viii); Cheryl was 'one of many informants in a study of youth culture from 1964 to 1969 in four urban communities' (Schwartz *et al.*, 1980); Stanley was one of 'a series of two hundred similar studies' of delinquent boys (cf. Shaw, 1966, p. 1; Snodgrass, 1978, p. 4); while Thomas initially discovered some of his letters when some garbage was thrown out of a window down a Chicago alley and landed at his feet! (cf. Janowitz, 1966, p. xxiv). In all these studies there is little sense of a sustained search for a suitable subject through explicit criteria; rather the feel is that the sociologist scooped a 'find' – someone who was congenial to the researcher, had a good story to tell and who could say it well. Given the overall value of such studies as the above, it may well be that the tacit criteria of a 'good find' should continue to guide research in the future. However, it would help to make such criteria more explicit.

The Formal Criteria
The above highlights a very practical guideline for the choice of informants – they are merely stumbled upon! Others, however, may try to find a subject on more explicit criteria (cf. Sellitz *et al.*, pp. 61–5). The choice here broadly is between three kinds of person: the marginal person, the great person and the common man.

The marginal person has probably been the most frequent and most fruitful choice of subject. Classically, the marginal person is one 'who fate has condemned to live in two societies, and in two, not merely different but antagonistic cultures' (Stonequist, 1961), while sociologically, it is Simmel and Schutz's 'Strangers' and Garfinkel's 'Practical Methodologist'. In each case the subject lives at a cultural crossroads. Experiencing contrasting expectations as to how he or she should live, the subject becomes aware of the essentially artificial and socially constructed nature of social life – how potentially fragile are the realities that people make for themselves. In this awareness the subject throws a much broader light on the cultural order, the 'OK world' that is routinely taken for granted by most (cf. Jansen, 1980).

Thus Don Talayesba, the Sun Chief, lies on the edge of Indian and American culture (Simmons, 1942), James Sewid experiences the culture conflict of a Kwakiutl Indian facing modernising Canada (Spradley, 1969), Wladek leaves Poland for Chicago, Victor – the Wild Boy of Aveyron – lives halfway between humanity and 'beast-hood' (Lane, 1977); Jane Fry and 'Agnes' travel from male worlds to female worlds (Garfinkel, 1967) and Frank Moore, an institutionalised alcoholic, lives on the margins of social respectability (Straus, 1974): all of these reveal the value of choosing a subject between two worlds. Agnes the hermaphrodite is perhaps the most explicit use of a case study in this fashion. Garfinkel, working with the psychiatrist Stoller, focused intensively upon the cultural productions of a hermaphrodite – of being born an ambiguous boy and later becoming self-defined as a girl and woman. Out of this highly atypical case, Garfinkel is able to clarify the artfully worked nature of gender meanings, showing how Agnes comes to sense a social, but taken-for-granted, world of gender expectations, and how she has to work hard to fit herself into them. Through this documentary study of one case, Garfinkel is able to produce a list of standardised expectations about gender as a social product in this society. Most people assume gender, but it is through the atypical case who finds such an assumption problematic that such a listing becomes possible. For most people gender is commonsensical and taken for granted, and the marginal case can highlight this (cf. Garfinkel, 1967; Kessler and McKenna, 1978).

The great person. Marginality can be fairly readily identified, greatness cannot. But it is this criterion which some historians use in order to throw light on *kultur* – socially significant events rather than routinely accepted ones. 'Great men' – Goethe, Luther, Napoleon, Gandhi, Hitler – are selected because in them, uniquely, are to be found certain values and crises which have a much wider bearing on the age in which they live than those of the common man. In this view, 'the average man is to Goethe as a lump of coal is to the Kohinoor diamond' (Mandelbaum, 1967, p. 124).

The sociological approach seems rarely to have espoused this view preferring instead to seek out the marginal or the commonplace. It is in 'psychohistory' that the great man approach has come most pivotally into its own, especially in Erikson's celebrated case histories of Luther, Gandhi and Hitler (e.g. Erikson, 1959). Erikson has a particular fascination with 'greatness', suggesting that the identity crises of great people mirror the identity crises of their time; such people have unusually powerful childhood consciences reflecting their periods (thereby commonly appearing old in their early years (cf. Roazen, 1979, p. 75)). Such people are usually marginal too, but their importance culturally helps throw light on grand historical concerns rather than commonplace ones.

The ordinary person seems to come closest to providing a source for generalisations to a wider population, but in effect it is notoriously difficult to locate such a person. Almost everyone stands 'out of the ordinary' on some dimension or the other. That is the essence of an intensive, ideographic approach. Nevertheless, with due caution, researchers have often focused upon samples of 'ordinary people' as a source (this is particularly true of oral history), or have sought a few people about whom initially there appeared little that was extraordinary – not too marginal, not too great. White's *Lives in Progress* is a good example perhaps of this latter approach, where volunteer students were the basis of selection.

(B) WHAT MAKES A GOOD INFORMANT?

Whatever may be the theoretical and methodological reasons for choosing a subject, there are also good logistical ones. A first criterion here is simple accessibility of place and time. Since meetings may take place each week for several years, and meetings may last each week for two to three hours, any subject must have a fair amount of spare time on their hands in order to participate in the research. Someone who is extraordinarily busy is unlikely to make a good informant. Likewise the subject should live within easy distance of the researcher: an excellent informant may be found who lives many miles away, hence making it very difficult to sustain the relationship and the research. A second criterion concerns the qualities of the informant: Spradley (1979a, pp. 45–54) suggests that a good informant should be thoroughly enculturalised (hence fully aware, deeply involved and informed in their particular cultural world), currently involved (their account is hence not simply a reinterpretation of past experiences but a statement of current practices) and non-analytic (informants that are overly intellectual and overly abstract are of less value than those who talk about their experiences in the raw). Clearly also the subject should be fairly articulate, able to verbalise and have a 'a good story to tell' – although, under the right conditions, all people will meet this bill. A third criterion centres around the relationship between the researcher and the subject. Life history research, perhaps more than any other, involves the establishment and maintenance of a close and intimate relationship with the subject, often for a number of years meeting regularly each week. Such a relationship cannot be sustained if there is an underlying dislike, lack of respect or hostility between the two people. Hence at the very outset it is crucial to establish that both researcher and subject have some broad common sympathies and basically like and respect each other sufficiently for the research to be sustained. I sometimes wonder just how many life history studies may have been started which have subsequently come to a sticky end because of hostilities developing in this highly intimate relationship.

(C)   WHAT NEEDS CLARIFYING AT THE EARLIER STATES OF THE RESEARCH?

Given that much life history research will simply evolve piecemeal – often out of a wider study – it is unlikely that the researcher will usually be able to sit down quietly for two or three hours to work out precisely all the questions that need going over with the life history subject. Living with ambiguity is a central feature of life history research and there is no easy way to plan it. Thus for instance very frequently the life history subject will not appear as such until after a few months of acquaintance, and the question concerning the subject's participation in a life history study may take a long time before it can be broached. In an ideal world of course, the subject will be located and a contract worked out between the researcher and subject which specifies the solutions to all kinds of problems; in practice the entire process is much more muddled and confused than that. Nevertheless, as a guide to issues that need to be considered the following is a brief checklist of worries that will invariably crop up.

First, *motivations* will need to be clarified. The subject will undoubtedly be curious as to why you, the researcher, are interested in him or her and you should be ready with an honest response: a response that will almost certainly include career and professional advantage side by side with some tangible political and/or moral concern for a social problem. At the outset it is necessary to come fairly clean with the subject who will very likely sense a whiff of exploitation unless you do. At the same time it is necessary for the researcher to try to grasp the motivation of the subject: why on earth should anybody be willing to let a social scientist into his/her life for a few years to hear all their intimate details? Allport suggests thirteen reasons why people might on occasions be willing to disclose themselves, ranging through special pleading (providing a self-justification), exhibitionism, a desire for order, literary delight, securing one's personal perspective, a relief from tension, monetary gain, filling in one's life, a therapeutic encounter, redemption and social reincorporation (a confession), a desire to help science or to further public service, a desire for immortality or simply as a course work assignment! (Allport, 1942, ch. 5).

In many instances, life history subjects will be paid small fees for their services, another issue which needs clarification with the subject at the outset. This may at times be the prime incentive, especially with marginal subjects, so that the whole enterprise may be based on a cash transaction. Frank Moore, for instance, the institutionalised alcoholic, received between one and five dollars for almost every letter that he wrote to Straus (Straus, 1974, pp. 20, and 306) and often the researcher 'sent tobacco, clothing, writing materials, books, candy, copies of articles on alcohol or other subjects of mutual interest, and copies of my own publications on descriptions of other professional activities' (p. 21). Frank Moore wrote a lot of letters and clearly got a lot of rewards; but helpful as this was to Frank Moore he strongly implies that this money was a debt that he built up to his researcher, not something that was rightfully and contractually his. Thus, Straus, had to reassure him: 'You have no financial obligations whatsoever to me' (p. 305). Money doesn't seem anything like as important as the intrinsic satisfaction derived from one's own self reflection. Consider Frank Moore again:

> Methinks I have received far more than I have contributed. My own evaluation of this correspondence is that it has been to me what the confessional box is to the Catholic, what the wailing wall is to the Hebrew, what the psychiatric couch is to the woman in menopause . . . with the added advantage you answer every time . . . Whatever this correspondence might have meant to you, it prevented me from laughing myself to death or murder. The correspondence was like the touchstone of alcohol to a man who had reached his particular peak of mental pain. (Straus, 1974, p. 371)

Here then the financial rewards, whilst present, do not seem to be as important as the emotional rewards. In general, it might be seen as a highly gratifying experience to know that somebody is sufficiently interested in one's life to be willing and bothered enough to take it down in great detail. It is rewarding that someone takes this interest; it is gratifying to clarify one's own view of one's life; and it is satisfying to finally obtain a document about oneself. Frequently of course these accounts will be little more than justificatory apologies. Motivations, therefore, need to be carefully reflected upon. The researcher needs to ask: what does the interviewee hope to gain from this? And as Sullivan comments:

> The quid pro quo which leads to the best psychiatric interview – as well as the best interview for employment or other purposes – is that the person being interviewed realises quite early he is going to learn something useful about the way he lives. (Sullivan, 1951, p. 18)

A second area to consider is that of *anonymity*. Whilst it is a commonplace in most social science research to guarantee the anonymity of the subjects, in the life history pure and proper so much intimate detail is likely to be revealed that it will not be too difficult for anybody dedicated to finding out who the subject is, actually to do so. I will discuss this issue further in the chapter on ethics, but suffice to say for the time being that the researcher needs to clarify with the subject (and in his or her own mind) the extent to which names, places and life events might need changing. For instance the selection of a subject who performs significant historically unique acts in his or her life might raise very serious problems as to the suitability of that subject. If only one person has led a particular battle, written a particular sort of book, been employed in a unique occupation, organised a particularly famous television programme, undergone a famous operation, then the inclusion of such a story in their life history will make them instantly recognisable. So it may not just be a matter of changing names or even places, but also sometimes changing the life history events. This, of course, could make a travesty of the issue of truth.

A third item that needs clarifying with the research subject is *the precise nature of the life history study*. Very often the subject will find it difficult to grasp what is entailed. It is important not to baffle and confuse your respondent by making the method sound too elaborate and complex. Often the most useful strategy is simply to give the informant some existing sociological life history works to look over – this will usually be quite sufficient to inform them of what is required. It will need to be clarified with the subject whether the life history research is simply going to depend upon the transcriptions of an interview situation or whether it will be combined with participant observation, talking to their friends, the reading of their letters, and the discussion of their photographs. Indeed if the latter techniques are going to be brought in, a much stronger sense of involvement and commitment will be required by the subject: the researcher will almost be trying to become a close friend of the subject and in doing this

the life history goals may lead to a potential tension between friendship and professionalism. Another issue that will need considering at
the outset is the *logistics of the interviewing situation.* Too frequently
this is left to chance. Once clear that a life history study is being
embarked upon, time should be taken with the subject to discuss in
detail many matters. These include the time and place of meeting; the
regular return of the transcripts for the subject to read over and
comment upon; the kinds of questions that will be asked at different
stages of the interview sessions; whether the subject is to read the
questions in advance or simply to talk at each session about the things
that interest him or her; what the final product might actually look
like and the degree of say that the subject will have over the contents;
and whether the final product will be published under the subject's
pseudonym or the researcher's name. Of course many of these issues
may change along the route, but some preliminary meeting to clarify
these things, while making the research a little bit formal, will help to
establish it as research and will give both the researcher and the
subject a clearer sense of where the enterprise is leading. One useful
checklist for thinking about the interview has been provided by
Gorden (1969, pp. 165–73). He suggests eight questions that should
be asked: How should I introduce myself? How should I explain the
purpose of the interview? How should I explain the sponsorship?
Should I explain why he was selected? How to discuss anonymity?
Should any extrinsic reward be mentioned? How should the interview be recorded? How open are we going to be?

One final feature that needs considerable thought before the work
starts is the *mode of recording* (cf. Thompson, 1978, pp. 173 *et seq.*).
The two major ways include either taking handwritten notes (as in
many of the earlier Chicago studies and in *The Professional Fence*
(Klockars, 1975)) or to tape-record. Each has a series of strengths and
weaknesses. But, on balance, provided one has mastered the
technicalities of tape-recording – a trite enough point but one which
really can lead to many researchers coming a cropper! – a tape-
recording is probably the most satisfactory since it is relatively
unobtrusive, and allows the material to be directly transcribed into a
manageable form. Careful choice of a tape-recorder and role play re-
hearsals into it before entering the field are basic prerequisites of good
life history research. For a machine that breaks down, a battery that
runs out, a tape that overruns, a microphone not switched on, an outside nosie that drowns the talk, and an overused tape can all cause havoc.

2 Gathering the Data

Three major methods have been established for getting at a person's
life. The first simply encourages people to write their life history

down following a guideline. This was true of many of the early pioneering studies, such as *The London Survey of the Poor* which asked Bermondsey housewives to write down their experiences (Smith, 1935) and the mass observation research of the 1930s and 1940s. It is also to be found in the classic Chicago studies of Shaw (1931), Thomas and Znaniecki (1958) and Sutherland (1937), as well as the anthropological studies of Simmons (1942) and Radin (1926), all of which were founded upon the simple expedient of getting the subject to write his or her own story down.

With the advent of a tape-recorder, however, the approach has shifted. Bogdan describes this new approach well for his study with Jane Fry:

> A few weeks elapsed between our first discussion of the project and the start of our work. Most of our meetings were held during the months of April, May and June of 1972 at my office, and consisted of unstructured interviews which were tape-recorded. We started with informal conversations, pursuing various topics and discussing different phases of her life as they came up. If Jane brought up topics during a taping session which she was unable to finish, I would mention them the next day. We did not attempt to record her life story chronologically, but skipped around from day to day. There was an advantage in this method: it allowed a relationship to develop between us so that the experiences that were difficult for her to talk about were dealt with at later sessions. I replayed certain tapes and at later taping sessions asked Jane questions regarding the chronology of events and so on. Early in the interviewing I asked her to list the main events in her life chronologically, and this listing was used as a guide in organising the material as well as in directing later taping sessions. During the three months period the material was recorded, we met from one to five times a week, and our meetings lasted from one to five hours. I did not keep an accurate count of the number of hours we spent recording our sessions; an estimate is about a hundred. Over 750 pages of transcribed material was the result of our effort. (Bogdan, 1974, p. 8)

Bogdan's account highlights both the dependency on a tape-recorder and the use of an interviewing style that is highly unstructured. A structured interview is a crutch: it pushes the researcher into a well-defined role (sitting there with a questionnaire in one's lap) and permits the relative security of knowing both what to ask and what is likely to be heard in reply. Without minimising the many difficulties to which researchers and research books testify, it is a comparatively technical exercise.

This is not true of the life history interview which has to be much more open and fluid. It is simply not what most people expect of an interview so that it makes the task difficult at the outset; there are no clear prescriptions as to how the subject is expected to behave. Often the subject is expected to take the lead rather than merely responding to a series of cues given by the questionnaire. Furthermore it is not like a simple conversation, an analogy that is sometimes made, for the researcher has to be too passive for that. The image which perhaps captures this interview method most clearly is that of the non-directive, phenomenologically aware counsellor. All the rules of non-directive counselling, espoused for example by Sullivan and Rogers, come into play here. Central to this view is the uniqueness of the person and the situation, the importance of empathy and the embodiment of 'non-possessive warmth' in the interviewer. The aim is 'to grasp the native's point of view, his relation to life, to realise his vision of the world' (Malinowski, 1922, p. 25). This phenomeno-logical (Lifton) or ethnographic (Spradley) form of interviewing may not always be what is required; sometimes a more structured form of life history may be taken in which the researcher works out a series of general guides at the outset. Typical of this may be the biographical approach described by Levinson (1978, pp. 14–15).

The third strategy is even less formal: it involves triangulation (Webb), a mixture of participant observation and almost casual chatting with notes taken. Klockars describes in detail his 'interview routine' with Vincent Swaggi, the professional fence:

Between January of 1972 and April of 1973 I interviewed Vincent once and occasionally twice a week. With the exception of the first few meetings, my weekly visits began in the late afternoon when I arrived at Vincent's store. I would watch him do business for an hour or so, and after he closed, we would go to dinner at a modest Italian restaurant. During dinner Vincent would recount the events and deals he had participated in since I last saw him. As we got to know one another better, Vincent would, in a relaxed fashion, review with me his options on pending deals and ask for my opinion on how he ought to proceed . . . From the restaurant we would drive to Vincent's home; there, in Vincent's consideration the 'real' interviewing would begin. This was signalled by my opening my briefcase and taking out my notebook and pencils. Vincent's part in the ritual was to settle in his large recliner chair and light a cigar. Quite often the topic we would begin with was carried over from our conversation at dinner.

By ten thirty Vincent would usually grow tired; he started his day at five thirty every morning except Sunday. Occasionally an especially productive interview would keep us going to midnight, but usually I would leave by eleven. As I drove home I would dictate my comments, recollections and impressions into a small battery operated tape-recorder. The lateness of the hour, the amount I had drunk during the interview and at dinner, and my attention to driving all took their toll on the quality of these comments. I was usually home in a few hours and always too tired to review my interviewing notes. This task was postponed until the following morning ... Once or twice we ate at Vincent's home where he prepared dinner with my assistance; once or twice his daughter made a special Italian dinner for us. But for fifteen months the pattern remained virtually the same; an hour at the store, two hours at dinner, three to four hours of real interviewing, an hour of variable quality dictation. In sum I spent roughly four hundred hours, watching, listening to and talking to Vincent over a period of fifteen months. (Klockars, 1975, pp. 218–19)

In most life history research the informal interview will usually have a key role to play. A great many volumes have been devoted to the different types and strategies of interviewing techniques and these need not be discussed in detail here. At base, however, it is useful to distinguish between techniques and tactics. Techniques are the specific forms of verbal and non-verbal behaviour in an interview which the interviewer must basically know, whereas tactics are ways of dealing with the specific problems that arise during the interview and which are much more unpredictable.

Gorden suggests several cornerstones of technique. The first rule is simply that silence is golden: one should never interrupt a respondent once they are under way. You are after what they have to say, and any interference by the interviewer prevents this. The second area to consider is the precise verbal forms that the interviewer should use. Talk should be geared to facilitating the respondent's ease and willingness to talk. Hence an emphasis should be given to stimulating the subject's motivation through the expression of interest; to reducing any form of threat to the subject by providing support and giving confidence; to preventing any form of falsification by the subject by mildly probing for further clarification which may reveal discrepancies; and by stimulating the memory of the respondent by providing minor probes which take them back further and further. A third issue entails the selection of the right vocabulary. A basic familiarity with the subject's argot and idiosyncratic linguistic forms is the prerequisite of a good interviewer – although that basic familiarity should not result in the researcher 'showing off' this inside knowledge and making the subject ponder, just who this 'smartarse' is. Another issue is grasping the different types of questions that could be asked. A fifth issue is the awareness of one's own attitude towards the subject, and an attempt to be generally unjudgemental.

The most generally useful *tactic* in interviewing is to see the entire enterprise as a funnel in which the researcher initially opens up a wide area with a broad statement or question allowing the subject to respond in as open and as general a way as possible. From this the researcher narrows down a series of specific probes involving further clarification, expansion or discussion of ideas raised by the general statements. To a large extent, as Gorden comments, 'most of the tactical problems of interviewing centre around the problem of using the right type of probe at the right time'.

Designing an interview schedule for an unstructured interview is very largely a matter of designing ideas about the right probe at the right time. Another important set of tactics to ponder upon are those which enable the researcher to break down the symptoms of resistance found in the respondent. When a respondent for example says, 'I don't know anything about that at all', 'I'm too busy now', or 'what do you mean?' the researcher may be awakened to an area that the subject is having difficulty talking about. Strategies need to be pondered as to ways to dig out such information – and of course the great advantage of the life history technique is that these areas need not be immediately followed through but can be re-raised at a later interview. It is one of the great advantages of life history research that one need never worry about getting it all at that moment (as with much survey research); certain issues can simply be shelved until a more appropriate time is arrived at. Another very important tactic mentioned by Gorden is the informal post-interview. After all the work is done, ostensibly, the relationship can be finally solidified by a casual chat about the interview with the subject. During this time particular attention could be paid to the subject's own feelings about the interview, the extent to which they feel that they got across what they wanted to say or didn't, and certain kinds of validity checks can be made.

Formal texts on interviewing – and even testaments by interviewers (cf. Converse and Schuman, 1974) – can alert the researcher to many issues of interview skill. So too can the replaying of video tapes of one's own interviewing. But, like so many of these tasks, I suspect they can only really be learnt through practice and personal mistake. I have found, for example, that despite all that the books say, when I commence a life history interview so much is dependent upon my mood and whether the interviewee and I get along or not – personal factors that books cannot really describe adequately. As Lofland (1971, p. 90) notes: 'successful interviewing is not unlike carrying on unthreatening, self-controlled, supportive, polite and cordial interaction in everyday life. If one can do that, one already has the main interpersonal skills necessary to interviewing.' Unfortunately, he concludes, such skills may be a little rare!

3   The Storage of Materials

Life history research notoriously produces a mass of data, and if careful thought is not given to the mode of storage at the outset of the study, the researcher may well be inundated with bits of paper that are quite unmanageable.

The first issue to be decided concerns the form in which the basic data are to be kept. In general the researcher will leave the research situation with one of two kinds of data: either a wad of handwritten notes or a tape (reel or cassette). The first task then is to ensure that the data are put into a manageable and retrievable form. The notes may require typing out clearly and systematically, and the tapes may need partial or whole transcription (depending upon how much material is required). Then the tapes may or may not have to be put into a storage system. In the transcription of tapes, several things should ideally be noted. The transcripts should be given as much space in typing as possible to allow for the researcher to scribble all kinds of comments upon them at a later stage. As many copies of the transcripts as is financially possible should be prepared at the outset – five or six copies will make it very easy for the final analysis to be done with scissors cutting up the transcripts into appropriate files. Transcripts ideally should be typed as soon as possible after the interview so that the process of analysis and data collection can proceed side by side. Instructions will have to be delivered to the typist concerning the extent to which a *literal* translation is required – for example, whether all the falterings, mumblings and confusions of everyday talk should be included or not, whether the text should be smoothed and rounded out by the typist, and whether issues of mood and feeling should be commented upon. All this will depend on the purpose. Ideally, too, the researcher on receiving the transcript will spend some time both checking the recording and analysis of the data. It is often good practice to send the transcript to the interviewees too, so that they may both enjoy re-reading their observations and provide stimulus for further comment and revision.

Once the data are put into a manageable form, the next obvious task is to develop records and filing systems which can make the data accessible. Lofland discusses a range of filing devices in his book *Analyzing Social Settings*; here it need just be noted that files should, at the very least, be of three forms. For constant reference there should be a *master file* which contains every transcript in its pure and richest unedited form and which is arranged and catalogued in strict chronological order (by date). Under no circumstances should such a file be tampered with; it is the ongoing and complete record of all the interview materials that are gathered and is most helpful if well indexed. In addition to this, however, there must also be a series of constantly changing *analytic files*: here the newly gained data are read with an eye to particular theoretical themes and concepts which have so far evolved in the research or which are found pristine and new in the transcript. These transcripts are then cut, referenced and placed in the appropriate analytic or thematic file. They will constantly have to be jiggled around but this does not matter as long as there always remains a master file containing the original documents. Often the analytic themes will slowly develop into the overarching structure of the life history book. A third set of files that can usefully be kept comprise *a personal log*. These are designed to convey the researcher's changing personal impressions of the interviewee, of the situation, of their own personal worries and anxieties about the research. These should be a necessary part of any interview situation, generally written up at the end of the interview transcript. Ideally these would also be kept in master files so there is a chronology – a diary if you like (cf. Palmer, 1928) – of the personal research experience; but they could also be arranged into analytic files, perhaps to help clarify the ethical and personal problems of the research enterprise as they occur.

Many other files will need to be kept in full-scale externally funded inquiries: many of these are discussed in Judith Fiedler's *Field Research* (1978). Suffice to say that one would want normally to keep correspondence files, financial files, bibliographical files and data files that are extraneous to the life history subject.

4 The Analysis of the Data

If there is one issue which requires much more discussion in the whole of life history methodology then it is the analysis of the data: a task that should invariably take considerably more time than the collection of data and which would invariably also proceed simultaneously (cf. Junker, 1960). In many ways this is the truly creative part of the work – it entails brooding and reflecting upon mounds of data for long periods of time until it 'makes sense' and 'feels right', and key ideas and themes flow from it. It is also the hardest process to describe: the standard technique is to read and make notes, leave and ponder, re-read without notes, make new notes, match notes up, ponder, re-read and so on.

Ultimately, though, there are two broad areas that have to be considered. The first is concerned with the quality of the data gathered: the three classic questions of reliability, validity and representativeness will thus be considered in this chapter. The second set of dilemmas concerns the move from data to conceptualisation and theorisation. I will deal with these issues in the next chapter.

THE QUALITY OF LIFE HISTORY RESEARCH

(1)   Representativeness

One of the most apparent attacks on life history research is that it fails to provide representative cases and thus hurls the reader into the eccentric world of the atypical – a story in itself, but no more. To avoid this accusation, the researcher must work out and explicitly state the life history's relationship to a wider population, and thus the issue of idiographic and nomothetic social science re-raises its head. Unfortunately, this is no easy task and researchers often display confusion over the issue. For example, in an examination of Oscar Lewis's study of the Rios family in *La Vida*, Valentine can show at least five contrasting positions concerning the characters. They are, he says, presented in turn as '(1) *typical* of the culture of the poor, (2) following a life style of *unknown* frequency and distribution, (3) deeply affected by a specialised occupational pattern confined to *one third* of their community, (4) characterised by an *extreme deviance* in their chronicler's experience and (5) *spanning the gap* between the upper and lower classes both in wealth and in family patterns' (Valentine, 1968, p. 54, my italics). Just where, then, is the reader to locate the Rios family given so many possibilities?

It would be helpful if researchers could appraise their subjects on a continuum of representativeness and non-representativeness. At one extreme, the study is meant to be typical of a known sample – a claim that Thomas and Znaniecki make without substantiation. Much better is the example of Stanley, *The Jack Roller*, who is firmly located as being being both typical and not typical of juvenile delinquency in Chicago in the 1920s. In clarifying his typicality, Burgess can show how the characteristics of Stanley 'match' the feature of their wider samples: he 'grew up in a delinquency area', 'lived in a broken home', 'began his delinquent career even before he started school', 'had institutional experiences in rapid succession', and became 'a jack roller' (cf. Shaw, 1966, pp. 184–5). Where it is possible to relate the characteristics of a 'case' to a 'sample', confidence in its generalisability may be considerably increased.

At the other extreme, the case history may explicitly be viewed (as Allport advocates) as a unique and necessary story to be told: the aim is to grasp one case for what it tells us about that case. Historians have no anxiety in doing this and neither, on occasions, should social scientists. They will, however, legitimately get into trouble if they naïvely push their claims too far (though they can of course *speculate* on wider implications) (cf. Allport 1942, chs 4 and 12).

Midway between these extremes is a possibility advocated by Blumer of seeking out key informants who have a profound and central grasping of a particular cultural world. As he says in commenting on *The Polish Peasant*:

A half dozen individuals with such knowledge constitute a far better 'representative sample' than a thousand individuals who may be involved in the action that is being formed but who are not knowledgeable about that formation. I put the matter in this startling way to call attention to the fact that the use of human documents sets a markedly new and unsolved methodological problem of representativeness. A problem which sociologists across the board do not recognise, much less address. (Blumer, 1979, p. xxxiii)

(2) *Reliability and Validity*

The other major problems which need to be addressed concern reliability and validity – two central issues of all research method which have a curious relationship to each other. Reliability is primarily concerned with technique and consistency – with ensuring that if the study was conducted by someone else similar findings would be obtained; while validity is concerned with making sure that the technique is actually studying what it is supposed to. A clock that was consistently ten minutes fast would hence be reliable but invalid since it did not tell the correct time. In general, reliability is the preoccupation of 'hard' methodologists – getting the attitude scale or the questionnaire design as technically replicable as possible through standardisation, measurement and control – while validity receives relatively short shrift. 'Attitude scales' may thus frequently be consistent but bear a highly tentative relationship to 'attitudes'. Indeed, as Frazier (1976, p. 129) remarks, 'it is probably safe to say that validity is more likely to decrease as the ease with which reliability is tested increases'. The closer one is to the phenomenon one wants to understand, the nearer one usually is to validity.

In life history research these two issues have been rarely discussed, perhaps because the problem of reliability is very hard to tap. Given that usually the virtue of life histories lies in the relatively free flowing babble of talk, to attempt standardisation of questionnaires is to invite invalidity. But without such standardisation and cross-checking, attacks become easy. As Blumer comments:

Many critics charge that the authors of personal accounts can easily give free play to their imagination, choose what they want to say, hold back what they do not want to say, slant what they wish, say only what they happen to recall at the moment, in short to engage in both deliberate and unwilling deception. They argue, accordingly, that accounts yielded by human documents are not trustworthy. (Blumer, 1979, p. xxxiv)

The problem, however, is really being tackled from the wrong end:

validity should come first, reliability second. There is no point in being very precise about nothing! If the subjective story is what the researcher is after, the life history approach becomes the most valid method – for reasons signposted at many points in this book. It simply will not do to classify, catalogue and standardise everything in advance, for this would be a distorted and hence invalid story.

The main concern, therefore, must lie with examining the possible sources of bias which inhibit the life history document from telling the researcher what is wanted, and employing techniques to reduce the possible sources of bias.

Sources of bias. In social science research generally three domains of bias are recognised; those arising from the subject being interviewed, those arising from the researcher and those arising from the subject–researcher interaction. In the first domain, the respondent may lie, cheat, present a false front or try to impress the interviewer in some way (cf. Douglas, 1976). Of particular importance may be the way in which the subject attempts to create a consistent and coherent story for the interviewer's benefit – even going to the extent of rehearsing it prior to the interview. It is indeed odd how, sometimes, respondents are able to repeat more or less in the same words a story told two months earlier – as if they had rehearsed and learnt a script. Of relevance here are all those features which psychologists have designated 'demand characteristics'; the respondent enters the situation, tries to work out what the interviewer is getting at, and proceeds to answer in accord with this (cf. Orne, 1962). And, most centrally, the subject may desire to please the researcher and gain positive evaluation (cf. Phillips, 1973, esp. ch. 3).

The second domain is concerned with the interviewer. Most blatantly, the researcher may hold prejudices and assumptions which structure the questioning; a 'non-directive' interviewer might be accused of harbouring the desire to encourage a person to tell the more outrageous and problematic things in his or her life, thereby encouraging a distortion of the more sensational episodes. The researcher may also bring biases into the situation by virtue of his or her age, class, gender and general background – not to mention pre-existing theoretical orientation. Sometimes, too, issues of mood may influence the researcher, as Webb *et al.* say:

> Just as a spring scale becomes fatigued with use, reading 'heavier' a second time, an interviewer may also measure differently at different times. His skill may increase. He may be better able to establish rapport. He may have learned necessary vocabulary. He may loaf or become bored. He may have increasingly strong expectations of what a respondent 'means' and code differently with practice.

Some errors relate to recording accuracy, while others are linked to the nature of the interviewer's interpretation of what transpired. Either way, there is always the risk that the interviewer will be a variable filter over time and experience. (Webb *et al.*, 1966, p. 22)

Finally, of course, bias may creep in through the very interactional encounter itself: the setting may be too formal to encourage intimacy or too informal to encourage an adequate response. All the inter-actional strategies discussed by writers like Goffman may well come into play here, and sometimes the life history interview may be seen as an elaborate dramaturgical presentation (cf. Denzin, 1978a, pp. 123–33).

Table 5.2   *A Brief Check List of Some Dimensions of 'Bias'*

Source One: The Life History Informant[1]
Is misinformation (unintended) given?
Has there been evasion?
Is there evidence of direct lying and deception?
Is a 'front' being presented?
What may the informant 'take for granted' and hence not reveal?
How far is the informant 'pleasing you'?
How much has been forgotten?[2]
How much may be self-deception?

Source Two: The Social Scientist–Researcher[3]
Could any of the following be shaping the outcome?
(a)   Attitudes of researcher: age, gender, class, race, etc.
(b)   Demeanour of researcher: dress, speech, body language, etc.
(c)   Personality of researcher: anxiety, need for approval, hostility, warmth, etc.
(d)   Attitudes of researcher: religion, politics, tolerance, general assump-tions.
(e)   Scientific role of researcher: theory held etc. (researcher expectancy).

Source Three: The Interaction[2]
The joint act needs to be examined. Is bias coming from
(a)   The physical setting – 'social space'?
(b)   The prior interaction?
(c)   Non-verbal communication?
(d)   Vocal behaviour?

---

[1] On this, see Douglas (1976, chs 4 and 5).
[2] On this, see Gittins (1979).
[3] On this, see Phillips (1971).

I have charted these three sources of bias in Table 5.2. A close examination of all bias in the researcher could only be possible if researcher and informant were mechanical robots. To purge research of all these 'sources of bias' is to purge research of human life. It presumes a 'real' truth may be obtained once all these biases have been removed. Yet to do this, the ideal situation would involve a researcher without a face to give off feelings, a subject with clear and total knowledge unshaped by the situation, a neutral setting, and so forth. Any 'truth' found in such a disembodied neutralised context must be a very odd one indeed. It is precisely through these 'sources of bias' that a 'truth' comes to be assembled. The task of the researcher, therefore, is not to nullify these variables, but to be aware of, describe publicly and suggest how these have assembled a specific 'truth'. It is just such accounting which lies at the heart of much ethno-methodology (cf. Silverman, 1973).

Validity checks. There have been several ways in which validity checks have been made on life documents. Sometimes the subject is asked to read the entire product and present an autocritique of it. Sometimes a comparison may be made with similar written sources – reading biographies of other criminals, for instance, can throw up points of major divergence or similarity. Sutherland thoroughly documents his account of a thief with other 'biographies of thieves' and no noticeable discrepancies were found. (Though at least one commentator is suspicious of this – see Snodgrass, 1973, p. 15.)

Another strategy for analysing validity is a comparison with official records; when the subject provides 'factual data' that are likely to have been recorded somewhere – births, deaths, marriages, divorces, imprisonment, operations, schools and so forth – it is possible to check up on the accuracy of the story. Shaw's delinquent boys were all matched up to the official records and where there were any inconsistencies they were pointed out to the boys. Nevertheless, given the problematic nature of official records – which makes it possible that official records are little more than sedimentation of the tacit assumptions and prejudices of statistic and record-keeping agencies – this could be an unreliable checkpoint (cf. Douglas, 1967). Indeed, in the case of Jane Fry her transsexual case records were directly at odds with her own perspective (Bogdan, 1974). On the records Jane is sick and disordered; in her account she is not. Who is to be believed? As I suggested in Chapter 4, this becomes an issue in the 'politics of perspective' – those at the bottom of the heap being less likely to have their voice heard or believed, those nearer the top, like psychiatrists, being more readily legitimated (cf. Becker, 1971). Cross-checking with physical data, therefore, is not always as straightforward as it may seem at first glance (cf. Frazier, 1976, pp. 233–4).

A final technique of validating the data is to make comparisons with other informants, either interviewing those in similar roles or else those who knew the subject well. Thus the stories of Frazier's black youth (Frazier, 1967) were checked through interviews with parents, and Jackson writes of Sam the Thief:

> Most of what he says is true. I have checked out what I could by talking with other thieves who knew him on the streets and with convicts who knew him in prison, and by spending considerable time with him in both prison and the free world. [It] was read by a number of consultants . . . a Texas warder, lawyers . . . (Jackson, 1972, p. 16)

The overarching problem in all this is to know precisely what it is that the life history research is purporting to obtain. Thus, for example, in oral history the aim is to gain information about the past; in the biographical life history, to gain information about a person's development; and in the sociological life history, to grasp the ways in which a particular person constructs and makes sense of his or her life at a given moment. The goal of the life history analysis will dramatically affect issues of validity. For instance, the oral historian's goal – of recapturing the past – is altogether more ambitious than the sociologist's goal, who is in a sense merely concerned with getting at the way a person sees his or her life history at the moment of the interview. For the oral historian the task is to dig up the truth of fifty or sixty years ago, and the validity checks required here are enormous since all kinds of more objective materials for that historical era need to be gathered for corroboration. In contrast, for the sociologist the account becomes 'a vocabulary of motive' – a set of linguistic devices drawn from the existing wider culture which can be used both to re-interpret the past, to fashion the present and to anticipate the future (cf. Mills, 1940). The linguistic constructs that people make about their lives at a given point in time are of interest sociologically in themselves. They can throw light on wider issues of ideology, context and language and they have become much studied by both sociologists of knowledge, motivational theorists and deviancy sociologists (cf. Marshall, 1981). However, these 'accounts' are no more than that. This indeed is precisely what Thomas recognised when challenged with the criticism that Wladek's story was not true; what is of interest, he remarked, was that it was true for him at that moment. It captured that person's subjective reality, his definition of the situation; this area should be a legitimate part of sociological investigation, and the personal document is the best tool for getting at it.

Yet, as Schwartz and Jacobs (1979, p. 72) have suggested, this very strategy of *believing what you are told* is very hard for social scientists trained to look for hidden and underlying reasons to follow through. Much more frequently they approach the subject's life from their point of view as if they 'know' the truth, proceed to read the subject's view as merely an 'interpretation' and then explain this 'interpretation' through their truth! When this is done the validity of life documents must be substantially reduced.

5   Writing a Life History

As for my experience with articles by experts in anthropology and sociology, it has led me to conclude that the requirement in my ideal university, of having the papers in every department passed by a professor of English, might result in revolutionizing these subjects – if indeed the second of them survived at all. (Edmund Wilson, 1956, p. 164)

The Children of Sanchez is not a literary work, but it renders a mass of literary works redundant. Why write a novel on its characters or their milieu? They tell us much more by themselves, with a much greater self-understanding and eloquence. (Jean-Paul Sartre, 1970)

Very little attention is usually paid to the techniques of writing up social science research. In the world of objectivist, positivist social science this is not surprising since such work generally parodies the style of the physical sciences; the tables, the findings, the tested hypotheses, simply speak for themselves and the exercise is merely one of *presenting* not *writing* 'the findings'. The style here is largely that of the external privileged reporter. But in the field of qualitative research there is much less clarity, consensus and coherence about the way in which research should finally be presented. The data, theory and hypothesis do not simply announce themselves, but usually have to be artfully woven into a literate text. Some researchers, for sure, try to bash and order 'the data' into a systematic technical report; but for many the underlying imagery for writing is derived from art not science. It is to the tools of the novelist, the poet and the artist that the social scientist should perhaps turn in the qualitative humanistic tradition.

Social science students – at both undergraduate and graduate levels – are rarely given any training in the issues of writing; it is almost presumed they will just 'know'. Yet for many of these students the task of writing is exceptionally daunting, and while their peers in literature departments may be rummaging through texts on 'creative writing' they are left alone in their struggle to produce good prose.

It may be helpful for such students to break this creative act into three components: purpose, intrusion and mechanics. I will discuss each briefly.

(1) PURPOSE

At the outset it is crucial to be clear who you are writing for and what you hope to achieve. Without this focus writing become diffuse, chaotic and undisciplined. As I write this book, for example, my reader is firmly in mind: a social science student who knows little about human documents but wants a grounding in this area, hopefully with a view to doing some research. I have to exclude from consideration the reader who knows nothing about social science, for that would mean that many more 'basics' should be explored; likewise I have to exclude from consideration the well-seasoned personal document researcher – he or she would want a significantly more detailed and complex treatment of many issues. Boundaries have to be set up to guide my flow of writing.

In sorting out the purposes behind writing a life history, Glaser and Strauss (1977) have suggested an important distinction to clarify: writers need to know whether they are to produce a *case history* or a *case study*. Some personal documents may be used for the value they have in themselves (they tell 'a good story'), having something interesting to say in depth about a certain social phenomenon be it a mining community (Bulmer, 1978) or a disastrous flood (Erikson, 1976). This is the case *history*. In contrast, a case *study* uses the personal document for some wider theoretical purpose. The documents are not of particular interest in themselves but only as they relate to some wider goal – Jack Douglas, for example, uses 'suicide accounts' in his book *The Social Meanings of Suicide*, but he is not interested in the stories as such but rather in using them to give credence to his phenomenological account of suicide definitions (see Douglas, 1967, ch. 17). As Glaser and Strauss put it:

> The research goal in a case history is to get the fullest possible story for *its own sake*. In contrast, the case study is based on analytic abstractions and constructions for purposes of description, or verification and/or generation of theory. There is no attempt at obtaining the fullest possible story for its own sake . . .
>
> In sum, the case history gives prominence to the story and to the story line – whereas in the case study the story is subordinated to abstract purpose. (Strauss and Glaser, 1977, p. 183)

It is not part of Glaser and Strauss's argument that case histories should never be interpreted with theory, for this must be the task of the social scientist. But in the case study the theory is there at the outset to weave together the documents whilst in the case history the theory is inductively evolved. For Glaser and Strauss, sociologists should pay more attention to producing case histories – good stories on which good theory can be based.

Having decided this issue, the next task is to be clear about the focus of the study. Some time ago Allport (1942) suggested three main forms of life history writing: the comprehensive, the topical, and the edited. Perhaps the most generally useful way of thinking about the focus is to consider whether the personal document is purporting to grasp the total *life*, or to grasp a particular *topic*. In each case life history may be either comprehensive or limited.

The *comprehensive life document* is the rarest document to come by: it purports to grasp the totality of a person's life. It has no sharp focus but tries to capture the essence of the development of a unique human being. Such a goal of course is strictly impossible: wholes and totalities must always be arranged from a particular perspective. Nevertheless the kind of work that approaches this is typified by Robert W. White and his study *Lives in Progress: A Study of the Natural Growth of Personality*. In this book he presents in considerable detail the lives of only three people. Hartley Hale, physician and scientist, Joseph Kidd, businessman, and Joyce Kingsley, housewife and social worker. He tries to bring together within the volume the perspectives of biology, psychology and sociology but the focus throughout is on the overall flow of the life. Among other studies which have produced this pattern are the Grant study of adaptation to life and the work of Kimmel (see White, 1975; Vaillant, 1977; Kimmel, 1980).

The *limited life document* does not aim to grasp the fullness of a person's life, but confronts a particular issue. Here are the most famous of all the life history documents: the study of Stanley in the late 1920s focuses throughout upon the delinquency of his life, the study of Janet Clark in the 1960s focuses throughout upon the theme of her drug use, and the study of Jane Fry in the early 1970s focused throughout upon her transsexuality (see Shaw, 1966; Hughes, 1961; Bogdan, 1974).

The *comprehensive topical personal document* organises the material around a special theme that is not related to an overall life. With these personal documents the full flow of a life is not necessary; the document is used to throw light upon a particular topic or issue. Sutherland's *The Professional Thief* is the classic instance of this – although it is often quite mistakenly called a life history. It was gathered during the early 1930s (through responses to a written questionnaire and long discussions) and tells neither the life story of its author, Chic Conwell, nor of his personal qualities; indeed, what it does provide on this score may even be false or fictitious (cf. Snodgrass, 1973). But this is not important. For its main concern lies with the detailed descriptions of the workings of professional theft – a picture further clarified and updated by *The Box Man* in the 1970s (cf. Chambliss, 1972). *The Professional Thief* details the strategies of various rackets like picking pockets, shoplifting, confidence tricks and passing illegal cheques; it describes the characteristics of the 'profession', including its understandings, agreements, rules, codes of behaviour and language; and reveals 'the fix', the widespread practice of arranging immunity for a thief on a criminal charge. As Chic Conwell says on the latter:

> In order to send a thief to the penitentiary, it is necessary to have the cooperation of the victim, witnesses, police, bailiffs, clerks, grand jury, prosecutor, judge, and perhaps others. A weak link in the chain can practically always be found and any of the links can be broken if you have pressure enough. There is no one who cannot be influenced if you go at it right and have sufficient backing, financially and politically. It is difficult if the victim is rich or important, it is more difficult in some places than others. But it can practically always be done. (Sutherland, 1967, pp. 82–3)

A topical life document then will usually have the task of throwing light on a highly focused area of life.

The *limited topical personal document* is very similar to the above, but covers much less ground. Normally studies containing limited topical personal documents will contain a number of these in one volume. For example, Dennis Marsden and Louanne Duff's book, *Workless*, rather than looking in depth at one individual case, details a number of responses to the problems of unemployment (Marsden and Duff, 1974, 1982).

(2) INTRUSION

Establishing the purpose of the study will also help to establish how far you – the researcher-cum-writer – should 'intrude' upon your gathered materials. This intrusion can occur in one of two major ways: one involves *editing*, and the other involves *interpretation*.

Editing is almost a *sine qua non* of any personal document research. I know of no research where the social scientist presents the material completely in its raw form. At the very least, as in Keiser's (1965) work, editors of life histories will have to eliminate 'excess verbiage and arrange the incidents in . . . sequence'. They will also find it 'necessary to change the names of all the individuals appearing in the narrative' for purposes of confidentiality. This is the minimal interference usually found in personal document research. Stoller, in the introduction to *Splitting*, suggests some rules that have governed his editing – albeit in a psychoanalytic life history:

> First, if there are multiple discussions of the same material usually

only one is used. Second, stumbling and broken speech is elimina-
ted where it adds no substance. Third, to make the material more
readable remarks made perhaps minutes apart and with other
sentences intervening are at times run together as if spoken that
way ... Fourth, almost invariably the quotations in each chapter
are in chronological order ... [Fifth, where a large proportion of an
hour is presented my remarks have usually been foreshortened for
the focus is on the subject ...] Sixth, details such as names and
places have been disguised, and – as an unfortunate necessity – data
have been left out for the sake of confidentiality. Finally, because
there are more themes than any one book could encompass, huge
chunks have been removed en masse simply to reduce its size.
(Stoller, 1974, p. xiv)

These guidelines are, perhaps, fairly widely in use amongst personal
document researchers. Sometimes the editing can involve more
extensive 'cutting'. Thus *The Polish Peasant* story was twice as long
in its original form, the *Letters from Jenny* were abridged to approximately one third of their original length (Allport, 1965) and Don, the
Sun Chief's 8,000 page diary was reduced (for publication purposes)
to one fifth of its original length (Simmons, 1942). It may well be
tedious to have an 8,000 page set of meanderings, but what, one
wonders, has been left out? Of course the extreme of cutting is found
in those kinds of surveys which reduce raw data to a minimum – the
style found for example in White's *Lives in Progress*. And it is most
unlikely that any maker of documentary film would be happy to
leave his footage 'raw'!

Just how much editing has taken place is often far from clear in
particular studies. Sutherland's *Thief*, for instance, wrote 'two thirds
of it' as a direct response to questions while the rest was gleaned
verbatim from joint discussions, and the whole was then 'organised'
by Sutherland. But just how much organisation did Sutherland do?
People have speculated that Sutherland's characteristic style is
embodied throughout the book. Did he, perhaps, write it all?
Snodgrass, reviewing Sutherland's private papers, came across letters
from 'the thief' which certainly seem to indicate Sutherland's over-
riding role. Thus the thief writes to Sutherland:

Many thanks for the copy of *The Thief*. I read it with a great
amount of interest and a great amount of confusion too. Sometime
I am going to ask you to take a copy and underline in red that which
the thief wrote and in blue that which you wrote. You have
accepted the philosophy of the thief so completely that it is
impossible to identify yours from his. If you had not done so it
would be easy to isolate sentences and say that the thief did not say

or write that . . . I shall read the book again in an effort to identify something familiar. Even though he did not write certain things, I am sure the thief felt that way and wished that he had. (Snodgrass, 1973, p. 8)

Here perhaps is the most common strategy for writing up life document research: get your subject's own words, come to really grasp them from the inside and then turn it yourself into a structured and coherent statement that uses the subject's words in places and the social scientist's in others but does not lose their authentic meaning.

Editing is frequently not the sole responsibility of the author, however: publishers and editors may be critical gatekeepers in determining the length, structure, style and even content of a study. Michael Frisch and Dorothy Watts (1980) have described an oral history study of unemployment in Buffalo, New York, commissioned by the *New York Times Magazine* ('Down and Out in America', 9 February 1975), and shown how various of their drafts came under the subtle scrutiny of the *Times* management. Initially it appeared that the editors were simply asking for cuts in length and academic style, but slowly it emerged that they were looking for a different kind of article (albeit implicitly). Thus the researchers had data which showed the rational reflections of their working-class respondents, but the *Times* seemed to prefer the more personal and unsubstantiated comments; the researchers had data which showed the subjects' articulate awareness of their wider social and class context, but the *Times* seemed to want to remove this and focus more upon emotional concerns. In the end, the researchers were able to sustain ultimate editorial responsibility (except for the title which they disliked intensely), but their account shows both how personal documents may be shaped by publishing gatekeepers as well as revealing quite clearly the researcher's own viewpoint in organising the data.

In addition to editing, there is always the problem of *interpreting*. Some personal documents are left without any interpretation: the interviews of Tony Parker and Studs Terkel leave the material in its edited form for the reader to ponder. Other documents are 'framed' by the interpretation: this is the technique of *The Polish Peasant* where Thomas and Znaniecki surround their letters and their life histories with commentary, in the introductions, in the footnotes and in the conclusions. A third way of treating the interpretation is to place it in a commentary at the end of the documents: this is the standard technique in nearly all the limited life history studies such as *Box Man* (Chambliss, 1972), *Being Different* (Bogdan, 1974), and *The Fantastic Lodge* (Hughes, 1961). A variant of this is in *Anguish* where in each chapter there is the document (the account of Mrs

Abel's dying) followed by a theoretical interpretation (Strauss and Glaser, 1977).

Finally, there is the more marginal case where the whole life history is interpreted through the researcher's writing so that in effect the original words of the personal document are more or less lost – except for illustrative purposes. A classic instance of this is in the study of personality development of black youth in the urban South conducted by Allison Davis and John Dollard in the late 1930s – *Children of Bondage*. This study (which Dollard partly uses to evaluate his 'criteria for a life history' listed in Chapter 2) presents eight portraits of black youth; only rarely are they allowed to speak for themselves, most of the book being devoted to interpretations of their lives, rather than the original document from the interviews. A similar technique is found in Wellman's more recent study of *White Racism* (1977), where he presents five in-depth character portraits drawn from his intensive interviewing. The people speak from time to time, but in the main it is interpretation. By the time we reach this style of work a very marginal zone has been entered.

A great deal of social science exists in this hinterland: in sociology, for example, there are the major case histories of David Riesman and his associates in the early 1950s on mass society and the individual (*The Lonely Crowd* and *Faces in the Crowd*), and the detailed interpretations of the experiences of class by R. Sennett and R. Cobb in *The Hidden Injuries of Class*; in psychology, the work of R. Coles on deprived children (*Children of Crisis*) and black women (*Women of Crisis*) is perhaps most central; in anthropology, Oscar Lewis likewise often loses the original statements in favour of his commentary; and, of course, in the domain of psychiatry, the standard approach, from Freud onwards, is to lose the first person account in favour of the third person interpretation (Stoller's *Splitting* being a good exception to this rule). Many of these interpreted documents rank amongst the classics of social science; but, important as they are, they are not personal documents in the sense used in this book. For they lack that central ingredient of disclosing the subject's own viewpoint, perspective and expression: this now has to be inferred from the researcher's comments alone. Often this is more insightful and more intellectually cogent than the subject's view, and often too it is an accurate presentation of the subject's world. But since the reader doesn't have access to the original documents, they are outside our discussion.

Since all data is always selective, the crucial problem (as Blumer commented forty years ago in his critique of *The Polish Peasant*), is this very matter of *interpretation*. 'This process of interaction between theory and inductive material ... is the essence of the methodological problem with personal documents' (Allport, 1942, p. 21).

To dissect this problem of the interpretation of personal documents it is useful to construct a continuum which locates the two major interpreters in any sociological life history: the subject under study and the sociologist. Both of these bring into any situation their own sets of assumptions. The sociologist is likely to use 'scientific' theories and concepts; the subject, on the other hand, is likely to use his or her 'world taken for granted views'. The problem of analysis is hence the extent to which the sociologist progressively imposes his or her 'theory' upon the understandings of the subject, or the extent to which the subject's own rational construction of the world is grasped and apprehended in its purest form. The 'ideal types' of a subject's interpretation and the sociologist's interpretation may be placed on a continuum of contamination as in Table 5.3.

Table 5.3   A Continuum of 'Contamination'

I The Subject's 'Pure Account' (raw)	II	III	IV	V The Sociologist's 'Pure Account'
e.g. original diaries, unsolicited letters, autobiographies, self-written books, sociologist's own experience	Edited personal documents	Systematic thematic analysis	Verification by anecdote (exampling)	e.g. sociological theories

This continuum locates the extent to which the sociologist imposes his or her own analytic devices upon the subject, or the extent to which the subject's own world is allowed to stand uncontaminated. Moving from right to left the extreme point of the continuum is armchair theory, where the sociologist may construct his or her account independently of the subject. Clearly this is an extreme form which should not be encountered in life history analysis (since presumably the material derived from the life history subject would always be incorporated at some point).

Moving a little further along the continuum, a common practice is for the sociologist to impose his or her own scheme upon the gathered data. Here the subject is hardly being allowed to talk for him or herself. It is a matter that is perhaps best called 'verification by anecdote' or 'exampling', in which the sociologist's own story is given support by selection of examples drawn from the subjects who were interviewed; and the sociologist provides little justification or accounting as to why he or she selects some quotations and not others. Further along the continuum, there comes a point when the subject is more or less allowed to speak for him or herself but where the sociologist slowly accumulates a series of themes – partly derived from the subject's account and partly derived from sociological theory. This method I would call *systematic thematic analysis*.

Moving further along the continuum, there is the life history document where the sociologist tries to intervene as little as possible. Some intervention, however, is usually necessary, if only to delete the (boring) repetition and stammering found in all people's verbal accounts. And finally, at the most extreme end of the continuum there is the simple publication of the subject's own accounts with no analysis attached. The most obvious examples of these would be the publication of their own *autobiographies*, diaries and unsolicited letters.

Researchers who use life histories can legitimately move through any stage on this continuum as long as they publicly acknowledge how far they are 'contaminating' the data. It is as useful to have 'raw data' as 'general theory'; and the sociologist should therefore acknowledge the degree of interpretation that has taken place.

(3)   MECHANICS

How you actually write a life history will clearly depend upon these earlier decisions of purpose and intrusion. If a decision has been made to produce a case history with minimum intrusion, the task becomes essentially one of an editor and commentator. If a case study with maximum intrusion is the goal much attention will have to be paid to writing technique.

The most general advice to be given here is the unremarkable suggestion *to practise writing regularly:* it will not do to see writing as a mere end point – it is an integral part of your work to communicate through the written word. As such it needs working at, and a daily drafting, revising and re-drafting is necessary: Spradley (1979a, pp. 212–15) has briefly described these stages in regular writing.

In writing, qualitative researchers need to become much more self aware of their 'point of view' and of the kind of imagery, metaphors and ironies that inform the overall writing of their work. Bruyn, for example, extracts eight different styles that can be found in the writings of participant observers; the romantic, the realistic, the poetic, the factual, the analytic, the satiric, the journalistic and the existential (see Bruyn, 1966). The romantic style is exemplified in the writings of Redfield on Tepoztlan. As Bruyn comments, 'Redfield's choice of metaphors leads the reader away from the realities of 'poverty' and the 'hardships' placed upon people who lack technical progress to a vaulted image of 'the culture'. He speaks of *time* in the village as not being determined by the 'clock in the tower or the placio municipal which strikes the hours'; rather, 'the metronome of human interests (Time)' is measured by the season and the 'waxing and waning of the moon'. It is through the 'cadence of nature' and the 'chronometers of sunset and sunrise' that the 'simpler peoples are more directly dependent'. He contrasts this with the realistic approach of Oscar Lewis studying the same area. For Lewis, the language highlights 'the dire effects of political and economic changes upon the lives of individuals by allowing the people to speak for themselves' (Bruyn, 1966, pp. 246–7).

Qualitative research differs not only in its literary style, but also in the nature of its conceptual analysis. John Lofland, in a review of several hundred unpublished articles and book-length reports of qualitative field research over a two-year period, extracts a number of dimensions. He suggests there is a 'generic style' looked for in most qualitative research, a style which 'delineates types of social structures and processes, their internal dynamics and their causes and consequences' (1974, p. 102). Most qualitative research will be concerned with an issue wider than the subject in hand – the frame ('a basic structural unit onto which or into which other constituents of a whole are fitted, with which they attach or with which they are integrated') (p. 103). In this view, specific instances of life histories will always be located in some wider 'frame'. The frame may be conceptual or substantive: thus the life history of Stanley, while of value in itself, will be located in the overall 'frame' of delinquency; and Mrs Abel's trajectory whilst again interesting in itself, will also be located within the 'frame' of status passages. All individual life histories, therefore, are finally located in some overarching problem.

But whilst this is a central dimension, Lofland can go on to outline eleven variants of this, four of which are crucial. Thus he suggests that reports may differ along the dimensions of 'novelty, elaboration, eventfulness and interpenetration'. The first one highlights the need for the researcher to bring out new, novel – and maybe even exotic – frames, ones that have not been hacked to death through earlier research. 'Elaboration' is concerned with the extent the researcher fills out the frame in considerable detail, rather than merely using it as an analytic device for two or three pages and then ignoring it. 'Eventfulness' is concerned with the extent the empirical material is amply and ably provided; too many qualitative researches engage in abstracted conceptualism by which the concepts become all important and the empirical material is lost in the text (or at the other extreme where there was nothing but empirical material and the conceptualisations become far too thin). The final dimension Lofland describes as an 'interpenetrated' frame. This is concerned with the way in which the conceptual text blends in with the empirical materials, the crucial distinction being between the segregated style (where the first and last chapters are given over to theory and the bulk in the middle given over to empirical data is made to fit some pre-existing conceptualisation). Life histories can be arranged on all these different dimensions.

A third issue to consider in writing up the research is the relationship of the researcher to the subject. Brown (1977, p. 58) drawing from Jean Pouillon's *Time and the Novel*, suggests three positions that the author may assume in relation to the subject: as superior, as equal, and as inferior. Parsons is cited as an example of the superior, Oscar Lewis as the equal, and Castaneda as an example of an inferior, the distinguishing mark being the extent to which the author permits the narrative of the subject to dominate the text. For Parsons clearly it is the sociological view that matters; for Lewis there is probably equal measurement between his perspectives on the Mexican family and the Mexican family's own perspective; for Castaneda his perspective is almost entirely subordinate to that of the Indian *Brujo*. Another distinction that Brown makes concerns the relative 'firmness of the boundaries between' the reported speech and the author's context. Thus at one extreme there is the study in which the boundaries are very lax indeed; subject and author's comments huddle together. At the other extreme the boundaries can be very tight; the author makes a clear demarcation between sections devoted to the subject's speech and those devoted to his analysis. All these matters need further explanation in personal document research.

Conclusion

The gathering of personal documents in social science is usually a long and complicated process, and only a few of the issues involved have been raised in this chapter – preparing, gathering, storing, analysing and presenting. There can be no rigid guidelines for this kind of work which essentially involves intensive absorption in first-hand accounts, with all the ambiguity and unpredictability that such experiences entail. Curiously, very few researchers have ever written about the 'doing' of life histories – probably because to do so is to give an order and a protocol to work that is thoroughly disorderly! I may therefore have performed a disservice to the method in this chapter. Yet this order is only for a writer's ease: my hope is to have sensitised the intending researcher to some of the issues to consider in doing such work wherever they may arise.

Suggestions for Further Reading

With the exception of a chapter in R. Bogdan and S. Taylor's *Introduction to Qualitative Research Methods* (1975, ch. 5) and two others in P. Thompson's

The Voice of the Past (1978, chs 6 and 7), there remains little explicit discussion on the techniques of doing life history research. The following suggestions hence deal with a wider literature, but should be of value.

Several studies by James P. Spradley provide systematic coverage of the research process, from selecting informants through to analysis and writing. See his *The Ethnographic Interview* (1979a) and *Participant Observation* (1980). Much of his material has direct relevance to 'doing life histories', and indeed some of his studies – *You Owe Yourself a Drunk* (1970) and *Guests Never Leave Hungry* (1969) – are examples of the method. John Lofland's work (*Analyzing Social Settings* (1971) and *Doing Social Life* (1976)) is significant for its attempt to bring rigour and a systematic approach to qualitative field work – the former also includes a section on 'filing'. L. Schatzman and A. Strauss's *Social Research in the Field* (1973) is a useful practical guide to field work and much of it is translatable to personal document research. It examines the stages of field research – entering, organising, watching, listening, recording, analysing and communicating. Of considerable practical value, too, is the Chicago manual *Field Work* by B. H. Junker (1960) which also contains an excellent bibliography (still well worth examining, even if a little outdated), and the methodological appendices in T. S. Bruyn's excellent *The Human Perspective in Sociology* (1966). Interestingly, all these texts are American: Britain has not, to date, produced a single qualitative text – although the Webbs (1932) *Methods of Social Study* is of interest and Robert Burgess's (1982) study in this series should rectify this glaring gap.

On interviewing, see Spradley (1979a); R. L. Gorden (1969) *Interviewing: Strategy, Techniques and Tactics* is good on actual strategies of interviewing; Richardson *et al. Interviewing* (1965) is good on interviewer and respondent effects; L. A. Dexter's *Elite and Specialised Interviewing* is helpful on in-depth interviews, and J. Converse and H. Schuman's *Conversations at Random* (1974) is an account of actual interviewers' experience and problems, and contains an excellent annotated bibliography compiled by practitioners of the art. Interviewing has much in common with therapeutic encounters, and on this H. S. Sullivan's classic *The Psychiatric Interview* (1954) may be of value. It can also be seen as an interactional encounter, and this view is elaborated upon in N. K. Denzin's *Research Act* (1978, ch. 4). Critical comments on interviewing may be found in A. Cicourel's *Method and Measurement in Sociology* (1964, ch. 3), and H. Roberts, *Doing Feminist Research* (1981, ch. 2 by Ann Oakley).

Problems of analysis, including validity and reliability, are featured in the articles of a special edition of *The Sociological Review* (November 1979, no. 4) which is a symposium on 'The analysis of qualitative data'. Two books by D. L. Phillips, *Knowledge from What?* (1971) and *Abandoning Method* (1973) are very helpful on issues of validity, as is E. J. Webb's *Unobtrusive Measures* (1966, ch. 1) and J. Douglas's *Investigative Social Research* (1976, chs 4 and 5). Many of the essays contained in W. J. Filstead, *Qualitative Methodology* (1970) and I. Deutscher's *What We Say/What We Do* (1973) are of value. H. Blumer's commentary on *The Polish Peasant* raises many key issues about representativeness and validity (Critiques of Research, 1939, 1979). The 'vocabulary of motive argument' has spawned a very substantial literature since the publication of C. W. Mills's classic paper 'Situated

Actions and Vocabularies of Motive' (1940). A good comprehensive review – with an excellent bibliography – is G. Marshall (1981).

On the 'writing' of research, an early account may be found in C. L. Fry's *The Technique of Social Investigation* (1934, ch. 11).

6

Theorising Lives

> I look forward to the day when the category of 'general
> methodologist' is a null class. Then, perhaps we can turn
> our attention to ridding the discipline of another
> anachronism: the 'general theorist'. (Hill, 1969, p. 29)

Life documents, more than any other sociological style, are open to
the accusation of neglecting theory, that grand *sine qua non* of
sociology; they are often charged with being no more than a few good
stories – art or journalism perhaps, but not science. Indeed, in the
hands of some of its practitioners like Terkel or Parker there is nil
concern with explicit theorisation, and no desire to engage in such an
enterprise: the stories speak for themselves, are of interest in themselves, and there is no reason to add to them. As Tony Parker can
comment at the start of his study of sex offenders, *The Twisting Lane*:

> These are personal statements made at unknown cost and with
> inestimable bravery and to try adequately to thank those who made
> them by allowing themselves to be subjected to persistent question-
> ing is beyond my power; I can only state my respect and admiration
> for their courage and dignity. There are no insights of interpreta-
> tions offered other than theirs. I am not competent to make any of
> my own. (Parker, 1969, Introduction)

Competent or not, and I suspect such researchers are often a lot more
competent than many who spend their time pontificating with
theory, they would seem to embody a healthy disdain for abstruse
theory or methodological meanderings: for them it is the findings –
the 'stories' – of their respondents that are all important. Theorising
can be left to others.

But amongst those others there is hardly agreement as to what their
task should be. There is no consensus on what theory is, how it should
be arrived at, what form it should take, or even what purposes it
should serve: the deductivists beat the inductivists and vie with the
abductionists; the 'grand theorisers' challenge the 'middle range'
theorisers; 'generators' criticise 'versificationists'; and textbooks

layer and order the various levels of 'theory work' – *ad hoc* classification systems, categorical taxonomies, conceptual frameworks,
theoretical systems, and empirical–theoretical systems.

A small test like this cannot enter these core domains of the
philosophy of science: suffice to say that the view of knowledge held
will shape the kind of 'theory' work engaged in. Thus, for the
positivist the usual requirement is to construct operationable
deductive hypotheses which are open to falsification and which can
enhance prediction. With this philosophy, personal documents in
their raw form can never be of much theoretical value. They will
either have to be viewed as a preliminary stage of knowledge development whereby hunches can be generated, ideas formulated and
hypotheses set up before the more critical stage of formal testing is
reached, or they will have to be rendered quantifiable. Thus an
individual case history may be 'hardened up' through a systematic
content analysis like that found in Bell and Hall's study of 1,368
dreams of a 'child molester' (see Bell and Hall, 1971); or an individual
case may be systematically gathered as part of a wider sample – in
effect, therefore, turning the case study into a survey! See, for
example, the coding suggestions in Carr-Hill and Macdonald (1973)
and Karweit (1973) and the discussion in T. Abel (1947). In any
event, the 'tale' in the document is not allowed to stand for itself.

In stark contrast, the sceptical philosophies discussed in Chapter 3
bring a much more limited approach to theorisation: Cole's study of
deprived and privileged children (e.g. Coles, 1968), Marsden and
Duff's concern with the unemployed (1974), Lewis's living with poor
families (1959), or Jane Fry's account of her transsexuality (Bogdan,
1974) are infused with theoretical insight from start to finish. But
nowhere is to be found the abstract theoretical schema. Such studies
differ from those of Terkel and Parker because the researcher here is
willing to comment upon, interpret and organise 'the stories' into a
more unified whole. Theorising becomes commentary, criticism,
synthesis, theme, metaphor. The concerns are always dual: a concrete case will have wider implications, and the outward manifestations must be apprehended from within. If there is one dominant
motif in this kind of study it is a naturalism that documents yet
comments, is faithful to reality yet critical of it, that appreciates
subjective diversity while aware of broader canvasses. In this general
sense, theorising is rarely far away. Grand theory – of the kind
espoused by a Parsons or an Althusser – is absent; and so too are the
more rigorous deductive systems associated with positivism.
(Although even these theories can on occasion be blended with
personal documents.) But it is important to see that a concern with
theorising, often in modest guise, is a feature of a great deal of this
documentary tradition.

The 'Polish Peasant' Revisited: A Theoretical Landmark

The accusation that personal documents ignore theory is even more surprising when one looks at the history of the technique. *The Polish Peasant* is far from simply being an empirical study of the immigration experience of Polish peasants, far from merely being the custodian of a range of personal documents, far from simply being the classic source of the life history method. It was written – the authors claim – to show the importance of sociological theorising (and the symbiosis of theory and method), and although the book is primarily composed of human documents it is wedged in by theorisations, many of which remain embodied in sociological thinking to the present day. And – at odds with some of my arguments – they even make it clear that their aim is scientific generalisation after the fashion of the physicist, the chemist and the biologist (cf. Thomas and Znaniecki, 1958, p. 63). Indeed, some of their claims hurl them towards a kind of positivism.

Amongst the most significant conceptualisations that their book introduces is the distinction (already outlined in Chapter 3) between values and attitudes; the introduction of the concept of 'the definition of the situation' whereby an individual 'has to take social meanings into account and interpret his experience not exclusively in terms of his own needs and wishes, but also in terms of the traditions, customs, beliefs, aspirations of his social milieu' (p. 1,852); the evolution of the concept of social personality, and with it a series of divisions – the Philistine, the Bohemian and the Creative Individual; and the clarification of the notions of social disorganisation and personal disorganisation (cf. p. 1,128) (see Carey, 1975). Each of these conceptualisations, and there are many others, has played a significant role in the development of sociological theory in America, particularly in social psychological theory. The 'definition of a situation', for example, was highly influential on Merton's work on the self-fulfilling prophecy and on McHugh's work in ethnomethodology (e.g. Merton, 1968, ch. XIII; McHugh, 1968).

The Polish Peasant is by no means an isolated example of the use of theory within personal documents – Angell's (1945) review of personal documents in sociology, for instance, devotes one chapter to showing their contributions to sociological theory, discussing eleven examples in some detail; and Dollard (1935), in devising his seven criteria for a life history, makes the importance of adequate conceptualisation and theorisation one of his key criteria. As he remarks:

Many workers seem to feel that if you can once get the subject to tell his own story that he will automatically give you material of scientific character. This can only very rarely be true because the material he gives naively is already conditioned and limited in a great number of ways . . . it is safe to accept the postulate that the naive material will never have scientific validity. Another way of stating the matter is that the life history material does not speak for itself; the subject is unable to give us explanatory theoretical paragraphs making sense of the material. He may, on the contrary, and usually does, do the very best he can to disguise it. This fact makes necessary that the life history worker plays an active role over against his material; he must do the critical work of fashioning the necessary concepts, of making the required connections and of piecing the whole life history together to make sense plain and scientific communication easy. (Dollard, 1935, pp. 33–4)

The Uses of Theory

I have so far spoken of theory as a modest but omnipresent force in personal document research, from its American inception onwards. In this section I wish briefly to examine some of the purposes to which such theorisations may be put. It may serve simply as a broad orientation in collecting materials; it may be formed and fashioned through documents; it may be 'tested' or 'falsified' through them; or it may simply illustrate them.

THEORY AS ORIENTATION

Theory is everywhere, and is intimately connected to issues of problem, method, and substance. Thus, any particular problem brings in its wake a most satisfactory theoretical approach and a preferred methodological stance. Freud's issues of defence and conflict for example, lead to a specification of concepts around the unconscious and appropriate tools for digging out their hidden processes – dream work, free association and psychoanalysis. The method, the problem and the theory are intimately meshed together.

The same is true of those who are interested in life history research. It stems from the problems of trying to understand how concrete people give meaning to their everyday lives (or some aspect of them), is thus highly connected to the theorisations of phenomenologists and symbolic interactionists, and in turn becomes the prime tool of such theoreticians (cf. Watson, 1976). This connection has been spelt out in a number of chapters, and it will suffice here simply to remark that a great deal of life document research is informed by these theorisations, and thus in the gathering of personal documents the kinds of questions that interest phenomenologists and interactionists come to the forefront. The concern with ambiguity, process, meaning, totality and history (outlined in Chapter 4) are likely to structure the kinds of questions the sociologist asks of the life history subject. One major use of theory, therefore, is in the selection of problems and materials for a life history presentation.

Although life history research often purports simply to 'tell it as it is' – to let the subject freely describe his or her own life – it is always likely to be shaped somewhat by the researcher's theory. At its most explicit, this will be seen in the researcher's broad check list of questions to be asked: if they do lack theoretical coherence, then the study is unlikely to be social science. Most frequently, the probes will in fact be designed to capture the phenomenology of the subject – a central rationale for life history research (cf. Watson, 1976).

A much more implicit orientation arises when the researcher claims *not* to probe, guide or ask questions but simply wants the subject to talk spontaneously and freely, revealing the flux and contradictions of everyday subjective reality. Yet this, of course, is itself a theoretical orientation (closely allied to symbolic interactionism) and will encourage ambiguities and contradictions to be found.

The trouble with this use of theory as an orientation, then, is that it can 'force the data'. It can do this in a very obvious way, by restricting issues of interest and only allowing the subject to talk about areas which fit the theory under consideration. Interactionism, however, poses a more subtle problem. Generally, a key debate in life history construction concerns whether the questions are focused and selective or open and permitting the subject to talk freely of his or her own life. Interactionism, in the main, would favour the latter strategy since it is concerned with capturing the ebb and flow and ambiguity of one individual's life. A central theoretical assumption of most interactionist writing is that the personal life is nowhere near as linear and clear as many social science accounts render it. It therefore, theoretically, leads one to seek out the diversity, ambiguity, negotiation and emergence in the construction of an individual's life. The trouble with this view is that it might encourage the researchers to seek ambiguity, flux, contradictions and diversity where there is none. The very process of allowing a subject to ramble on about his or her own life will confirm the tenets of interactionist theory about the rambling and negotiable aspects of life.

In the early days of some of my research I did not see this obvious problem. I thought, simply and crudely, that by allowing the subjects to ramble over their lives and by not focusing the issues I would be able to demonstrate the ambiguity of life. The problem is that, in fact, the theory was shaping the way the interviews were conducted which led in turn to a self-confirmation of theory.

In general, it would seem there is no way round this problem. Either one has a rigidly tight questionnaire schedule which focuses upon pre-selected issues – in which case the role of the subject will become much clearer than it possibly is; or, following interactionism, one allows the subject to talk freely over a long period of time and to display the diversity and flux of his or her life – but in this case one is only confirming the principles of interactionism through the style of questioning adopted.

BUILDING THEORY FROM LIFE HISTORIES

Glaser and Strauss, in their now classic work *The Discovery of Grounded Theory* (1967), have argued that in sociology too high a premium is placed on verifying pre-existing theories: certainly one common use of life histories is precisely this. The Life is 'made sense of' through the theory. But what is equally required is the pursuit of a new and relevant theory that directly fits a known body of data –indeed for Glaser and Strauss, this task of *generating sociological theory* is an activity 'that *only* sociologists can do' (1967, p. 6). Can life histories be of value here?

One answer is very general and suggests that many detailed stories from the past embody the ideas of later-to-be-formulated theories. The life history here provides a whiff of theory: it provokes, suggests, anticipates – but it does not formulate. Who today, for example, could read the following quote from Stanley, a delinquent, in the later 1920s, and not anticipate the subsequent more formal development of 'the labelling theory of deviance':

> The cell was bare, hard and drab. As I sat on my bunk thinking, a great wave of feeling shook me, which I shall always remember because of the great impression it made on me. There, for the first time in my life, I realised that I was a cirminal. Before, I had been just a mischievous lad, a poor city waif, a petty thief, a habitual runaway; but now, as I sat in my cell of stone and iron, dressed in a grey uniform, with my head shaved, small skull cap, like all the other hardened criminals around me, some strange feeling came over me. Never before had I realised that I was a criminal. I really became one as I sat there and brooded. At first I was almost afraid of myself, ebbing like a stranger to my own self . . . (Shaw, 1966, p. 103)

It was only a few years after this that the first explicit formulation of labelling theory was made by Tannenbaum in his *Crime and the Community* (1938) and some forty years later it was something of an orthodoxy (cf. Plummer, 1979). Now I am obviously not suggesting that Stanley 'generated' labelling theory – only that life histories can often provoke, suggest and anticipate later theorisations.

Sutherland's work on *The Professional Thief* provides another illustration. Quite early in his career Sutherland gathered the case materials from Chic Conwell (1930), certainly well before he had developed the theories with which he later became identified – differential association, social disorgansiation and 'white collar crime'. Now although these *concepts* are nowhere to be found in Conwell's story, a close reading will show the ideas to be firmly present. At base, crime is an ordinary, learnt phenomenon. It could well be that the story of Chic Conwell was instrumental in later generating the more full-blown theoretical accounts (cf. Schuessler, 1973; Snodgrass, 1973; Vasoli and Terzola, 1974).

These are very general and unsystematic ways of building theories, and some interactionists have attempted to make the process much more rigorous by developing explicit logics to deal with it. The two most frequently discussed are analytic induction and grounded theory – and while both could be used with life history research, in practice this has been rare.

Analytic induction was introduced to sociology by Znaniecki (although not used by him; 1934, ch. VI), in contrast to enumerative induction (whereby statistical generalisations are made from a limited, but known, sample of cases). In most respects analytic induction is the logic most suited to case studies and life histories because it is quite happy, initially, not to have pre-existing formulations or large samples. Rather, it proceeds from scrutiny of one case to produce a low-level generalisation which then starts to define and characterise a given phenomenon. As Znaniecki says, 'In analytic induction certain particular objects are determined by intensive study, and the problem is to define the logical classes which they represent . . . [it] abstracts from the given concrete case characters that are essential to it, and generalises them, presuming that in so far as they are essential, they must be similar in many cases' (1934, pp. 249–51).

The method has been defined by Manning as 'a non-experimental, qualitative sociological method which employs an exhaustive examination of cases in order to prove universal, causal generalisations' (Manning, forthcoming). From such a definition, the affinity between analytic induction and case study methods should be apparent. Typical examples are Lindesmith's work on opiate addiction, (Lindesmith, 1947), Becker's work on marijuana smokers (Becker, 1963) and Cressey's work on embezzlement (Cressey, 1953). Yet none of these deal with one case alone; they deal with many. Nevertheless, the method proceeds by the intensive inspection of one case out of which a definition of the field to be investigated and a tentative explanation of it is derived; from this the procedure is to examine another case in great detail, and this may involve a possible reformulation of both definition and explanation to create a new generalisation which holds for both cases; a third case will then be inspected and likewise modified so that the statements made about it also hold for the preceding two cases. Slowly a statement is built up which is applicable to a number of cases and which constitutes a generalisation. More specifically, Cressey describes the research procedures as follows:

> The complete methodological procedure, then, has essentially the following steps. First a rough definition of the phenomenon to be explained is formulated. Second a hypothetical explanation of that phenomenon is formulated. Third one case is studied in the light of the hypothesis with the object of determining whether the hypothesis fits the facts in that case. Fourth, if the hypothesis does not fit the facts, either the hypothesis is reformulated or the phenomenon to be explained is redefined so that the case is excluded. This definition must be more precise than the first one. Fifth, practical certainty may be obtained after a small number of cases have been examined, but the discovery by the investigator or any other investigator of a single negative case disproves the explanation and requires a reformulation. Sixth, this procedure of examining cases, re-defining the phenomena and reformulating the hypothesis is continued until a universal relationship is established, each negative case calling for a redefinition or a reformulation. Seventh for purposes of proof, cases outside the area circumscribed by the definition are examined to determine whether or not the final hypothesis applies to them. This step is in keeping with the observation that scientific generalisations consist of descriptions of conditions which are always present when the phenomenon is present but which are never present when the phenomenon are absent. (Cressey, 1953, p. 16).

The second major qualitative logic introduced by Glaser and Strauss is known as grounded theory (Glaser and Strauss, 1967). Its concern is to move around a chosen empirical field sampling items that emerge as theoretically relevant until 'a dense' analysis is completed. The goal is to produce theories out of the data rather than from some *ad hoc* prior conceptualisation; it involves an intimate, first hand acquaintance with the empirical world. Such a familiarity, however, is nevertheless rigorously ordered: the researcher moves from one particular sampling source to another according to theoretically relevant criteria that have evolved in the previous source. It hence involves both 'theoretical sampling' and 'constant comparison' and such strategies may not always be feasible in the execution of life history research. Thus, where a life history means a long examination of one case, it would not usually permit one to make comparisons or to adequately theoretically sample (except, perhaps, within the one life). On the other hand, if an examination occurred of personal documents such as letters, photographs, diaries, then the strategy may work very well. Nevertheless, although the grounded theory strategy does not of itself immediately facilitate life history research, Glaser and Strauss do believe that the case history study may be of value in bring out constant comparisons: at the end of their study of Mrs Abel, a dying cancer patient mentioned in Chapter 4, they write:

> To achieve ... theoretical integration he [the researcher] can sample theoretically for his case histories. This means that if he has a case history, and a theory to explain and interpret it then he can decide – on theoretical grounds – about other possible case histories that would provide good contrasts and comparisons. For example, our case history of Mrs. Abel, a hospital dying trajectory, might well be compared to a recovering trajectory in a tuberculosis hospital: thus we will be comparing two kinds of hospital careers. The resulting comparative analysis is different from that used in case studies for description, verification or generation. In the case studies, one analyses similarities and differences to establish empirical generalisations and variations and to verify and generate theory. (Glaser and Strauss, 1977, p. 184)

These two logics are rather formal; it is more common in life history research for the analysis to proceed in an intuitive and hidden way. Indeed, this practice invites precisely the kind of criticism that Blumer makes of Thomas and Znaniecki's *Polish Peasant* – there is no clear statement as to how these researchers moved from the data to the construction of analytical frameworks and theories. At the same time Blumer is quick to point out that there is a large amount of internal consistency. The data does seem valid and the concepts do seem to make sense, but there is no account of how that move from data to theory was finally completed. This, surely, is the most difficult task in all social science research – even quantitative. It is that moment of intellectual imagination when the data turns itself into generalisation, concepts and theoretical hunches; and it is that very moment which is most difficult to document and put down on paper. As life history research proceeds, this process will hopefully become clearer.

FALSIFICATION AND THE 'NEGATIVE CASE'

Life histories and personal documents provide rich data which can be used to cast doubt on received theories and to throw light on future directions for theoretical research. As Becker comments, 'it can be a negative case that forces us to decide a proposed theory is inadequate' (Becker, 1966, p. xi). Dukes goes so far as to suggest that while individual case studies are very limited in establishing generalisations, 'an N of 1 when the evidence is "negative", is as useful as an N of 1,000 in rejecting an asserted or assumed universal relationship' (1965, p. 77). If the search is on for falsification, then a case study may be just as good as a massive survey, although in practice it would be only an extremist who would reject a theory on the basis of one refuting case. It is much more likely that it would lead to either a revision of the theory (as in analytic induction) or a return to larger samples for probabilistic statements.

Charles Frazier's (1976) study *Theoretical Approaches to Deviance* puts this approach to use. He starts his study by outlining three of the dominant approaches to deviance – socialisation theories, labelling theories and control theories – which are then teased through fifty 'self-perceived life histories' gathered through interviews with inmates from state prisons in Florida and Illinois. In some ways, Frazier comes closer to large-scale interviewing than providing deep life histories : but the numbers are in a sense immaterial here – what matters is the matching of a life with a theory. For the study is primarily concerned with showing the fit, lack of fit, and mixture that the theories displayed when matched against concrete lives – Hubert, Don, Albert, Ken. The interviewees were not directed into theories but were allowed to free float around six broad topics – memorable events, relations with others, self conceptions, deviant acts, perceptions and reactions of others and appraisals of life circumstances – and the 'story' of the emergent deviance, its patterning and change is then analysed through the contrasting theories. As Frazier comments:

> The procedure involves looking at the life-history case not only to see that it is consistent with hypotheses derived from the theory under consideration, but also to see whether anything else that is important in the case fits the theory or not. In other words, the life history researcher should inquire as to whether what is supposed to be present and operating in the cases is there in fact, and whether all that is present and operating causally in the development of behaviour patterns can be explained by the theory. If something is at work in the development of criminal or delinquent behaviour patterns that is outside the explanatory range of the test theory, or is not consistent with it, the theory is less than completely reliable and must be considered generally less credible. (Frazier, 1976, p. 136)

He sees his approach as following in the tradition of Lindesmith who, after Znaniecki, championed the use of analytic induction in his study of *Opiate Addiction* (1947) (later to be emulated in the more famous study of marijuana use by Howard Becker, *Outsiders*, 1963). This basic logic of qualitative research has been discussed earlier: it sees the need to scrutinise a case in detail to modify the general theory to fit it, and then for a rigorous pursuit of further cases to be examined and subsequently to generate further theoretical modification. Hence it both generates and tests theory. Out of such an approach it is possible for life history research to return to the search for universals and not simply to examine the negative, falsifying case. (For a critique of this approach, though, see Turner (1953), in Denzin (1970).)

ILLUSTRATING THEORY

'It would,' says Allport, 'be a pedant indeed who would prefer the collections of facts and strings of abstractions that psychology offers to the vivid portraits presented by gifted writers' (Allport, 1965, p. 158), and amongst these gifted writers he includes Mrs Jenny Masterson whose letters have been introduced in Chapter 2. These letters, and many other personal documents, certainly tell a rich and rewarding story to the reader: but left in their original 'raw' state they demand interpretive work from the social scientist. Thus (and this is probably the most frequent function of theory in life documents) when the story is told, the social scientist sets forth with his or her theories, speculating on their relevance, comparing rival accounts, filtering the data through concepts and hypotheses that science has constructed. Jenny's letters, for example, are sifted through three psychological approaches; the existential which takes seriously her own world view – 'its major motifs and themes', the structural – dynamic which looks behind this to identify 'the traits and dispositions that motivate her', and the depth analysis which focuses upon the unconscious source of motivation in childhood and family. The reader is then left to 'consider the arguments, weigh them and render his [sic] own verdict' (p. 211). Maybe, speculates Allport, from such eclecticism 'a true synthesis of theories' may be derived.

A similar goal is to be found in Rettig's commentary upon *Manny: a Criminal Addict* (Rettig, Torres and Garrett, 1977). This rich first-person account shows us a Puerto Rican lad's entry into his 'ganging days' in the Bronx, the graduation into more organised hustling and crime ('In my head I thought I was a big time gangster'), the drift to heroin mainlining and onwards through Sing Sing Prison, Synanon and the California Rehabilitation Center: a life of crime, hustling, dope and 'connections'. The story is told, and the reader is taken on a lightning tour of deviancy theorisation: Merton is evoked to explain

Manny's 'socially obstructed goal attainments' (p. 207); 'Manny's self-report data supports the central assumption of Sutherland and Cressey's theory' (p. 208); and the structural–functional and sequential development accounts of prison life are compared through Manny's experience with the latter being found to be more adequate (p. 216). Hence, the story comes to serve as a prop in illustrating the relevance of a wide range of deviancy theorising and to make steps towards 'an integrated theoretical perspective in the final chapter'. The authors conclude:

> We will advance the notion that the broad, general run of street-criminal careers similar to his can best be understood be referring to theories of social strain, differential opportunity, and institutional labelling processes rather than by casting them within a pathological frame of reference (Rettig *et al.*, 1977, p. 239)

Here, then, as so frequently, theory plays a multiple role: illustrative purposes are pushed to a more general theory.

The Object of Theory

Personal documents may become linked through theory to any substantive topic – although deviance has been a very popular topic, perhaps because of the affinity that life histories have to marginality (see Bennett, 1982). Fairly recently, life histories have become popular amongst those – like Kimmel, Vaillant and Levinson – who seek to understand the stages of a person's life. But in all such cases the document is taken to mirror or reflect an extant problem in the empirical world – unemployment or deviance, life stages or sexual divisions. The object of investigation is to be found in the empirical world and the personal document addresses this problem.

There is, however, a wholly different tradition which uses personal documents not as a resource to explain the world but as a topic to be investigated in its own right. The theoretical object becomes the life history which is then seen as a 'text'.

LIFE HISTORY AS 'TEXT'

Sometimes 'life histories' and 'biographies' arouse interest in theoreticians whose 'denial of the subject' and search for realist structures makes them strange bedfellows indeed. For these theoreticians, life histories would be of little interest if they just played the roles that I have outlined above – in orientating, generating, falsifying and illustrating theory – for in all these cases the recorded life history is taken as a relatively unproblematic given: it is not a problem in itself. Thus

'Stanley the delinquent' may be used to illustrate theories of delinquency, or to falsify them, or to generate new ideas: it is not the 'object' of theoretical investigation intrinsically.

The contrasting approach, however, would see 'The Jack Roller' as a 'text' and would make it and its byproducts the object of theory. There are varying schools and problems that can be drawn upon, but two interesting questions will be raised here. The first, akin to the sociology of knowledge, would perceive the 'text' as an historically produced discourse embodying the power relations of a certain moment (between, for example, social scientists and subjects). The second would perceive the text as an ensemble that is of interest primarily through the interpretations of its readership; the author becomes lost.

The work of Michel Foucault provides a good illustration of this first usage. Foucault is most renowned for his theoretical writings, but he has produced two book-length case studies (1978, 1980). The first, *Pierre Rivière*, tells the story of a 20-year-old peasant who slaughtered his pregnant mother, 18-year-old sister and 7-year-brother in 1835 and the second, *Herculine Barbin*, tells the story of a nineteenth-century French hermaphodrite. In both cases (though in much more detail in the former than in the latter) we are provided not only with the subject's memoires but also with accounts from legal, psychiatric and wider sources. The books provide a mass of original documentation, but must all be seen as firmly embedded in Foucault's own theoretical tradition of the analysis of 'power-knowledge spirals' and 'discourses'. Thus, for example, in the introduction to the Rivière study Foucault can comment:

> Documents like those in the Rivière case should provide material for a thorough examination of the way in which a particular kind of knowledge (e.g. medicine, psychiatry, psychology) is formed and acts in relation to institutions and the roles prescribed within them (e.g. the law with respect to the expert, the accused, the criminally insane and so on). They give us the key to the relations of power, domination and conflict within which discourses emerge and function and hence provide material for a potential analysis of discourse (even of scientific discourses) which may be both tactical and political and, therefore, strategic . . . they furnish the means for grasping the power of derangement peculiar to a discourse of either a madman or a criminal. (Foucault, 1978, pp. xi–xii)

This case study needs to be placed in the context of Foucault's wider study of *Discipline and Punish* (1977). Likewise the case of Herculine Barbin can be seen to connect closely with Foucault's much wider study of *The History of Sexuality* (1979), a study which is detailedly concerned with the construction of sexuality and sexual types through discourses – and here an exemplar discourse is available. In both cases, and given Foucault's marked anti-humanism and denial of the subject, there is no concern here with either Rivière or Barbin as individuals; apart from avowing an interest in the documents' sheer original beauty, they are merely a means to an end – the end being his wider analysis of power, discourse and social control in France during the nineteenth century.

Foucault's use of documents is as 'a text' where the human authorship is of no interest, where the subject is denied and where the informational value of the document is of little concern. It is merely an independent discourse through which power relations are constituted, and the text hence comes simply to exemplify this wider theory.

To make this point clear it may be useful to contrast Bogdan's *Jane Fry* with Foucault's *Herculine Barbin*. The former, a sociological product, is the story of a transsexual which is taken seriously on its own terms – a strong personal account (see Chapter 2, pp. 16–17), which speaks of personal suffering and throws light upon the problems of gender in American society in the early 1970s. We can read it to *understand* Jane, to glean information about her social world and to make sense of her transsexual predicament. Whilst Herculine Barbin could be read in this way, it is certainly not what Foucault intends. His theory places this text at the crossroads of a discursive formation: the people who made it do not matter and the historical information it contains are of little concern. It does, however, reveal, like many other documents, the search for 'truth' and the power to shape life through the medical profession. These are interesting ideas, but the text is merely the embodiment of wider processes: it is of no interest in itself.

A related tradition of textual analysis was signposted by Barthes in his now celebrated comment on the 'Death of an Author':

> A text is made of multiple writings, drawn from many cultures and entering into mutual relations of dialogue, parody or contestation, but there is one place where this multiplicity of focuses converge and that place is the reader, not, as was hitherto said, the author. A text's unity lies not in its origin but in its delineation . . . The birth of the reader must be at the cost of the death of the author. (Barthes, 1977, p. 148)

In this view, therefore, the life history subject's intentions, purposes and meanings are rendered null and void: what matters is the product which now comes to have a life of its own in the mind of the reader. It is how the reader interprets the text that becomes the object of theorisation.

Conclusion

Theorising comes in many forms, from the operational deductive statements to the grand and global system. And it is generally seen to be the *sine qua non* of social science: without it, no real advance in human understanding can be made. The claim is sometimes advanced that personal documents are inherently atheoretical, and hence of little value. In this chapter I have tried to show that historically theory has frequently been a key part of the tradition, and have outlined a number of uses and objects to which it can be put in contemporary work. Once again, I hope to have shown the role that personal documents can play in social science: no longer should we plead theoretical ignorance in using them.

Suggestions for Further Reading

There is a huge literature available on theory and types of theory work. The best interactionist introduction is N. K. Denzin's, *The Research Act* (1978a). Otherwise, debates are helpfully opened in Julienne Ford's eccentric *Paradigms and Fairy Tales* (1975) and George Homans's more orthodox – but brief – *The Nature of Social Science* (1967). On the relationship between differing epistemologies, theory work and qualitative research I think Peter Halfpenny's 'The Analysis of Qualitative Data' (1979) is especially valuable.

The role of theory in life histories and personal documents is not frequently discussed, although Robert Angell's classic review (1945) does see theory as one of three key contributions in life history research (the other two being 'history' and 'method') and hence devotes a full chapter to it (ch. 3, pp. 201–22). Both L. Watson's 'Understanding a life history' (1976) and Charles Frazier's 'The use of life histories in testing theories' (1978) are useful recent articles; while H. Becker's 'Photography and sociology' (1974) has much to say on theory and photography.

Many examples of studies using theory are given in this chapter, but A. Strauss and B. Glaser's *Anguish* (1977) should be highlighted as it stresses five dimensions of theory work in case histories: amount, source, degree of systematisation, density of formulation and level of generality (which when cross-linked provide thirty-two cells!). This should be located within their wider work, notably their classic of qualitative method *The Discovery of Grounded Theory* (Glaser and Strauss, 1967), and their empirical studies (1967a and 1968).

Analytical induction is introduced by Florian Znaniecki in his *The Method of Sociology* (1934). The most useful overview is the essay by Peter Manning (forthcoming) in which he cites four key exemplars of the tradition: Angell (1936), Lindesmith (1947), Cressey (1953) and Becker (1963). An attempt to show its relevance to life history research may be found in Frazier (1976, 1978).

The study of life stages has spawned a substantial literature, and D. C. Kimmel's *Adulthood and Ageing* (1980) is an excellent introduction to the field and the literature. (J. T. Mortimer and R. G. Simmons, 'Adult

Socialization' (1978) is a shorter but less readable introduction). Classics in this field are R. White's *Lives in Progress* (1975), G. Vaillant's *Adaptation to Life* (1977) and D. J. Levinson's *The Seasons of a Man's Life* (1978). A 'popular' English account – which has a television series to accompany it – is J. Nicolson's *Seven Ages* (1980).

Theorising in biography is a central feature of the work of R. Harré and his colleagues at Oxford University. See, for example, his *Personality* (1976, esp. ch. 7). It is also of value to examine the work of 'personality' theorists, a good guide to this being L. A. Hjelle and D. J. Ziegler's *Personality* (1976). Finally, in clarifying the work of Foucault, a very helpful and sympathetic introduction is Alan Sheridan's *Michel Foucault – The Will to Truth* (1980) which provides introductions to the studies referred to in the chapter. His classic paper is Foucault's 'What is an author?' (1979). A more wide-ranging discussion of all these issues may be found in Janet Wolff's *The Social Production of Art* (1981). See also the work of the Griffith Institute for Modern Biography (e.g. Walter, 1981).

7

The Personal Face of Personal Documents

It seems to me curious, not to say obscene and thoroughly terrifying, that it could occur to an association of human beings drawn together through need and chance and for profit into a company, an organ of journalism, to pry intimately into the lives of an undefended and appallingly damaged group of human beings, an ignorant and helpless rural family, for the purpose of parading the nakedness, disadvantage and humiliation of these lives before another group of human beings, in the name of science, of 'honest journalism' (whatever that paradox may mean), of humanity, of social fearlessness, for money, and for a reputation for crusading and for unbias which, when skillfully enough qualified, is exchangeable at any bank for money (and in politics, for votes, job patronage, abe-lincolnism, etc.); and that these people could be capable of meditating this prospect without the slightest doubt of their qualification to do an 'honest' piece of work, and with a conscience better than clear and in the virtual certitude of almost unanimous public approval. It seems curious, further that the assignment of this work should have fallen to persons having so extremely different a form of respect for the subject, and responsibility toward it, that from the first and inevitably they counted their employers, and that Government likewise to which one of them was bonded, among their most dangerous enemies, acted as spies, guardians, and cheats, and trusted no judgement, however authoritative it claimed to be, save their own: which in many aspects of the task before them was untrained and uninformed. It seems further curious that realizing the extreme corruptness and difficulty of the circumstances and the unlikelihood of achieving in any untainted form what they wished to achieve, they accepted the work in the first place. And it seems curious still further that, with all their suspicion of and contempt for every person and thing to do with the situation, save only for the tenants and for themselves, and their own intentions, and with all their realization of the seriousness and mystery of the subject, and of the human responsibility they undertook, they so little questioned or doubted their own qualifications for this work. (J. Agee, 1965, pp. 7–8)

Until recently, research reports have often been written as if they had been executed by machines: not a hint of the ethical, political and personal problems which routinely confront the human researcher and the researched subject can be found. Indeed from the inception of modern social research in the nineteenth century (Oberschall, 1972), the prevailing philosophy of the natural sciences has led the researchers to take their 'subjects' as 'objects' – probing and prodding, poking and peeking, testing and measuring as if they were studying molecules or mice rather than ethically-engaged human beings. There were, of course, notable exceptions – such as some of the Chicago work in the 1920s – but in the main the attitude of social scientists is pointedly put by George Homans: 'People who write about methodology often forget it is a matter of strategy not of morals' (Homans, 1949, p. 330).

All this, thankfully, is starting to change: many studies now take it as a matter of course to depict not just the formal research strategies (like those outlined in Chapter 5) but also the more personal issues of actually doing research – with all the ethical and practical angst this entails. Such a change may be decried by some as a narcissistic pre-occupation with the researcher – an introspective navel gazing that deflects from *what* is being argued to *who* is arguing it. Indeed, in its most extreme form, all research comes to be seen as little more than the elaborate projections of the researcher's own unconscious needs! (cf. Devereux, 1967). But it can perhaps be viewed more fruitfully as part of a wider growth in pluralism and 'people-based power' since the ethnocentric absolutism of the nineteenth century. As Barnes says:

> The recent increase in concern about what topics shall be investigated, where support for the inquiry shall come from, how the data shall be collected and aggregated, and how the results of the inquiry shall be published has not come about accidentally. It springs from an historical shift in the balance of power between the four parties to the research process [sponsor, gatekeeper, scientist and subject], and from the institutionalisation of social inquiry in the ambient culture of industrialised societies. It is one outcome of a movement away from positivism towards a hermaneutic view of knowledge and from an evaluation of knowledge as a source of enlightenment to an evaluation in terms of power and property. (Barnes, 1979, p. 22)

The social researcher is not a mere medium through which know-ledge is discovered; he or she can also be seen as a 'constructor' of 'knowledge'. And with this view it is vital to delve both into how the researcher's personal and social worlds lead to these constructions, and how such constructions are subsequently used in the social world. This is not to deny that there may be some independent truth content in such research; it is merely to state the obvious truism that issues of personal experience, social morality and public politics are an ever present feature of reasearch and need to be firmly confronted. Agee's observation about journalism at the start of this chapter surely poses similar questions for the social scientist using personal documents: by what right can an academic enter the subjective worlds of other human beings and report back to the wider world on them? In this chapter, I propose to examine a few of these more personal issues.

Personal Worlds

In a rather candid set of observations about his life, posthumously published, Malinowski has charted his personal angst in conducting field work amongst the Trobriand Islanders. Whatever 'knowledge' is to be found in his *Sexual Life of Savages in North Western Melanesia* (1929), there is another tale to be told. And this can be gleaned from his personal diaries. Thus on 26 November 1917, Malinowski can write:

Yesterday I had what is usually called an attack of feverishness, a touch of fever. Physical and mental sluggishness. Yesterday, for instance, I felt no desire and was not strong enough to take a walk, not even around the Island. Nor had I the energy to get to work, not even write letters to ERM, or even look over my ethnographic notes. Moreover, I am extremely irritable and the yells of the boys and other noises get horribly on my nerves. The moral tonus is also considerably lower. Emotional bluntness – I think of ERM less intensely than usual. Resistance to lecherous thought weaker. Clarity of metaphysical conception of the world completely dimmed: I cannot endure being with myself, my thoughts pull me down to the surface of the world. I am unable to control things or be creative in relation to the world. Tendency to read *rubbish* . . . (Malinowski, 1967, p. 131)

All this – and more – from the great social anthropologist who challenged the universality of Freud's Oedipus complex? But he is not alone in this personal angst: all researchers have their trials and tribulations. Paul Roazen (1979), for example, has interviewed over a hundred people who knew Freud and managed to convey something of the way his personal life bore upon his intellectual discoveries (and Watson (1968) – co-discoverer of DNA – has described his own frailties in *The Double Helix*), and there now exist a number of biographies and anthologies which relay these experiences (e.g. Adams and Preiss, 1960; Berreman, 1962; Vidich *et al.*, 1964; Powdermaker, 1967; Freilich, 1970; Wax, 1971; Bell and Newby, 1977; Shaffir, Stebbins and Turowetz, 1980; and Roberts, 1981).

Few accounts exist of this in the world of personal documents and life histories. Yet here the propensity for entangling subjects' and researchers' lives is possibly at its greatest. It is true that some 'styles' of this research can be detached and aloof: when Allport (1965) gathered Jenny's letters and Erikson studied Luther (1959) there was clearly no personal interaction (although there almost certainly was personal involvement, cf. Coles 1973), but the same cannot be said, surely, of Shaw's involvement with Stanley (1966), of Strauss's twenty-year relationship with Frank Moore (1974), or of Klockars's friendship with Vincent Swaggi (1975). Here is almost a methodology of friendship, of building a quite special relationship founded partly on research goals but equally on friendship. While there remains little documentation of these involvements, they surely existed and need understanding.

A formal way of examining these relations is to return to the classic paper by Gold (1958) on participant observation where he suggested four 'ideal' type researcher roles, ranged along a continuum from *complete participant* through *participant as observer* and *observer as participant* to *complete observer*. The continuum captures nicely the delicate balance needed between the relatively objective observer and the relatively subjective participant: in life document research the latter, more subjective, view is stressed – and to gain this, intensive involvement of the researcher has to be encouraged. Simply getting respondents to write 'raw' letters or simply flicking on a tape recorder for a subject to 'tell their story' will certainly provide a subjective tale, but it will lack the depth and detail that could be gleaned if the researcher was immersed in the subject's world for a long time and tried to build up a depth description from the inside. Redesigning Gold's continuum for personal documents, four stages of involvement could be designated from the very passive 'Nil Involvement Role', through the 'Stranger Role' and the 'Acquaintance Role' to the most active 'Friendship Role'.

At the most passive end of this continuum, then, is the life historian who gathers personal documents from subjects (living and non-living) with nil intrusion or involvement, and who uses these to assemble the subject's own life account: Allport's *Letters from Jenny* (1965) provides an account of Jenny's problems entirely from the correspondence she addressed to two people; and Foucault's *'I Pierre Rivière'* (1978) gathers materials from interrogation transcripts in the early nineteenth century. In both accounts there is nil direct involvement of the researcher. A little further along the continuum is the life historian who enters a person's life for a brief interview and then departs, the relationship being defined entirely as a professional interview. Presumably many of the interviews conducted by Studs Terkel for his books *Hard Times* and *Working* must be of this form; he interviewed so many that it is hard to see how he could really get to know them well (but see his *Talking to Myself*, 1978). Further along the continuum is the life historian who wants to obtain a casual working relationship with his or her subject – possibly, therefore, having a drink after the interview in a pub with the person who was interviewed to facilitate rapport and ease. Sometimes this will be taken much further and common interests and points of overlap in life will become a basis for an acquaintance relationship. But at the most extreme this can result in the individual becoming a close and intimate friend over the period of time. This can create an enormous tension between the professional role of the researcher and the personal commitments of friendship. Oscar Lewis's work on Mexican families captures this last mood very clearly:

> What began as a professional interest in their lives turned into warm and lasting friendships. I became deeply involved in their problems and often felt as though I had two families to look after, the Sanchez family and my own. I have spent hundreds of hours with members of the family; I have eaten in their homes, attended their dances and festive occasions, have accompanied them to their places of work, have met their relatives and friends, have gone with them on pilgrimages to church, to the movies, and to sports events. The Sanchez family learned to trust and confide in me. They would call upon me and my wife in times of need or crisis and we helped them through illness, drunkenness, trouble with the police, unemployment and family quarrels. I did not follow the common anthropological practice of paying them as informants (nor informers) and I was struck by the absence of monetary motivation in their relationship with me. Basically it was their sense of friendship that led them to tell me their life stories. (Lewis, 1961, p. xx)

Closely linked to these researcher roles must be the time spent with the subject. In some cases, for instance, the subject need not be met at all, as in much psychohistory (Erikson did not, one presumes, meet Martin Luther). Most commonly, the life history will be taken in a few interview sessions and hence the subject will be seen probably no more than ten hours in all – possibly the case with Tony Parker's (1969) sex offenders study; sometimes the subject will be seen for intensive periods and then recontacted at later periods in life – as in White's (1975) *Lives in Progress*; and sometimes a subject will be studied over a long period of time. Sutherland (1967) for example knew his thief for five years and maintained a friendship afterwards, while Strauss (1974) first met Frank Moore in 1948 and continued to know him until his death in 1972. During the 1970s Jon Snodgrass revisited the materials for two of the most famous sociological personal documents – Shaw's *Jack Roller* (1966) and Sutherland's *Professional Thief* (Snodgrass, 1973, 1978). In each case, it is clear that the researcher had a fairly lengthy and complex relationship with the subject. Shaw seems to have met Stanley in 1921 – as 'a graduate student and resident settlement worker in a Polish neighbourhood' (Snodgrass, 1978, p. 5), but *The Jack Roller* was not published until 1930. Sutherland had a much lengthier relationship with Chic Conwell – the thief:

> They became lifetime friends and corresponded and visited one another after Sutherland left the University of Chicago for Indiana University in 1935. Jones stayed in Sutherland's home at times and Sutherland took him to class to entertain and educate his students. Some people thought that in subsequent years Jones 'hustled' or continued to 'hustle' 'The Doctor', as Sutherland was affectionately called by Jones. Their relationship seems much more substantial than this. (Snodgrass, 1973, p. 9)

If they had this 'relationship' all kinds of questions need asking of it. Did Sutherland's personal sympathies toward a friend bias his theoretical interpretations? How did Sutherland relate with Jones when with his personal friends and family? What reciprocal obligations were built up between the two men? What tensions existed? Was a divide between public work and private involvements sustained? How did their relationship develop and end? Little is known about this and yet surely much light could be thrown on personal documents by being able to answer such questions.

A Research Morality?

Closely bound up with these personal issues are matters of morality. Recent research has talked a great deal about ethical issues – with professional bodies establishing their own moral codes (e.g. Diener and Crandall, 1978, pp. 221–31), with specialisations (the 'ethicist' etc.) being developed to deal with the problems, and with many reports on explicit problems of ethics in research (e.g. Klockars and O'Connor, 1979).

At the broadest level, two positions have been suggested in relationship to ethics: the ethical absolutist and the situational relativist (cf. Denzin, 1978a; Klockars and O'Connor, 1979, pt 1). The first view seeks to establish firm principles which should guide all social research – 'the risks to subjects must be outweighed by potential benefits', for example, or there must be 'informed consent' (cf. Klockars, 1977, p. 203); such principles should be encoded in professional charters and are absolutely necessary to protect both the community and the researcher. All professionals should have their code of ethics. In contrast, the second view suggests that the ethical dilemmas of the social scientist are not 'special' but co-terminous with everyday life, and there can be no absolute guidelines: ethics have to be produced creatively in the concrete situation at hand, and any attempt to legislate this morality could simply degenerate into mindlessness, rigidity or – as with many professionals – a monopolistic front that perpetuates privileges and elites (those with a higher morality (!) than ordinary mortals). Douglas captures the generality of the dilemmas when he remarks:

> Anyone with friends knows a great deal about their private lives, information which these friends are normally trying to keep away from potential enemies who might use it against them. At the same time, anyone with friends needs to share some of the private information about each friend with other friends, especially mutual friends. But what do you share and what do you keep secret? Even worse, when is it appropriate to probe for private information from a friend or acquaintance, and what methods of probing are appropriate? The answers have to be constructed out of the vastly complex feelings, ideas, values, and experience we have. And they have to be constructed in the concrete situations we face at any given time. (Douglas, 1979, p. 29)

The argument here suggests that researchers are familiar with ethical decisions in their daily lives and need no special guidance. This view thus smacks of an individualistic *laissez-faire* approach with no wider accountability than the researcher's conscience, while the former smacks of a collective responsibility that harbours a potential for a dogmatic sterility.

Both sides have their weaknesses. If, for instance, as the absolutists usually insist, there should be 'informed comment', it may leave relatively privileged groups under-researched (since they will say 'no') and underprivileged groups over-researched (they have nothing to lose and say 'yes' in hope) (cf. Lofland, 1976; Duster, Matza and Wellman, 1979). If the individual conscience is the guide, as the relativists insist, the door is wide open for the unscrupulous – even immoral – researcher. On balance, I suggest, some broad guidelines should be presented collectively by professional bodies, but these should always allow plenty of room (but not absolute room) for personal ethical choice by the researcher.

It is not my place in this book to suggest ethical guidelines for life document research, but I can suggest a few of the dilemmas that are likely to be encountered by anyone embarking upon life history research.

A first dilemma highlights the issue of *confidentiality*. While some life histories explicitly reveal their informants – Samuel's (1981) Arthur Harding has his photograph on the cover of the book (as well as many others inside) and Allport's (1965) Mrs Masterson has the photographs of the participants opposite the title page – most make a clear claim to guarantee anonymity. Thus names are changed, places are shifted and sometimes a few 'fictional' events are added to prevent intimates of the subject suspecting. Just how far one can go in such modifications without making a nonsense of the goal of authenticity is a moot point. Nevertheless, such blanket guarantees of confidentiality are rarely enough to prevent a dedicated pursuer of identity tracking the original subject down. Fifty years after the original study, Shaw's *Jack Roller* could be located for a re-interview (Snodgrass, 1978) and after only a month's detective work could Oscar Lewis's *Children of Sanchez* (1961) be tracked down by a reporter (Diener and Crandall, 1978, p. 103).

The research guarantee of confidentiality to the subject may, ironically, also be threatened by the subject's own self publicity. One subject of mine, for example, would repeatedly remind me of my need to safeguard his security and confidences – only to proceed to tell his friends and acquaintances all about his involvement in the research! Indeed these friends would then talk to me about this involvement, and I would be placed in the curious position of pretending not to know what they meant. My wall of silence was constantly threatened by the subject's babbling declarations. In the end, I had to stop researching this subject as confidentiality was an impossibility. A similar problem befell Klockars with Vincent Swaggi, the fence:

> I told Vincent that I would not reveal his identity unless it meant that I was going to jail if I did not, and he told me that he really could not expect me to do more. These contingencies notwithstanding Vincent could just not resist a little advance publicity. He told everybody – judges, lawyers, politicians, prosecutors, thieves, hustlers and most of his good customers. He started this word of mouth publicity campaign a full year before the book was released. (Klockars, 1977, p. 214)

Confidentiality may appear to be a prerequisite of life history research; it frequently becomes an impossibility.

Closely allied to this dilemma is the whole issue of *honesty*. It would seem to be a minimal canon of 'science' that the researcher should be as accurate, painstaking and honest as possible. Life histories, for example, should just not be 'made up' – this may be the novelist's domain, but the social scientist should accurately describe a real life. Yet in science generally there is enough evidence to suggest that outright falsification does occur sometimes, the most recent controversy here centring around the work of Sir Cyril Burt on intelligence testing where it has been suggested that the world-renowned scientist faked most of his data, invented co-authors and fabricated results to negate critics! A huge controversy followed (cf. Diener and Crandall, 1978, ch. 9).

There is no clear case of a falsified life history in social science, but there have certainly been hints that the studies by Castaneda of Don Juan, a Yacqui Indian magician, are untrue, even fictional. Murray (1979), in a review of a number of evaluations of Castaneda's work, certainly leaves ground for considering that all his work is a fictional hoax: although he was awarded a Ph.D for his studies, nobody seems to have seen the original material and many experts reviewing the book (Edmund Leach and Weston Le Barre among them) have been scathing and dismissive, suggesting little connection between the book and the Yacqui tradition. Yet, curiously, while this is undoubtedly ethically unacceptable – for some analytic purposes it could still be of value. Silverman (1975), for example, has analysed the 'text' as a case of cultural construction independent of its truth content, and even Blumer has hinted that truth may not be the ultimate arbiter! (Blumer, 1979, p. xxxv) I am clearly neither advocating dishonesty nor suggesting social scientists should invent life histories. But even if this does happen, it does not leave the study without any merit.

A related form of dishonesty arises with *deception*. In social science this dilemma raises its head most frequently in experimental psychology where subjects are not told the true nature of the experiment – such lies occur in between 19 and 44 per cent of all cases (Diener and Crandall, 1978, p. 74) – and in sociology where the researcher conceals his or her identity and 'cons' his way into a new group – the overt/covert debate (see Erikson, 1967).

Life history research can rarely involve such direct and blatant deceptions – it is hard to see how a subject could be persuaded to hand over his or her letters, diaries, or provide a detailed life story without being told about the research in some way (albeit death may lead to their posthumous abuse!). But deceptions for a lesser nature can and will occur all along the way. Thus, for example, the general description given of the research may leave out some key issues – indeed to tell the subject precisely what it is you are looking for may bias the outcome quite substantially. Further, different accounts of the research may have to be presented to different groups. In my own study, for example, of sexual minorities we produced four different statements about the goals and aims of the research – for the subjects, colleagues, general inquiries and outside friends. None of these accounts actually lied, they merely emphasised different aspects of the research.

For issues of confidentiality, sometimes the researcher must partially deceive his readership. Thus two of our respondents had occupations that were unique and rendered them as 'minor celebrities': to reveal this would be to reveal their identity, yet not to reveal it would be to distort the picture. Sutherland's thief, Chic Conwell, is for example described as having died in 1933 (Sutherland, 1967, p. vii) but it appears that he lived at least until the 1940s remaining friendly with 'the Doctor' (as he called Sutherland). Again, little lies like this may help to protect the subject from possible legal or social hassles. Klockars faced a similar problem when he discovered this his professional fence (Vincent Swaggi) was also an informant – 'the greatest undercover agent in the country' – and that through this informant role he had received some police protection. To have explicitly revealed this in the book would have been to expose Swaggi to his own underworld: as Swaggi remarked, 'you tell about that and I'll have every gang in the country gunning for me' (Klockars, 1977, p. 212). To get round this problem, Klockars made oblique references in the text and footnotes – 'I felt obliged to make the truth opaque to all but the most vigorous readers'. Ironically, by 1977 Klockars did seem willing to reveal all. So perhaps a case can be made for such deceptions providing the social scientist keeps documentation of them, and makes them public when the risk of informant damage has ceased.

Perhaps the most crucial ethical problem in life history research is that of *exploitation*. Consider again what life histories are usually about: a subject is asked by a sociologist to give up hours – often hundreds of hours – of his or her life to tell their story. It might be very painful and involve a great deal of effort. At the end of it all – for reasons of confidentiality – the subject must remain anonymous while the sociologist publishes. Hence *The Jack Roller* is 'by Clifford Shaw', *The Professional Fence* is by Carl B. Klockars, and *Being Different* is 'collected, compiled, and edited with an introduction and conclusion by Robert Bogdan'. Worse, it may even be the case that the researcher takes all the royalties. Certainly there have been prosecutions over such alleged abuses: the mother of one 'case study' – that of Genie, a 'wild child' found at the age of 13 to be living in complete isolation and subsequently studied in detail by psychologists – filed a suit against the researchers on the grounds that private and confidential information had been disclosed for 'prestige and profit' and that Genie had been subjected to 'unreasonable and out-rageous' testing (Curtiss 1977; Pines, 1981, p. 34). It is estimated that total damages could be around $500,000! In this case, exploitation of the subject has clearly become an issue and maybe it is time for the researchers to confront the problem of their subject's rights. For, unlike the researcher, the respondents will not usually be able to gain status or prestige for their story, since it will usually be published anonymously. It seems fair, therefore, that for their work they should be entitled to material reward. This might be through informal means (buying meals, giving presents and so forth) but it is perhaps advisable to establish their rights more formally. Spradley, for example, explicitly contracted one of his life history subjects (James Sewid):

> When it became apparent that the edited transcripts might become a published book, I decided to safeguard Mr. Sewid's rights by making him a full partner who signed the contract with Yale University Press. He shared equally in all royalties and, with me, had the right to decide on crucial matters of content. (Spradley, 1979a, p. 36)

With such explicit 'contracts' the risk of exploitation is reduced.

One of the most frequently named ethical criteria for research is that of '*informed consent*' (cf. The British Sociological Association in Barnes, 1979, p. 105): respondents in research should know that they are invovled in a research undertaking and roughly what this research is about. With sociological life histories this is usually the case, and although it is perfectly possible for a researcher to listen to some-body's tale and record it secretly, I am unaware of this happening. With raw documents, however, like letters and diaries, the chances of an invasion of privacy do increase. Were Mrs Masterson's letters given by her to Allport for analysis? The answer is no (Allport, 1965, p. vi). So how, if she were alive, would she feel about her private letters being published and discussed? (The reader would do well to ask how they would feel about their own private letters being treated like this.)

In photography and documentary film the right to comment would appear paramount, since respondents are immediately recognisable and irrevocable damage could thus be done to them. But to ask them for permission is surely also to invite them to pose, to present a good front for the camera? (Barnes, 1979, p. 144; cf. Harper, 1978). Wiseman poses a solution to this dilemma: he always takes pictures without asking permission. Then, as he says,

> I go up to someone and say, 'We just took your picture and it's going to be for a movie . . . Do you have any objection?' If they have

any objection, I don't use the material. I either ask just before the shooting or immediately after. (Wiseman, 1971, p. 320)

A final ethical dilemma to be briefly raised is that of *betrayal*. When I speak of betrayal in life history research, I am not simply speaking of deception or the breaking of confidences – though it will usually incorporate both of these. I am referring to the act of 'giving up treacherously; of being disloyal to; of revealing treacherously' (*Concise Oxford Dictionary*). The old-fashioned word 'treachery' serves to sensitise us to matters of serious humanistic importance. For if life history research is built out of humanistic principles, to violate the trust of one's subjects and to directly inflict suffering through this makes such principles a mockery.

In everyday political life such betrayals seem commonplace enough – witness the diaries of Richard Crossman and Barbara Castle, two Labour Cabinet Ministers. The differ, of course, from sociological studies because presumably no utter commitment through friendship and loyalty is necessarily made to political peers, and, of course, higher 'duties', 'principles' (or profits) may call. But in sociology, there is something slightly awry when a sociologist can enter a group or a person's life for a lengthy period, learn their most closely guarded secrets, and then expose all in a critical light to the public.

Conclusion

It should by now be widely recognised that social science is shot through with personal and ethical dilemmas – and life history research is no exception to this general rule. Yet voices have been mute on such issues. My aim in this chapter has simply been to suggest areas for consideration and further development.

Suggestions for Further Reading

Ethical dilemmas in life' history research have scarcely been mentioned. C. Klockars's (1977) 'Field ethics for the life history' is the most explicit formal commentary, and A. Faraday and K. Plummer's (1979) 'Doing life histories' has a section on the ethics of their research. Otherwise, the reader should examine the introduction to various studies, such as Ruth Lewis's introduction to *Living the Revolution* (1977), and James Agee's *Let Us Now Praise Famous Men* (1965).

In contrast, the general literature on both the personal experiences of research and the ethics of social research is now enormous. On the former, I have found Arthur Vidich *et al.*'s *Reflections on Community Studies* (1964) to be most valuable, while C. Bell and H. Newby's *Doing Sociological Research* (1977) provides a contrasting set of English 'stories'. A listing of others is contained in the text. See also M. Bulmer, *Social Research Ethics* (1982).

On ethics, two excellent concise guides are E. Diener and R. Crandall's *Ethics in Social and Behavioural Research* (1978), and J. A. Barnes's *Who Should Know What?* (1979). Field reports which examine concrete ethical problems may be found in C. B. Klockars and F. W. O'Connor (eds), *Deviance and Decency* (1979), and M. Glazer's *The Research Adventure* (1972). J. Johnson's *Doing Field Research* (1975) contrasts some of the more formal canons of research practice and morality with those of actual practice, drawing from his own field work in two large metropolitan departments of social welfare.

8

In Conclusion:
The 'Other Side' of Social Science

___

> Lewis's books, just because they are not what we are
> pleased to call fiction, have made another thing quite
> clear: the writing of social, political, military history, the
> whole machinery of historical research, is a narrowly
> specialised, conceptualised, intellectual business which
> has little more immediate application to life than
> metaphysics or mathematics ... The historical writing
> capable of recreating the qualitative 'feel' of historic,
> social–individual existence has not yet been discovered.
> Lewis was a sociologist whose sociological labours com-
> pelled him to give up sociology as heretofore practised. His
> works are an explicit critique of sociology and history, all
> the more searching for not consciously being intended as
> such. (Pelz, 1974, pp. 261–2)

A critic may charge this book with dishonesty: for while it seeks to
establish the neglect and marginality of a particular method, it is so
besotted with examples and references to this very method that the
claim becomes absurd. Just look at the bibliography to the book, the
critic would say; so many references must testify to a well-used and
even well-worn method. And to an extent the critic would be
correct – in practice, as I argued in Chapter 1, it does constitute a
huge underbelly of social research.

But my point is that it remains unacknowledged and undiscussed.
Whilst writing this book it has sometimes been easy, in the midst of
reading and references, to agree with the critic and forget just how
marginal my concerns were to mainstream methodology. To remind
myself of this I kept returning to the standard methods texts of the
day – very rarely are human documents paid much attention, a brief
page or two of discussion is as much as one could expect, and many
just ignore it altogether. A massive 884 page collation of all post-
graduate methodology in the UK makes seven fleeting references
(Burgess, 1979) to it. I looked at the American Sociological Association's annual review publication *Sociological Methodology* where no
allusion has ever been made to the existence of such a method since

its inception in 1969 (indeed, there was only one article on 'soft' methods – by Reiss in 1971 – and even this was advocating the 'hardening' of such data!). I pondered why I was aware of only four books published on life histories during the past forty years, and three of these were extraordinarily recent (Langness, 1965; Thompson, 1978; Paul, 1979; Bertaux, 1981). No, I was right: the method is downright peripheral to the concerns of most methodologists. The debates that were so rife in Chicago during the 1920s seem to have been won – hands down – by the hard-line positivistic methodologists or the equally hard-line theoretical abstractionists. The works that I have mentioned in this book thus get relegated to the dustbins of journalism and the most marginal social science journals. They can hardly be taken seriously. My claim in this book is that the method has a history and a value, and that it is neglected at our peril.

This is not, however, to suggest that life documents should be the central tool of social science. On the contrary, as I hope to have indicated throughout, sociology should be far too concerned with the changing nature of social structures and the suffering they generate to focus primarily on individuals: by its very logic sociology is drawn to the collective, the comparative and the structural. But as I also hope to have indicated, sociology was twin born: the problem of determined structure can never make sense without a complementary focus upon creative individuality.

All disciplines can gravitate towards an abstracted and moribund reductionism: sociology can try to make its students believe that all is ultimately social; biologists can suggest the paramountcy of genetics and evolution; psychologists can explain societies through a preoccupation with individual traits. They all have much to say, but each has a tendency to degenerate into self-absorption, to argue that their mode of work is *prima facie* the better. I have heard enough academics argue to realise that generally they speak primarily only to those who will hear.

And hence the role of personal documents. In social science this has clearly been a crucial debate of the past (cf. Ch. 3), and it seems to have been taken for granted that the debates were won some time ago. I am not at all sure this is so.

This book seeks only to sustain the debate – re-open the wounds if you like. The approaches discussed in this book should be recognised for what they are: a persistent and nagging critique of grander tendencies, an endless confrontation of theory with life, a sense of the ambiguity that is ultimately present in all social science. It is indeed the underground, the 'other side' of sociology.

Bibliography

Abel, T. (1947), 'The nature and use of biograms', *American Journal of Sociology*, vol. 53, pp. 111–18.

Abrams, M. (1951), *Social Surveys and Social Action* (London: Heinemann).

Adams, R. N., and Preiss, J. J. (1960), *Human Organization Research: Field Relations and Techniques* (Homewood, Ill.: Dorsey Press).

Adler, A. (1929), *The Case of Miss R: The Interpretation of a Life Story* (New York: Greenberg).

Agee, J., and Evans, W. (1965), *Let Us Now Praise Famous Men: three tenant families* (London: Peter Owen).

Akeret, R. V. (1973), *Photoanalysis: How to Interpret the Hidden Psychological Meaning of Personal and Public Photographs* (ed. T. Humber) (New York: Wyden).

Allport, G. W. (1937), *Pattern and Growth in Personality* (New York: Holt, Rinehart & Winston); first published in Britain in 1963.

Allport, G. W. (1942), *The Use of Personal Documents in Psychological Science* (New York: Social Science Research Council).

Allport, G. W. (1962), 'The general and the unique in psychological science', *Journal of Personality*, vol. 30, no. 3, pp. 405–22.

Allport, G. W. (ed.) (1965), *Letters from Jenny* (London: Harcourt Brace Jovanovich).

Althusser, L. (1969), *For Marx*, translated by Ben Brewster (Hardmondsworth: Penguin).

Althusser, L. (1976), 'Reply to John Lewis', in *Essays in Self Criticism* (London: New Left Books).

Altick, R. D. (1965), *Lives and Letters* (New York: Knopf); reprinted in 1979 by Greenwood Press, Inc., Westport, Conn.

Anderson, N. (1961), *The Hobo* (Chicago: University of Chicago Press); first published in 1923.

Anderson, N. (1975), *The American Hobo: An Autobiography* (Leiden: E. J. Brill).

Angell, R. C. (1936), *The Family Encounters the Depression* (New York: Scribners).

Angell, R. C. (1945), 'A critical review of the development of the personal document method in sociology 1920–1940', in Gottschalk *et al.* (1945), pp. 177–232.

Angell, R. C., and Freedman, R. (1953), 'The use of documents, records, census materials and indices', in L. Festinger and D. Katz, *Research Methods in the Behavioural Sciences* (New York: Holt, Rinehart and Winston), 1st ed., ch. 7, pp. 300–26.

Atkins, T. R. (1976), *Frederick Wiseman* (New York: Simon & Schuster).

Aune, B. (1970), *Rationalism, Empiricism and Pragmatism: An Introduction* (New York: Random House).

Bailey, K. D. (1978), *Methods of Social Research* (London: Collier-Macmillan).

Bakan, D. (1967), *On Method* (San Francisco, Calif.: Jossey-Bass).

Banish, R. (1976), *City Families: Chicago and London* (New York: Pantheon).

Banish, R., and Milgram, M. (1977), 'City families', *Psychology Today*, January 1977, vol. 10, pp. 58–65.

Barker, R., and Wright, H. (1951), *One Boy's Day* (New York: Harper and Row).

Barnes, J. A. (1979), *Who Should Know What? Social Science, Privacy and Ethics* (Harmondsworth: Penguin).

Barsam, M. (1974), *Non Fiction Film: A Critical History* (London: Allen & Unwin).

Barthes, R. (1977), 'The death of the author', in *Image-music-text* (Glasgow: Fontana/Collins); originally published in French, 1968.

Barzun, J., and Graff, H. F. (1977), *The Modern Researcher* (London: Harcourt Brace Jovanovich).

Bateson, G., and Mead, M. (1942), *Balinese Character* (New York: New York Academy of Science, Vol. II).

Baxter, A. K., Stein, L., and Welter, B. (advisory eds) (1980), Signal Lives: *Autobiographies of American Women*, 51 books (New York: Arno Press).

Beals, R. L. (1969), *Politics of Social Research: An Inquiry into the Ethics and Responsibilities of Social Scientists* (Chicago: Aldine).

Becker, H. S. (1963), *Outsiders: Studies in the Sociology of Deviance* (New York: Free Press of Glencoe).

Becker, H. S. (1966), '*Introduction*' to The Jack Roller, by Clifford Shaw (Chicago: University of Chicago Press), in H. S. Becker (1971), *Sociological Work* (London: Allen Lane).

Becker, H. S. (1971), *Sociological Work: Method and Substance* (London: Allen Lane).

Becker, H. S. (1974), 'Photography and sociology', *Studies in the Anthropology of Visual Communication*, Vol. 5, pp. 3–26.

Becker, H. S. (1979), 'Do photographs tell the truth?' in Cook and Reichardt (1979), pp. 99–117.

Bell, A. P., and Hall, C. S. (1971), *The Personality of a Child Molester: an Analysis of Dreams* (Chicago: Aldine).

Bell, C., and Newby, H. (eds) (1977), *Doing Sociological Research* (London: Allen & Unwin).

Bennett, J. (1982), *Oral History and Delinquency: The Rhetoric of Criminology* (Chicago: University of Chicago Press).

Benton, T. (1977), *Philosophical Foundations of the Three Sociologies* (London: Routledge & Kegan Paul).

Berger, J. (1972), *Ways of Seeing* (Harmondsworth: Pelican).

Berger, M. (1977), *Real and Imagined Worlds: The Novel and Social Science* (London: Harvard University Press).

Berger, P. (1966), *Invitation to Sociology* (Harmondsworth: Penguin).

Berger, P., and Berger, B. (1976), *Sociology: A Biographical Approach* (Hardmonsworth: Penguin).

Bernstein, R. J. (1976), *The Restructuring of Social and Political Theory* (Oxford: Oxford University Press).

Berreman, G. (1962), *Behind Many Masks* (New York: Cornell University, Ithaca, NY: Society for Applied Anthropology).

Bertaux, D. (ed.) (1981), *Biography and Society. The Life History Approach in the Social Sciences* (Beverly Hills; Calif.: Sage).

Bertaux, D., and Bertaux-Wiame, I. (1981), 'Life stories in the Bakers' trade', in D. Bertaux (1981), pp. 169–90.

Biersted, R. (ed.) (1969), *Florian Znaniecki on Humanistic Sociology* (Chicago: University of Chicago Press).

Blos, I. A. *The Adolescent Personality: A Study of Individual Behaviour* (New York: Appleton-Century).

Blumer, H. (1939), *Critiques of Research in the Social Sciences: I: An Appraisal of Thomas and Znaniecki's The Polish Peasant in Europe and America* (New York: Social Science Research Council).

Blumer, H. (1969), *Symbolic Interactionism* (Englewood Cliffs, NJ: Prentice-Hall).

Blumer, H. (1979), 'Introduction to the *Transaction* edition', in *Critiques of Research in the Social Sciences: An Appraisal of Thomas and Znaniecki's The Polish Peasant in Europe and America* (New Brunswick, NJ: Transaction Books).

Blumer, H. and Hughes, E. C. (1980), 'Reminiscences of classic Chicago', *Urban Life*, no. 9 (ed. L. Lufland), pp. 251–81.

Blythe, R. (1969), *Akenfield* (London: Allen Lane).

Blythe, R. (1979), *The View in Winter* (London: Allen Lane).

Bogardus, E. S. (1926), *The New Social Research* (Los Angeles: Press of Jesse Ray Miller).

Bogdan, R. (1974), *Being Different: The Autobiography of Jane Fry* (London: Wiley).

Bogdan, R., and Taylor, S. J. (1975), *Introduction to Qualitative Research Methods: A Phenomenological Approach to the Social Sciences* (London: Wiley).

Bogue, D. J. (ed.) (1974), *The Basic Writings of Ernest W. Burgess* (Chicago Community and Family Study Center, University of Chicago).

Borenstein, A. (1978), *Redeeming the Sin: Social Science and Literature* (New York: Columbia University Press).

Boswell, J. (1950), *London Journal 1762–3* (New York: McGraw Hill).

Bouchard, T. (1976), 'Unobtrusive methods: an inventory of uses', *Sociological Method and Research* vol. 4, pp. 267–300.

Bramson, L. (1961), *The Political Context of Sociology* (Princeton, NJ: Princeton University Press).

Brittan, A. (1977), *The Privatised World* (London: Routledge & Kegan Paul).

Brown, R. H. (1977), *A Poetic for Sociology: Toward a logic of discovery for the human sciences.* (Cambridge: Cambridge University Press).

Brown, R. H., and Lyman, S. M. (1978), *Structure, Consciousness and History* (Cambridge: Cambridge University Press).

Bruyn, S. T. (1966), *The Human Perspective in Sociology: The Methodology of Participant Observation* (Englewood Cliffs, NJ: Prentice-Hall).

Bucher, R., Fritz, C., and Quarantelis, E. (1956), 'Tape recorded interviews in social research', *American Sociological Review*, vol. 21, pp. 359–64.

Buhler, C., and Massarik, F. (eds) (1968), *The Course of Human Life* (New York: Springer).

Bullock, A. (1962), *Hitler: A Study in Tyranny* (Harmondsworth: Penguin).

Bulmer, M. (ed.) (1977), *Sociological Research Methods* (London: Macmillan).

Bulmer, M. (ed.) (1978), *Mining and Social Change: Durham County in the Twentieth Century* (London: Croom Helm).

Bulmer, M. (1981), 'The Society for Social Research: an institutional under-pinning to the Chicago School of Sociology in the 1920's', *Urban Life* 11 (No. 4) January.

Bulmer, M. (ed.) (1982), *Social Research Ethics* (London: Macmillan).

Burgess, E. W. (1925), 'What social case records should contain to be useful for sociological interpretation', *Social Forces*, no. 6, pp. 524–32.

Burgess, E. W. (1941), 'An experiment in the standardization of the case study', *Sociology*, vol. 4, pp. 329–48.

Burgess, E. W. (1945), 'Research methods in sociology', ch. 2 of Gurvitch and Moore (1945), pp. 20–40.

Burgess, R. (ed.) (1979), *Teaching Research Methodology to Postgraduates: a Survey of Courses in the U.K.* (Coventry: Department of Sociology, University of Warwick (mimeo). Copies may be ordered from the author or loaned from the British Library).

Burgess, R. (ed.) (1982), *Field Research: a Sourcebook and Field Manual* (London: Allen & Unwin).

Burnett, J. (1974), *Useful Toil* (Harmondsworth: Penguin).

Butterfield, H. (1973) (1st ed. 1931), *The Whig Interpretation of History* (Harmondsworth: Penguin).

Byers, P. (1964), 'Still photography in the systematic recording and analysis of behavioural data', *Human Organization*, vol. 23, pp. 78–84.

Calder-Marshall, A. (1963), *The Innocent Eye: The Life of R. J. Flaherty* (London: W. H. Allen).

Capote, T. (1966), *In Cold Blood* (London: Hamish Hamilton).

Capote, T. (1981), *Music for Chameleons* (London: Hamish Hamilton).

Carey, J. T. (1975), *Sociology and Public Affairs: The Chicago School; Sage Library of Social Research*, vol. 16 (Beverly Hills, Calif.: Sage).

Carr, E. H. (1964), *What is History?* (Harmondsworth: Penguin Books).

Carr-Hill, R. A., and Macdonald, K. I. (1973), 'Problem in the analysis of life histories', *Sociological Review Monograph 19*, pp. 57–89.

Carroll, J. (1980), *Sceptical Sociology* (London: Routledge & Kegan Paul).

Castaneda, C. (1968), *The Teachings of Don Juan* (Harmondsworth: Penguin).

Cavan, R. S. (1928), *Suicide* (New York: Russell & Russell).

Cavan, R. S. (1929), 'Topical summaries of current literature: interviewing for life history material', *American Journal of Sociology*, vol. 15, pp. 100–15.

Cavan, R. S., Hauser, P. M., and Stouffer, S. A. (1930), 'A note on the statistical treatment of life history material', *Social Forces*, vol. 9, pp. 200–3.

Chambliss, B. (1972), *Box Man; A Professional Thief's Journal* (by Harry King as told to and edited by Bill Chambliss) (New York: Harper and Row).

Chapin, F. (1920), *Field Work and Social Research* (New York: Century Co.).

Chessman, C. (1954), *Cell 2455* (Englewood Cliffs, NJ: Prentice-Hall).

Chiari, J. (1975), *Twentieth Century French Thought: From Bergson to Levi-Strauss* (London: Elek).

Cicourel, A. V. (1964), *Method and Measurement in Sociology* (New York: The Free Press).

Cleaver, E. (1968), *Soul on Ice* (New York: McGraw-Hill).

Clifford, J. L. (1970), *From Puzzles to Portraits* (London: Oxford University Press).

Cohen, S. (1977), 'Introduction' and 'Commentary' to Probyn (1977), *Angel Face.*

Cohen, S. (1979), 'The Last Seminar', *Sociological Review*, vol. 27, pp. 5–20.

Cohen, S., and Taylor, L. (1972), *Psychological Survival* (Harmondsworth: Penguin).

Cole, S. (1980), *The Sociological Method*, 3rd edn (Chicago: Rand McNally).

Coles, R. (1968), *Children of Crisis* (London: Faber).

Coles, R. (1973), *Erik H. Erikson: The Growth of his work* (London: Souvenir Press).

Coles, R., and Coles, J. H. (1978), *Women of Crisis: Lives of Struggle* (New York: Delacorte Seymour Lawrence).

Collier, J., Jr (1967), *Visual Anthropology: Photography as a Research Method* (London: Holt, Rinehart & Winston).

Converse, J. M., and Schuman, H. (1974), *Conversations at Random: Survey Research as Interviewers See it* (London: Wiley).

Cook, T. D., and Reichardt, C. S. (eds) (1979), *Qualitative and Quantitative Methods in Evaluation Research* (Beverly Hills, Calif.: Sage).

Cooley, C. H. (1926), 'The roots of social knowledge' *American Journal of Sociology*, vol. 32 (July), pp. 59–79.

Cooley, C. H. (1930), *Sociological Theory and Social Research* (New York: Holt, Rinehart & Winston).

Cooley, C. H. (1956), *Human Nature and the Social Order* (Glencoe, Ill.: The Free Press).

Cottle, T. J. (1973), 'The life study: On mutual recognition and the subjective inquiry', *Urban Life and Culture,* vol. 2, pp. 344–60.

Cottle, T. J. (1978), *Private Lives and Public Accounts* (London: Franklin Watts/New Viewpoints).

Cottrell, L. S., Hunter, A., and Short, J. F. (1973), *Ernest Burgess on Community, Family and Delinquency* (Chicago: University of Chicago Press).

Cressey, D. R. (1953), *Other People's Money* (Glencoe, Ill.: The Free Press; 2nd ed. (1973) NJ: Patterson Smith).

Crisp, Q. (1977), *The Naked Civil Servant* (London: Fontana).

Curry, T., and Clarke, A. C. (1977), *Introducing Visual Sociology* (Dubuque: Kendall/Hunt).

Curtiss, S. (1977), *Genie: A Psycholinguistic study of a Wolf Child* (London: Academic Press).

Daley, A. (1971), *Assessment of Lives: Personality Evaluation in a Bureaucratic Society* (London: Jossey-Bass).

Davis, A., and Dollard, J. (1940), *Children of Bondage* (Washington: American Council on Education).

Dawe, A. (1973), 'The role of experience in the construction of social theory: an essay in reflexive sociology', *Sociological Review*, vol. 21, no. 1, pp. 25–55.

Dawe, A. (1978), 'Theories of social action', in R. Bottomore and R. Nisbet (eds), *A History of Sociological Analysis* (London: Heinemann), ch. 10, pp. 362–417.

Denfield, D. (ed.) (1974), *Streetwise Criminology* (Cambridge, Mass.: Schenkman Pub. Co.).

Denzin, N. K. (1970), *Sociological Methods: A Sourcebook* (London: Butterworth).

Denzin, N. K. (1978a), *The Research Act*, 2nd edn (Chicago: Aldine).

Denzin, N. K. (1978b), *Studies in Symbolic Interaction: A Research Annual* – vol. 1 (Greenwich, Conn.: J.A.I. Press).

Denzin, N. K. (1979), *Studies in Symbolic Interaction: A Research Annual* – vol. 2 (Greenwich, Conn.: J.A.I. Press).

Deutscher, I. (1973), *What we Say/What we Do: Sentiments and Acts* (Brighton: Scott, Foresman and Co.).

Deva, I. (1974),'Oral tradition and the study of peasant society', *Diogenes*, no. 85, pp. 112–27.

Devereux, G. (1967), *From Anxiety to Method in the Behavioural Sciences* (The Hague: Mouton & Co.).

Dexter, A. (1964), 'Goodwill of important people: more on the jeopardy of the interview', *Public Opinion Quarterly*, vol. 28, no. 4, pp. 556–63.

Dexter, L. A. (1970), *Elite and Specialised Inteviewing* (Evanston: Northwestern University Press).

Dharamasi, F. *et al.* (1979), *Caring for Children: A Diary of A Local Authority Children's Home* (West Yorkshire: Owen Wells, 166 The Grove, Ilkley).

Diener, E., and Crandall, R. (1978), *Ethics in Social and Behavioural Research* (Chicago: University of Chicago Press).

Diesing, P. (1972), *Patterns of Discovery in the Social Sciences* (London: Routledge & Kegan Paul).

— Ditton, J. (ed.) (1980), *The View from Goffman* (London: Macmillan).

Dollard, J. (1935), *Criteria for the Life History: with Analysis of Six Notable Documents* (New Haven, Conn.: Yale University Press).

Dollard, J. (1938), 'The life history in community studies', *American Sociological Review*, vol. 3, pp. 724–37.

Douglas, J. D. (1967), *The Social Meanings of Suicide* (Princeton, NJ: Princeton University Press).

Douglas, J. D. (1972), *Research on Deviance* (New York: Random House).

Douglas, J. D. (1976), *Investigative Social Research: Individual and Team Field Research* (Beverly Hills, Calif.: Sage).

Douglas, J. D. (1979), 'Living morality versus bureaucratic fiat', in Klockars and O'Connor (1979).

Drake, M. (1973), *Applied Historical Studies* (London: Methuen).

Dukes, W. F. (1965), 'N = 1', *Psychological Bulletin*, vol. 64, no. 1, pp. 74–9.

Duster, T., Matza, D., and Wellman, D. (1979), 'Field work and the protection of human subjects', *American Sociologist*, vol. 14, pp. 136–42.

Dyk, W. (1938), *Son of Old Man Hat* (New York: Harcourt Brace Jovanovich).

Easthope, G. (1974), *History of Social Research Methods* (London: Longman).

Edgerton, R. B., and Langress, L. L. (1974), *Methods and Styles in the Study of Culture* (San Francisco, Calif.: Chandler & Sharp).

Ekman, P., Friesen, W. V., and Ellsworth, P. (1972), *Emotion in the Human Face* (New York: Pergamon).

Elbow, P. (1973), *Writing Without Teachers* (Oxford: Oxford University Press).

Elder, G. H. (1974), *Children of the Great Depression: Social Change in Life Experience* (Chicago: University of Chicago Press).

Ellison, R. (1952), *Invisible Man* (New York: Random House).

Erikson, E. H. (1959), *Young Man Luther* (London: Faber).

Erikson, E. H. (1968), *Identity: Youth and Crisis* (London: Faber).

Erikson, E. H. (1977), *Childhood and Society* (St Albans: Triad/Paladin).

Erikson, K. T. (1967), 'A comment on disguised observation in sociology', *Social Problems*, vol. 14, pp. 366–73.

Erikson, K. T. (1973), 'Sociology and the historical perspective', in M. Drake (1973), pp. 13–30.

Erikson, K. T. (1976), *Everything in its Path: Destruction of Community in the Buffalo Creek Flood* (New York: Simon and Schuster).

Ermarth, M. (1978), *William Dilthey: The Critique of Historical Reason* (Chicago: University of Chicago Press).

Faraday, A., and Plummer, K. (1979), 'Doing life histories', *Sociological Review*, vol. 27 (November), pp. 773–92.

Farberman, H. (1979), 'The Chicago School: continuities in urban sociology', in N. K. Denzin (ed.), *Studies in Symbolic Interaction*, vol. 2 (Greenwich, Conn.: J.A.I. Press).

Faris, E. (1937), *The Nature of Human Nature and Other Essays in Social Psychology* (London: McGraw-Hill).

Faris, R. E. I. (1970), *Chicago Sociology: 1920–1932* (Chicago: University of Chicago Press).

Fest, J. C. (1977), *Hitler* (Harmondsworth: Pelican).

Festinger, L., and Katz, D. (eds) (1953), *Research Methods in the Behavioural Sciences* (New York: Holt, Rinehart and Winston).

Fiedler, J. (1978), *Field Research: A Manual for Logistics and Management of Scientific Studies in Natural Settings* (London: Jossey-Bass).

Filstead, W. J. (ed.) (1970), *Qualitative Methodology: Firsthand Involvement with the Social World* (Chicago: Markham Publishing Co.)

Filstead, W. J. (1979), 'Qualitative methods: a needed perspective in evolution research', in Cook and Reichardt (1979), pp. 33–48.

Finestone, H. (1976), *Victims of Change* (Westport, Conn.: Greenwood Press).

Fischer, D. H. (1971), *Historians' Fallacies* (London: Routledge & Kegan Paul).

Fisher, B. M., and Strauss, A. (1978), 'Interactionism', in T. Bottomore and R. Nisbet (eds) (1978), *A History of Sociological Analysis* (London: Heinemann).

Fletcher, C. (1974), *Beneath the Surface: An Account of Three Styles of Sociological Research* (London: Routledge & Kegan Paul).

Ford, C. S. (1941), *Smoke from Their Fires* (New Haven, Conn.: Yale University Press).

Ford, J. (1975), *Paradigms and Fairy Tales*, 2 vols (London: Routledge & Kegan Paul).

Fothergill, R. A. (1974), *Private Chronicles: A Study of English Diaries* (London: Oxford University Press).

Foucault, M. (1977), *Discipline and Punish* (London: Allen Lane).

Foucault, M. (1978), *I, Pierre Rivière, having Slaughtered my Mother, my Sister and my Brother* . . . (Harmondsworth: Peregrine).

Foucault, M. (1979a), 'What is an author?' *Screen*, vol. 20, pp. 13–35.

Foucault, M. (1979b), *The History of Sexuality*, vol. 1 (London: Allen Lane).

Foucault, M. (1980), *Herculine Barbin: Being the Recently Discovered Memoirs of a Nineteenth Century French Hermaphrodite* (New York: Pantheon).

Fraser, R. (1968), *Work* (Harmondsworth: Penguin).

Frazier, C. E. (1976), *Theoretical Approaches to Deviance* (Columbus, Ohio: Charles E. Merrill).

Frazier, C. E. (1978), 'The use of life histories in testing theories of criminal behaviour: toward reviving a method', *Qualitative Sociology*, vol. 1, pp. 122–42.

Frazier, E. F. (1967), *Negro Youth at the Crossways: their Personality Development in the Middle States* (New York: Schocken Books); originally published in 1940.

Freilich, M. (ed.), (1970), *Marginal Natives: Anthropologists At Work* (London: Harper & Row).

Freud, S. (1925), 'Analysis of a phobia in a five year old boy', *Collected Papers* vol. 2 (London: Hogarth Press), pp. 149–289.

Freud, S. (1976), *The Interpretation of Dreams*, vol. 4, The Penguin Freud Library (Harmondsworth: Pelican).

Freud, S. (1977), *Case Histories: 'Dora' and 'Little Hans'*, vol. 8, The Penguin Freud Library (Harmondsworth: Penguin).

Friday, N. (1976), *My Secret Garden* (New York: Pocket Books).

Frisch, M., and Watts, D. L. (1980), 'Oral history and the presentation of class consciousness: the *New York Times* versus the Buffalo unemployed', *International Journal of Oral History*, vol. 1, pp. 88–110.

Fry, C. L. (1934), *The Technique of Social Investigation* (New York: Harper & Bros).

Garfinkel, H. (1967), *Studies in Ethnomethodology* (Englewood Cliffs, NJ: Prentice-Hall).

Garraty, J. A. (1958), *The Nature of Biography* (London: Jonathan Cape)

Genet, J. (1964), *The Thief's Journal* (New York: Grove Press).

Gerth, H., and Mills, C. W. (1954), *Character and Social Structure* (London: Routledge & Kegan Paul).

Giddens, A. (1976), *New Rules of Sociological Method* (London: Hutchinson).

Gittings, R. (1978), *The Nature of Biography* (London: Heinemann).

Gittins, D. (1979), 'Oral history, reliability and recollection', in L. Moss and H. Goldstein, *The Recall Method in Social Surveys* (London: University of London, Institute of Education), pp. 82–99.

Glaser, B. G., and Strauss, A. (1967a), *The Discovery of Grounded Theory* (Chicago: Aldine).

Glaser, B. G., and Strauss, A. (1967b), *Awareness of Dying* (London: Weidenfield & Nicholson).

Glaser, B., and Strauss, A. (1968), *Time for Dying* (Chicago: Aldine).

Glassner, B., and Freedman, J. A. (1979), *Clinical Sociology* (London: Longman).

Glazer, M. (1972), *The Research Adventure: Promise and Problems of Fieldwork* (New York: Random House).

Gold, R. L. (1958), 'Roles in sociological field observation', *Social Forces*, vol. 36, pp. 217–23.

Golden, M. P. (ed.) (1976), *The Research Experience* (Ithaca, Ill.: Peacock).
Goode, W. J., and Hatt, P. K. (1952), *Methods in Social Research* (London: McGraw-Hill).
Gorden, R. L. (1969), *Interviewing: Strategy, Techniques, and Tactics* (Homewood, Ill.: Dorsey Press).
Gottdiener, M. (1980), 'Field research and video tape', *Sociological Inquiry*, vol. 49, no. 4, pp. 59–66.
Gottschalk, L. (1942), 'The historian and the historical document', in L. Gottschalk *et al.* (1942), pp. 3–78.
Gottschalk, L., Kluckhohn, C., and Angell, R. (1942), *The Use of Personal Documents in History, Anthropology and Sociology* (New York: Social Science Research Council).
Gouldner, A. W. (1962), 'Anti-minotaur: the myth of a value-free sociology', *Social Problems*, vol. 9, no. 3, pp. 199–213.
Gouldner, A. (1973), *For Sociology: Renewal and Critique in Sociology Today* (London: Allen Lane).
Grele, R. (ed.) (1975), *Envelopes of Sound: Six Practitioners Discuss the Method, Theory and Practice of Oral History and Oral Testimony* (Chicago: Precedent Publishing).
Griffin, J. (1961), *Black Like Me* (Boston: Houghton-Mifflin).
Gurvitch, G., and Moore, W. E. (1945), *Twentieth Century Sociology* (New York: The Philosophical Library Inc.).
Haley, A. (1968), *The Autobiography of Malcolm X* (Harmondsworth: Penguin).
Haley, A. (1977), *Roots* (London: Hutchinson).
Halfpenny, P. (1979), 'The analysis of qualitative data', *Sociological Review*, vol. 27, pp. 799–825.
Halmos, P. (1978), *The Personal and The Political* (London: Hutchinson).
Hammond, P. E. (ed.) (1964), *Sociologists at Work: Essays on the Craft of Social Deviance* (New York: Basic Books).
Hanlan, A. J. (1979), *Autobiography of Dying* (New York: Doubleday & Co.).
Hardy, F. (ed.) (1946), *Grierson on Documentary* (London: Collins).
Harper, D. (1978), 'At home on the rails: ethics in a photographic research project', *Qualitative Sociology*, vol. 1, pp. 61–77.
Harré, R. (ed.) (1976), *Personality* (Oxford: Basil Blackwell).
Hawthorn, G. (1976), *Enlightenment and Despair: A History of Sociology* (Cambridge University Press).
Heider, K. (1976), *Ethnographic Film* (Austin: University of Texas).
Helling, I. (1976), 'Autobiography as self-presentation: the carpenters of Konstanz', in R. Harré, *Life Sentences; Aspects of the Social Role of Language* (London: Wiley), ch. 6, pp. 42–8.
Henderson, B. (1980), *A Critique of Film Theory* (New York: E. P. Dultz).
Henry, J. (1972), *Pathways to Madness* (New York: Random House).
Hersey, J. (1972), *Hiroshima* (Harmondsworth: Penguin).
Hewitt, J. P. (1979), *Self and Society* (2nd edn) (Boston: Allyn and Bacon).
Heyl, B. S. (1979), *The Madam as Entrepreneur: Career Management in House Prostitution* (New Jersey: Transaction Books).
Hill, J. (1969), 'On the relevance of methodology', repr. in N. K. Denzin (1970), pp. 12–19.

Hinkle, R. C. (1980), *Founding Theory of American Sociology 1881–1915* (London: Routledge & Kegan Paul).

Hjelle, L. A., and Ziegler, D. J. (1976), *Personality: Theories, Basic Assumptions, Research and Applications* (New York: McGraw Hill).

Homans, G. C. (1949), 'The strategy of industrial sociology', *American Journal of Sociology*, vol. 54, pp. 330–7.

Homans, G. C. (1967), *The Nature of Social Science* (New York: Harcourt, Brace and World Inc.)

Howard, A. (ed.) (1979), *The Crossman Diaries* (London: Magnum Books; Methuen Paperbacks).

Hughes, H. M. (ed.) (1961), *The Fantastic Lodge: The Autobiography of a Girl Drug Addict* (Boston: Houghton-Mifflin).

Hughes, J. A. (1976), *Sociologcial Analysis: Method and Discovery* (London: Nelson).

Humphries, S. (1981), *Hooligans or Rebels? An Oral History of Working Class Childhood and Youth 1889–1939* (Oxford: Basil Blackwell).

Illich, I. (1980), *Toward a History of Needs* (New York: Bantam Books).

Jackson, B. (1972), *Outside the Law: A Thief's Primer* (New Jersey: Transaction Books).

Jackson, B. (1977), *Killing Time: Life in the Arkansas Penitentiary* (New York: Cornell University Press).

Jackson, B. (1978), 'Killing time: life in the Arkansas Penitentiary', *Qualitative Sociology*, vol. 1, pp. 21–32.

Jacobs, J. (1974), *Fun City: An Ethnographic Study of a Retirement Community* (New York: Holt, Rinehart & Winston).

Jacobs, R. H. (1970), 'The journalist and sociological enterprise as ideal type', *American Sociologist*, vol. 5, pp. 348–50.

Jahoda, M., Lazarsfeld, P., and Zeisel, H. (1972), *Marienthal: The Sociography of an Unemployed Community*, 2nd edn (London: Tavistock).

James, W. (1913), *Talks to Teachers on Psychology: And to Students on some of Life's Ideals* (London: Longman's, Green), first pub. 1899.

James, W. (1952), *The Varieties of Religious Experience* (London: Longman).

James, W. (1955), *Pragmatism* (New York: Meridian Books).

Janowitz, M. (ed.) (1966), *W. I. Thomas on Social Organization and Social Pesonality* (Chicago: University of Chicago Press).

Jansen, S. C. (1980), 'The stranger as seer or voyeur: a dilemma of the peep-show theory of knowledge', *Qualitative Sociology*, vol. 2, no. 3, pp. 22–55.

Jelinek, E. C. (ed.), (1980), *Women's Autobiography: Essays in Criticism* (Bloomington, Ind.: Indiana University Press).

Johnson, J. M. (1975), *Doing Field Research* (New York: The Free Press; Macmillan).

Junker, B. H. (1960), *Field Work: An Introduction to the Social Sciences* (Chicago: University of Chicago Press).

Karweit, N. (1973), Storage and retrieval of life history data', *Social Science Research*, vol. 2, pp. 41–50.

Keat, R., and Urry, J. (1975), *Social Theory as Science* (London: Routledge & Kegan Paul).

Keller, H. (1954), *The Story of My Life* (with an introduction by Ralph Barton Perry and an account by John Albert Macy) (Garden City, NY: Doubleday).

Kessler, S. J., and McKenna, W. (1978), *Gender: An Ethnomethodological Approach* (London: Wiley).

Kiki, A. M. (1968), *Kiki: Ten Thousand Years in a Lifetime – A New Guinea Autobiography* (London: Cheshire Paperback).

Kimmel, D. C. (1974), *Adulthood and Ageing: An Interdisciplinary, Developmental view* (2nd edn 1980) (London: Wiley).

Kinsey, A. C., Pomeroy, W. B., and Martin, C. E. (1948), *Sexual Behaviour in the Human Male* (London: W. B. Saunders).

Klockars, C. B. (1975), *The Professional Fence* (London: Tavistock).

Klockars, C. B. (1977), 'Field ethics for the life history', in R. S. Weppner (ed.) (1977) *Street Ethnography* (London: Sage), pp. 201–27.

Klockars, C. B., and O'Connor, F. B. (eds) (1979), *Deviance and Decency: The Ethics of Research with Human Subjects* (London: Sage).

Kluckhohn, C. (1942), 'The personal document in anthropological science', in L. Gottschalk *et al.* (1942), pp. 79–176.

Kriseberg, B. (1975), *Crime and Privilege: Toward a New Criminology* (Englewood Cliffs, NJ: Prentice-Hall; Spectrum).

Lane, H. (1977), *The Wild Boy of Aveyron* (London: Allen & Unwin).

Langness, L. L. (1965), *The Life History in Anthropological Science* (London: Holt, Rinehart & Winston).

Lasch, C. (1979), *The Culture of Narcissism* (New York: Norton).

Lazarsfeld, P., and Robinson, W. S. (1940), 'The quantification of case studies', *Journal of Applied Psychology*, vol. XXIV, pp. 817–25.

—— Lee, A. M. (1978), *Sociology for Whom?* (New York: Oxford University Press).

Lemert, E. (1951), *Social Pathology* (New York: McGraw-Hill).

Lesy, M. (1973), *Wisconsin Death Trip* (New York: Pantheon).

Lesy, M. (1976), *Real Life: Louisville in the Twenties* (New York: Pantheon).

Levi-Strauss, C. (1966), *The Savage Mind* (London: Weidenfeld).

Levi-Strauss, C. (1977), *Structrual Anthropology*, vol. 2, (London: Allen Lane).

Levin, G. Roy (1971), *Documentary Explorations: 15 Interviews with Film-makers* (New York: Doubleday).

Levine, D. N. (ed.) (1971), *George Simmel on Individuality and Social Forms* (Chicago: University of Chicago Press).

Levinson, D. J., Darrow, C. N., Klein, E. B., Levinson, M. H., and McKee, B. (1978), *The Seasons of a Man's Life* (New York: Knopf).

Lewis, D. J., and Smith, R. L. (1980), *American Sociology and Pragmatism: Mead, Chicago Sociology and Symbolic Interaction* (Chicago: University of Chicago Press).

Lewis, L. (1950), 'An anthropological approach to family studies', *American Journal of Sociology*, vol. LV, no. 5 (March) pp. 468–75.

Lewis, O. (1951), *Life in a Mexican Village: Tepotzlan Restudied* (Urbana, Ill.: University of Illinois Press).

Lewis, O. (1959), *Five Families* (New York: Basic Books).

Lewis, O. (1961), *Children of Sanchez: Autobiography of a Mexican family* (New York: Random House).

Lewis, O. (1964), *Pedro Martinez: A Mexican Peasant and his Family* (London: Secker & Warburg).

Lewis, O. (1965), *La Vida: A Puerto Rican Family in the Culture of Poverty* (New York: Random House).

Lewis, O. (1970a), *A Death in the Sanchez Family* (London: Secker & Warburg).

Lewis, O. (1970b), *Anthropological Essays* (New York: Random House).

Lewis, O., Lewis, R., and Rigdon, M. (1977), *Living the Revolution: An Oral History of Contemporary Cuba*, vol. 1, *Four Men*; vol. 2, *Four Women*; vol 3, *Neighbours* (London: University of Illinois Press).

Liebow, E. (1967), *Tally's Corner* (Boston, Mass.: Little, Brown).

Lifton, R. J. (1968), *Death in Life* (New York: Random House).

Lifton, R. (1972), 'Experiments in advocacy research', in J. H. Masserman (ed.), *Research and Relevance*, vol. XXI of *Science and Psychoanalysis* (New York: Grune and Stratton).

Lifton, R. J. (1973), *Home from the War* (New York: Simon & Schuster).

Lifton, R. J., with E. Olsen (ed.) (1974), *Explorations in Psychohistory: the Wellfleet Papers* (New York: Simon & Schuster).

Light, D., Jr (1975), 'The sociological calendar: an analysis tool for fieldwork applied to medical and psychiatric training', *American Journal of Sociology*, vol. 80, no. 5, pp. 1145–64.

Lindesmith, A. (1947) (rev. 1968), *Opiate Addiction* (Chicago: University of Chicago Press).

Lofland, J. (1966), *Doomsday Cult* (Englewood Cliffs, NJ: Prentice-Hall).

Lofland, J. (1971), *Analyzing Social Settings: A Guide to Qualitative Observation and Analysis* (Belmont, Calif.: Wadsworth).

Lofland, J. (1974), 'Styles of reporting qualitative field research', *American Sociologist*, vol. 9, pp. 101–11.

Lofland, J. (1976), *Doing Social Life* (London: Wiley).

Lukes, S. (1973), *Individualism* (Oxford: Blackwell).

Lundberg, G. A. (1926), 'Case work and the statistical method', *Social Forces*, vol. 5, pp. 61–5.

Lundberg, G. A. (1929), *Social Research: A Study in Methods of Gathering Data* (London: Longmans).

Lundberg, G. A. (1941), 'Case studies v. statistical methods – an issue based on misunderstanding', *Sociometry*, vol. 4, pp. 379–83.

Lurie, A. (1967), *Imaginary Friends* (New York: Coward, McCann and Geoghegan).

Lyman, S. M., and Scott, M. B. (1975), *The Drama of Social Reality* (Oxford: Oxford University Press).

Lynd, A., and Lynd, S. (1973), *Rank and File: Personal Histories by Working Class Organisers* (Boston: Beacon Press).

Lynd, R. S. (1939), *Knowledge for What?* (Princeton, NJ: Princeton University Press).

Lyons, N. (1966), *Photographers on Photography* (Englewood Cliffs, NJ: Prentice-Hall).

Maas, S., and Kuypers, J. A. (1974), *From Thirty to Seventy: a 40 Year Longitudinal Study of Adult Life Styles and Personality* (London: Jossey-Bass).

McCall, G. J., and Simmons, J. (1969), *Issues in Participant Observation: A Text and Reader* (Reading, Mass.: Addison-Wesley).

McHugh, P. (1968), *Defining the Situation* (New York: Bobbs-Merrill).

McPhail, C., and Rexroat, C. (1979), 'Mead vs. Blumer: the divergent methodological perspectives of social behaviourism and symbolic interactionism', *American Sociological Review*, vol. 44, pp. 449–67.

McVicar, J. (1974), *McVicar by Himself* (London: Hutchinson).

Madge, C. (1963, *The Origin of Scientific Sociology* (London: Tavistock).

Madge, J. (1953), *The Tools of Social Science* (London: Longman's, Green).

Mailer, N. (1968), *The Armies of the Night: History as a Novel. The Novel as History* (New York: New American Library).

Mailer, N. (1979), *The Executioner's Song* (London: Hutchinson).

Makkreed, R. (1975), *Dilthey: Philosopher of the Human Studies* (Princeton, NJ: Princeton University Press).

Malinowski, B. (1922), *Argonauts of the Western Pacific* (London: Routledge & Kegan Paul).

Malinowski, B. (1929), *Sexual Life of Savages in North Western Melanesia* (New York: Harcourt, Brace & World).

Malinowski, B. (1967), *A Diary in the Strict Sense of the Term* (London: Routledge & Kegan Paul).

Mandelbaum, M. (1967), *The Problem of Historical Knowledge: An Answer to Relativism* (London: Harper & Row).

Manis, J. G., and Meltzer, B. N. (1978), *Symbolic Interactionism: A Reader in Social Psychology*, 3rd edn. (Boston: Allyn and Bacon).

Manning, P. (forthcoming), 'Analytic induction', in R. Smith (ed.), *Social Science Methods* (New York: Irvington/Wiley Press).

Mariampolski, H., and Hughes, D. (1978), 'The use of personal documents in historical sociology', *American Sociologist*, vol. 13 (May), pp. 104–13.

Marsden, D., and Duff, E. (1974), *Workless: Some Unemployed Men and Their Families* (Harmondsworth: Penguin; repr. with new intro., 1982).

Marshall, G. (1981), 'Accounting for deviance', *International Journal of Sociology and Social Policy*, vol. 1, no. 1, pp. 17–45.

Mason, M. (1980), 'The other voice! autobiographies of women writers', in J. Olney (1980), pp. 207–35.

Matthews, F. (1977), *Quest for an American Sociology: Robert E. Park and the Chicago School* (Montreal: McGill-Queens University Press).

Matza, D. (1969), *Becoming Deviant* (Englewood Cliffs, NJ: Prentice-Hall).

Mead, M. (1964), 'Anthropology and the camera', in W. Morgan (ed.), *The Encyclopaedia of Photography*, Vol. 1 (New York: Greystone).

Meehl, P. (1951), *Clinical v. Statistical Prediction: A Theoretical Analysis and Review of the Evidence* (Minneapolis: University of Minnesota).

Merton, R. K. (1968), *Social Theory and Social Structure* (London: Collier-Macmillan).

Milgram, S. (1977), 'The image freezing machine', *Psychology Today*, vol. 10, no. 5 (January), pp. 50–9.

Miller, R., and Miller, A. Seiden (1976), 'The student's sociological diary', *Teaching Sociology*, vol. 4, no. 1, pp. 67–82.

Mills, C. W. (1940), 'Situated actions and vocabularies of motive', *American Science Review*, vol. V, pp. 904–13.

—— Mills, C. W. (1970), *The Sociological Imagination* (Harmondsworth: Penguin).

Minton, R. J. (1971), *Inside: Prison American Style* (New York: Random House).

Misch, G. (1951), *A History of Autobiography in Antiquity*, trans. E. W. Dickes, 2 vols (Cambridge: Harvard University Press; Mars).

Morris, C. (1972, *The Discovery of the Individual 1050–1200* (London: SPCK).

Mortimer, J. T., and Simmons, R. G. (1978), 'Adult socialization', in *Annual Review of Sociology* (1978), vol. 4, pp. 421–54.

Moser, C., and Kalton, G. (1971), *Survey Methods in Social Investigation*, 2nd edn (London: Heinemann).

Moss, L., and Goldstein, H. (eds) (1979), *The Recall Method in Social Surveys* (London: University of London, Institute of Education).

Mowrer, E. R. (1927), *Family Disorganization* (Chicago: University of Chicago Press).

Murray, D. (1968), *A Writer Teaches Writing* (Boston: Houghton-Mifflin).

Murray, S. O. (1979), 'The scientific reception of Castaneda', *Contemporary Sociology*, vol. 8, (March), pp. 189–92.

Musello, C. (1979), 'Family photography', in J. Wagner (1979), pp. 101–18.

National Press Photographers Association (1978), *The Best of Photojournalism* (London: Orbis Publishing).

Nicolson, J. (1980), *Seven Ages* (London: Fontana).

Nisbet, R. (1976), *Sociology as an Art Form* (London: Heinemann).

Oberschall, A. (ed.) (1972), *The Establishment of Empirical Sociology* (London: Harper & Row).

Odum, H., and Jocher, K. (1929), *An Introduction to Social Research* (New York: Henry Holt & Co.).

Olney, J. (ed.) (1980), *Autobiography: Essays Theoretical and Critical* (Princeton, NJ: Princeton University Press).

Orlans, H. (1967), 'Ethical problem in the relation of research sponsors and investigation', in Sjoberg (1967), pp. 3–25.

Orne, M. T. (1962), 'On the social psychology of the psychological experiment', *American Psychologist*, vol. 17, pp. 776–83.

Palmer, V. M. (1928), *Field Studies in Sociology: A Student's Manual* (Chicago: University of Chicago).

Park, R. E. (1930), 'Murder and the case study method', *American Journal of Sociology*, vol. 36 (November), pp. 447–54.

Park, R. E., and Burgess, E. W. (1969), *Introduction to the Science of Sociology: Including the Original Index to Basic Sociological Concepts* (Chicago: University of Chicago Press); originally pub. 1921.

Parker, T. (1963), *The Unknown Citizen* (London: Hutchinson).

Parker, T. (1965), *Five Women* (London: Hutchinson).

Parker, T. (1967), *A Man of Good Abilities* (London: Hutchinson).

Parker, T. (1969), *The Twisting Lane* (London: Hutchinson).

Parker, T., and Allerton, R. (1962), *The Courage of his Convictions* (London: Hutchinson).

Pascal, R. (1960), *Design and Truth in Autobiography* (London: Routledge & Kegan Paul).

Paul, S. (1979), *Begegnungen: Zur Geschichte persönlicher Dokumente in Ethnologie, Soziologie, Psychologie. (Encounters: Contribution to the History of Personal Documents in Ethnology, Sociology, Psychology)*, 2 vols (Hohenschäftlarn, Austria).

Pelz, W. (1974), *The Scope of Understanding in Sociology* (London, Routledge and Kegan Paul).

Pepys, S. (1970, *The Diary of Samuel Pepys: A New and Complete Trans-cription Edited by R. Latham and W. Matthews*, vols 1–9 (London: Bell).
Peterson, D. M., and Truzzi, M. (eds) (1972), *Criminal Life: Views from the Inside* (Englewood Cliffs, NJ: Prentice-Hall).
Phillips, D. L. (1971), *Knowledge from What? Theories and Methods in Social Research* (Chicago: Rand McNally).
Phillips, D. L. (1973), *Abandoning Method* (London: Jossey-Bass).
Pines, M. (1981), 'The civilizing of Genie', *Psychology Today*, vol. 15, no. 9 (September), pp. 28–34.
Pitt, C. (1972), *Using Historical Sources in Anthropology and Sociology* (New York: Holt, Rinehart & Winston).
Platt, J. 'Whatever happened to the case study?' (unpub. paper, School of Social Sciences, University of Sussex).
Plummer, K. (1979), 'Misunderstanding labelling perspective', in D. Downes and P. Rock (eds) (1979), *Deviant Interpretations* (Oxford: Martin Robertson).
Plummer, K. (1981), 'Social change, personal change and the life history method: researching the social construction of sexuality', in *An Introduction to Sociology*, pp. 15–27 (Open University Media Booklet No. 1).
Polansky, N. (1941), 'How shall a life history be written?', *Character and Personality*, vol. 9, pp. 188–207.
Ponsonby, A. (1923), *English Diaries: A Review of English Diaries from the sixteenth to the twentieth century with an introduction on diary writing* (London: Methuen).
Powdermaker, H. (1967), *Stranger and Friend: The Way of an Anthropologist* (London: Secker & Warburg).
Probyn, W. (1977), *Angel Face: The Making of a Criminal* (London: Allen & Unwin).
Rabinowitz, D., and Nielsen, Y. (1971), *Home: A Story of Old Age* (London: Macmillan).
Radin, P. (ed.) (1926), *Crashing Thunder: The Autobiography of an American Indian* (New York: D. Appleton & Co.).
Raushenbush, R. W. (1979), *Robert E. Park: Biography of a Sociologist* (Durham, NC: Duke University Press).
Rawick, G. P. (ed.) (1978), *The American Slave: A Composite Auto-biography* (London: Greenwood Press, Westport).
Reckless, W. (1929), *Six Boys in Trouble* (Chicago: University of Chicago Press).
Reinharz, S. (1979), *On Becoming a Social Scientist* (San Francisco, Calif.: Jossey-Bass).
Rettig, R., Torres, M., and Garrett, G. (1977), *Manny: A Criminal Addict's Story* (Boston: Houghton-Mifflin).
Rice, S. A. (ed.) (1931), *Methods in Social Science: A Case Book* (Chicago: Chicago University Press).
Richardson, S. A., Dohrenwend, B., and Klein, D. (1965), *Interviewing: Its forms and functions* (New York: Basic Books).
Riemer, J. W. (1977), 'Varieties of opportunistic research', *Urban Life*, vol. 5, no. 4, pp. 467–77.
Riesman, D., with Denney, R., and Glazer, N. (1950), *The Lonely Crowd: A*

Study of the Changing American Character (New Haven, Conn.: Yale University Press).

Riesman, D., with Glazer, N. (1952), *Faces in the Crowd: Individual Studies in Character and Politics* (New Haven, Conn.: Yale University Press).

Riis, J. A. (1971), *How the Other Half Lives* (New York: Dover) (Original publication, 1890).

Riley, M. W. (1963), *Sociological Research: (1) A Case Approach* (New York: Harcourt, Brace and World).

Roazen, P. (1979), *Freud and his followers* (Harmondsworth: Peregrine); originally published by A. Knopf in 1975.

Roberts, H. (ed.) (1981), *Doing Feminist Research* (London: Routledge & Kegan Paul).

Rock, P. (1976), 'Some problems of interpretative sociology', *British Journal of Sociology*, vol. 27, pp. 353–69.

Rock, P. (1979), *The Making of Symbolic Interactionism* (London: Macmillan).

Rogers, C. R. (1945), 'The non-directive method as a technique for social research', *American Journal of Sociology*, vol. 50, pp. 279–382.

Rosenblatt, R. (1980), 'Black autobiography: life as the death weapon', in J. Olney (ed.), (1980), pp. 169–80.

Rosenthal, A. (1971), *The New Documentary in Action: A Casebook in Film Making* (Berkeley, Calif.: University of California Press).

Rucker, D. (1969), *The Chicago Pragmatists* (Minneapolis: University of Minnesota Press).

Rynkiewich, M. A., and Spradley, J. P. (eds) (1967), *Ethics and Anthropology: Dilemmas in Fieldwork* (New York: Wiley).

Samuel, R. (1981), *East-End Underworld: Chapters in the Life of Arthur Harding* (London: Routledge & Kegan Paul).

Sarbin, T. R. (1942), 'A contribution to the study of actuarial and individual methods of prediction', *American Journal of Sociology*, vol. 48, pp. 593–602.

Sartre, J. P. (1970), 'Jean Paul Sartre: an interview', *New York Review of Books*, vol XIV, no. 6 (26 March), pp. 22–31.

Schatzman, L., and Strauss, A. (1973), *Social Research in the Field: Strategies for a Natural Sociology* (Englewood Cliffs, NJ: Prentice-Hall).

Scheffler, I. (1974), *Four Pragmatists: A Critical Introduction to Peisce, James, Mead and Dewey* (London: Routledge & Kegan Paul).

Schuessler, K. F. (ed.) (1973), *On Analysing Crime* (Chicago: University of Chicago Press).

Schwartz, G., Merten, D., Behan, F., and Rosenthal, A. (1980), *Love and Commitment* (Beverly Hills, Calif.: Sage).

Schwartz, H., and Jacobs, J. (1979), *Qualitative Sociology: A Method to the Madness* (London: Collier-Macmillan).

Scimecca, J. A. (1977), *The Social Theory of C. Wright Mills* (Port Washington, NY: Kennikat Press).

Scott, R. A., and Shore, A. R. (1979), *Why Sociology does not Apply: A Study of the Use of Sociology in Public Policy* (New York: Elsevier).

Seabrook, J. (1967), *The Unprivileged* (London: Longman).

Seabrook, J. (1971), *City Close Up* (London: Allen Lane).

Seabrook, J. (1973), *Loneliness* (London: Temple Smith/New Society).

Seabrook, J. (1976), *A Lasting Relationship: Homosexuals and Society* (London: Allen Lane).

Sechrest, L. (1979), *Unobtrusive Measurement Today* (San Francisco, Calif.: Jossey-Bass).

Sellitz, C., Jahoda, M., Deutsch, M., and Cook, S. W. (1962), *Research Methods in Social Relations* (rev. edn) (London: Methuen).

Sennett, R., and Cobb, R. (1972), *The Hidden Injuries of Class* (New York: Random House).

Sennett, R. (1974), *The Fall of Public Man* (London: Cambridge University Press).

Shaffir, W. B., Stebbins, R. A., and Turowetz, A. (1980), *Fieldwork Experience; Qualitiative Approaches to Social Research* (New York: St Martin's Press).

Shaw, C. R. (1927), 'Case study method', *Publication of American Social Science*, vol. 21, pp. 149–57.

Shaw, C. R. (1931), *The Natural History of a Delinquent Career* (Chicago: University of Chicago Press).

Shaw, C. R. (1938), *Brothers in Crime* (Chicago: University of Chicago Press).

Shaw, C. R. (1966), *The Jack Roller: A Delinquent Boy's Own Story* (Chicago: University of Chicago Press); originally published 1930.

Shaw, C., and McKay, H. D. (1969), *Juvenile Delinquency and Urban Areas* (rev. edn) (Chicago: University of Chicago Press).

Shelston, A. (1977), *Biography* (London: Methuen).

Sheridan, A. (1980), *Michel Foucault: The Will to Truth* (London: Tavistock).

Shils, E. (1948), *The Present State of American Sociology* (Glencoe, Ill.: The Free Press).

Shils, E. (1980), *The Calling of Sociology* (Chicago: University of Chicago Press).

Shipman, M. D. (1972), *The Limitations of Social Research* (London: Longman).

Short, K. R. M., and Fledelius, R. (eds) (1980), *Film and History: Methodology, Research and Education* (Copenhagen: IAMHIST/Eventus).

Short, K. R. M. (ed.) (1981), *Feature Films as History* (London: Croom Helm).

Silverman, D. (1973), 'Interview talk: bringing off a research instrument', *Sociology*, vol. 7, no. 1, pp. 31–48.

Silverman, D. (1975), *Reading Castaneda: A Prologue to the Social Science* (London: Routledge & Kegan Paul).

Simmel, G. (1977), *The Problems of the Philosophy of History: An Epistemological Essay* (ed. G. Oakes) (New York: The Free Press, Macmillan).

Simmons, W. (ed.) (1942), *Sun Chief: The Autobiography of a Hopi Indian* (New Haven, Conn.: Yale University, Institute of Human Relations).

Simon, J. (1978), *Basic Research Methods in Social Science: The Art of Empirical Investigation* (2nd edn) (New York: Random House).

Sjoberg, G. (ed.) (1967), *Ethics, Politics and Social Research* (Cambridge, Mass.: Schenkman Publishing).

Sjoberg, G., and Nett, R. (1968), *A Methodology for Social Research* (London: Harper & Row).

Smith, H. L. (Director) (1935), *The New Survey of London Life and Labour: Vol. IX Life and Leisure* (London: P. S. King).

Smith, T. V., and White, L. D. (1968), *Chicago: An Experiment in Social Science Research* (New York: Greenwood Press); originally published in 1929 by University of Chicago Press.

Snizek, W. E. (1975), 'The relationship between theory and research: a study in the sociology of sociology', *Sociological Quarterly*, vol. 16, pp. 415–28.

Snodgrass, J. (1973), 'The criminologist and his criminal: the case of Edwin H. Sutherland and Broadway Jones', *Issues in Criminology*, vol. 8, no. 1, pp. 1–17.

Snodgrass, J. (1976), 'Clifford R. Shaw and Henry D. McKay: Chicago criminologists', *British Journal of Criminology*, vol. 16 (July), pp. 1–19 and (April) pp. 289–93.

Snodgrass, J. (1978), 'The Jack Roller at seventy: a fifty year follow-up of the delinquent boy's own story' (Paper presented at the American Society of Criminology meetings in Dallas, November 1978).

Sontag, S. (1978), *On Photography* (Harmondsworth: Penguin).

Sorlin, P. (1980), *The Film in History: Restaging the Past* (Oxford: Oxford University Press).

Sorokin, P., and Berger, C. (1938), *Time Budgets of Human Behaviour* (Cambridge, Mass.: Harvard University Press).

Speier, M. (1973), *How to Observe Face-to-Face Communication: A Sociological Introduction* (Pacific Palisades: Goodyear Publishing).

Spindler, G. (ed.) (1970), *Being an Anthropologist* (New York: Holt, Rinehart & Winston).

Spradley, J. P. (1969), *Guests Never Leave Hungry: The Autobiography of James Sewid, a Kwakiutl Indian* (London: Yale University Press).

Spradley, J. P. (1970), *You Owe Yourself a Drunk: An Ethnography of Urban Nomads* (Boston: Little, Brown).

Spradley, J. P. (1979), *The Ethnographic Interview* (London: Holt, Rinehart & Winston).

Spradley, J. (1980), *Participant Observation* (New York: Holt, Rinehart & Winston).

Stacey, M. (1969), *Methods of Social Research* (Oxford: Pergamon).

Stannard, D. (1980), *Shrinking History: On Freud and the Failure of Psychohistory* (Oxford: Oxford University Press).

Stasz, C. (1979a), 'Texts, images and display conventions in sociology', *Qualitative Sociology*, vol. 2, no. 1 (May), pp. 29–44.

Stasz, C. (1979b), 'The early history of visual sociology', in J. Wagner (1979), pp. 119–36.

Steel, D. (1980), *Discovering Your Family History* (London: British Broadcasting Corporation).

Stein, G. (1938), *Everybody's Autobiography* (London: Heinemann).

Stewart, J. (1977), 'Oral history is beyond the stage of talking', *New York Times* (22 May).

Stoller, R. (1974), *Splitting: A Case of Female Masculinity* (New York: Delta Books).

Stonequist, E. V. (1961), *The Marginal Man: A Study in Personality and*

Culture Conflict (New York: Russell and Russell); originally published in 1937.

Stott, W. (1977), *Documentary Experience and Thirties America* (Oxford: Oxford University Press).

Stouffer, S. A. (1930), 'Experimental comparison of statistical and case history methods in attitude research, unpub. Ph.D (Chicago University).

Stouffer, S. A. (1941), 'Notes on the case study and the unique case', *Sociometry*, vol. 4, pp. 349–57.

Straus, R. (1948), 'Some sociological concomitants of excessive drinking as revealed in the life history of an itinerant inebriate', *Quarterly Journal Studies of Alcohol*, vol. 9, pp. 1–52.

Straus, R. (1974), *Escape from Custody* (New York: Harper & Row).

Strauss, A. (ed.) (1964), *George Herbert Mead on Social Psychology* (Chicago: University of Chicago Press).

Strauss, A. (1969), *Mirrors and Masks: The Search for Identity* (San Francisco, Calif.: The Sociology Press).

Strauss, A., and Glaser, B. (1977), *Anguish: A Case History of a Dying Trajectory* (Oxford: Martin Robertson).

Sullivan, H. S. (1954), *The Psychiatric Interview* (New York: Norton).

Sutherland, E. H. (1937), *The Professional Thief by a Professional Thief* (2nd edn 1967) (University of Chicago: Phoenix Books).

Taft, J. (1933), *Thirty One Contacts with a Seven Year Old Boy* (New York: Macmillan).

Tannenbaum, F. (1938), *Crime and the Community* (New York: Columbia University Press); reprinted in New York in 1963.

Terkel, S. (1968), *Division Street: America* (London: Allen Lane).

Terkel, S. (1970), *Hard Times: An Oral History of the Great Depression* (London: Allen Lane).

Terkel, S. (1977), *Working* (Harmondsworth: Penguin).

Terkel, S. (1978), *Talking to Myself: A Memoir of My Times* (New York: Pocket Books).

Terkel, S. (1981), *American Dreams: Lost and Found* (London: Hodder & Stoughton).

Thomas, E. A. (1978), 'Herbert Blumer's critique of the Polish Peasant: a post mortem on the life history approach in sociology', *Journal of the History of the Behavioural Sciences*, vol. 14, pp. 124–31.

Thomas, W. I., and Znaniecki, F. (1958), *The Polish Peasant in Europe and America* (New York: Dover Publications); original editions published 1918–20.

Thompson, E. P. (1978), *The Poverty of Theory and Other Essays* (London: Merlin Press).

Thompson, K. S., and Dinitz, S. (1974), 'Reactions to My Lai: a visual verbal comparison', *Sociology and Social Research*, vol. 58, pp. 122–9.

Thompson, P. (1978), *The Voice of the Past: Oral History* (Oxford: Opus Books; Oxford University Press).

Thompson, T. (1981), *Edwardian Childhoods* (London: Routledge & Kegan Paul).

Thrasher, F. (1926), *The Gang: A Study of 1,313 Gangs in Chicago* (abridged edn, 1963) (Chicago: University of Chicago).

Trilling, L. (1972), *Sincerity and Authenticity* (London: Oxford University Press).

Truzzi, M. (ed.) (1973), *The Humanities as Sociology: An Introductory Reader* (Ohio: Charles E. Merrill).

Turner, R. (1953), The quest for universals in sociological research', *American Sociological Review*, vol. 2A (June), pp. 605–11, and in N. K. Denzin (1970), pp. 264–77.

Turner, R. E. (ed.) (1967), *Robert E. Park on Social Control and Collective Behaviour* (Chicago: University of Chicago Press).

Vaillant, G. E. (1977), *Adaptation to Life* (Boston, Mass.: Little, Brown).

Valentine, C. A. (1968), *Culture and Poverty: Critique and Counter Proposals* (Chicago: University of Chicago Press).

Vasoli, R. H., and Terzola, D. (1974), 'Sutherland's professional thief', *Criminology*, vol. 12, pp. 131–54.

Vidich, A. J., Bersman, J., and Stein, M. J. (eds) (1964), *Reflections on Community Studies* (New York: Wiley).

Wagner, J. (ed.) (1979), *Images of Information: Still Photography in the Social Sciences* (Beverly Hills, Calif.: Sage).

Wakeford, J. (1968), *The Strategy of Social Inquiry* (London: Macmillan).

Wallace, A. F. C. (1965), 'Driving to work', in Melford E. Spiro (ed.), *Context and Meaning in Cultural Anthropology* (New York: The Free Press), pp. 277–94.

Walter, J. (ed.) (1981), *Reading Life Histories* (Brisbane: Institute for Modern Biography, Griffith University).

Ward, R. H. (1957), *A Drug-Taker's Notes* (London: Gollancz).

Washington, B. T. (1965), *Up From Slavery* (New York: Dodd, Mead).

Watson, J. (1968), *The Double Helix* (New York: Atheneum).

Watson, L. C. (1976), 'Understanding a life history as a subjective document: hermeneutical and phenomenological perspectives', *Ethos*, vol. 4, no. 1, pp. 95–131.

Wax, R. H. (1971), *Doing Fieldwork* (Chicago: University of Chicago Press).

Webb, B., and Webb, S. (1932), *The Methods of Social Study* (London: Longman's, Green).

Webb, E. J., Campbell, D. T., Schwartz, R. D., and Sechrest, L. (1966), *Unobtrusive Measures: Non-reactive Research in the Social Sciences* (Chicago: Rand McNally).

Weber, R. (1981), *The Literature of Fact: Literary Non Fiction in American Writing* (Athens: Ohio University Press).

Weber, G. H., and McCall, G. J. (1978), *Social Scientists as Advocates: Views from the Applied Disciplines* (London: Sage).

Webster, F. (1980), *The New Photography: Responsibility in Visual Communication* (London: Platform Books).

Weinberg, M. S., and Williams, C. J. (1974), *Male Homosexuals: Their Problem and Adaptations*. (Oxford: Oxford University Press).

Weintraub, K. J. (1978), *The Value of the Individual: Self and Circumstance in Autobiography* (Chicago: University of Chicago Press).

Wellman, D. T. (1977). *Portraits of White Racism* (Cambridge: Cambridge University Press).

Wells, H. G. (1934), *Experiment in Autobiography*, 2 vols (New York: Macmillan).

White, R. R. (1975), *Lives in Progress: A Study of the Natural Growth of Personality* (3rd edn) (New York: Holt, Rinehart & Winston).

White, R. (1976), *The Enterprise of Living: A View of Personal Growth* (2nd edn) (New York: Holt, Rinehart & Winston).

Williams, C. (1980), *Realism and The Cinema* (London: Routledge & Kegan Paul).

Williamson, H. (1965), *Hustler edited by R. Lincoln Keiser with a commentary by Paul Bohannon* (Garden City, NY: Doubleday).

Wilson, E. (1956), *A Piece of My Mind* (New York: Farrow, Straus & Cudahy).

Winslow, R. V. (1974), *Deviant Reality: Alternative World Views* (Boston: Allyn and Bacon).

Wiseman, F. (1971), 'Interview with Wiseman', in G. Roy Levin, *Documentary Explorations*, pp. 313–28 (New York: Doubleday).

Wolff, J. (1981), *The Social Production of Art* (London: Macmillan).

Wolff, K. H. (1960), 'The collection and organization of field materials: a research report, in R. N. Adams and J. J. Preiss (1960), pp. 240–54.

Young, P. (1939), *Scientific Social Surveys and Research* (1st edn; 4th edn, 1966) (New York: Prentice-Hall).

Zavarzadeh, M. (1976), *The Mythopoeic Reality: The Post War American Non Fiction Novel* (Urbana: University of Illinois Press).

Zetterberg, H. L. (ed.) (1956), *Sociology in the United States of America: A Trend Report* (Paris: UNESCO, Documentation in the Social Sciences).

Zijderveld, A. (1970), *The Abstract Society* (London: Allen Lane).

Zimmerman, D. H., and Wieder, D. L. (1977) 'The diary diary-interview method', *Urban Life*, vol. 5, no. 4 (January), pp. 479–97.

Znaniecki, F. (1934), *The Method of Sociology* (New York: Farrar & Rhinehart).

Zorbaugh, H. (1965), *The Gold Coast and The Slum* (Chicago: University of Chicago Press).

Index